A HISTORY OF THE
GREAT
WESTERN
RAILWAY

COLIN MAGGS

AMBERLEY

First published 2013
This edition first published 2015

Amberley Publishing
The Hill, Stroud
Gloucestershire, GL5 4EP

www.amberley-books.com

British Library Cataloguing in Publication Data.
A catalogue record for this book is available from the British Library.

ISBN 978 1 4456 4428 8 (paperback)
ISBN 978 1 4456 1300 0 (ebook)

Typesetting and Origination by Amberley Publishing
Printed in Great Britain

Contents

1
Birth:
1824–1835

Once there was no Great Western Railway. Goods between Bristol and London were subject to long delays in summer if the water level on the Kennet & Avon Canal was low, or in winter if it was frozen. Delays, apart from being frustrating for traders, gave more opportunity for the dishonest fraternity to steal, such as abstracting wine from casks and substituting water. Cattle and sheep lost weight when being driven to market and would have achieved higher prices if they could have been transported.

Passenger transport left much to be desired. Although stagecoaches connected the cities, the speed was slow, the ride uncomfortable and the risk of accident always present. The Industrial Revolution brought demand for faster passenger movement and speedier and more reliable carriage for the increasing commercial traffic. The answer was a railway.

The first proposal for a Bristol to London line was by the London & Bristol Rail-Road Company promoted by Bristol merchants in 1824. This scheme proved abortive, but the success of the Stockton & Darlington Railway, opened the following year, encouraged similar proposals, none of which came to fruition. Then, in the autumn of 1832, four Bristolians met in a small office in Temple Back, a site later covered by Temple Meads goods depot, and formed a committee of fifteen prominent citizens representing Bristol's interests. It first met on 21 January 1833 and all the representatives reported that their organisations looked favourably on the undertaking and would supply funds for a preliminary survey.

The post of engineer was offered to the twenty-seven-year-old Isambard Kingdom Brunel, well known in the city for his improvements to Bristol Harbour and for having submitted designs for Clifton Suspension Bridge.

A detailed report was presented at a public meeting at the Guildhall, Bristol, on 30 July 1833 and it was resolved that a company should be formed for building a railway from Bristol to London and that one set of directors should look after the Bristol end and a similar body, based in London, should supervise the eastern end. Due to the distance between the two cities and the difficulties of communication, this was a sensible move.

The first joint meeting of the two committees took place on 19 August 1833 when the title 'Great Western Railway' was adopted. This was preferred to the alternative 'Bristol and London Railroad' because it was believed that, as Bristol's trade was thought to be declining in favour of Liverpool, having Bristol in the title could raise apprehension among potential investors.

Having 'great' in the title was brilliant as it rolled off the tongue easily and gave confidence to investors, passengers and those seeking carriage of their goods. Quite a few other railways eventually adopted the word in their titles: the Great Central Railway; Great Northern Railway; Great North of England Railway and the Great North of Scotland Railway.

The GWR required an Act of Parliament in order to obtain power for the compulsory purchase of land. The parliamentary committee to consider the Bill first met on 16 April 1834 and evidence was given of the great benefit a railway would offer to the transport of goods: three hours by rail from Bath to London instead of at least three days and Bristol to Bath in an hour instead of a whole day. Eggs, butter and cheese were imported from the Continent in large quantities for London consumption, whereas the GWR could carry home-produced food to the capital thus benefiting western farmers.

On the fifty-seventh day of the hearing, the committee approved the Bill and it passed the Commons with 182 for and 92 against, but the Lords rejected it on 25 July 1834 by 47 to 30. All was not lost; the plan was slightly modified and on 28 August 1835 the GWR Bill passed the Lords on a vote of 49 to 27, receiving royal assent on 31 August 1835.

The Bill itself is 250 feet in length, weighs over 9 lb and consists of 130 parchment skins sewn with twine. The Act 5 & 6 William IV c. 107 stipulated that eight directors should be resident within 20 miles of Bristol and eight within a similar distance of London though, due to the company's subsequent expansion, this ruling was annulled in 1849.

The GWR did not build the line itself, but placed the work in the hands of contractors. It was not always wise to select the cheapest contractor, as in trying to cut his costs that contractor might go bankrupt, thus delaying construction.

The GWR usually offered landowners a fair price for the property it required. For example, an inquiry was held on 19 September 1837 at Bath to assess the value of property required. The company offered £1,600, the owner claimed £2,800 and the jury's verdict was £1,150. Had the owner accepted the GWR's offer he would have been £450 better off.

Brunel supervised the whole undertaking, dashing between the London and Bristol sections, seemingly delegating little responsibility to his residential engineers in the various areas.

His ideal concept of a railway was a straight, level line. This was possible from London to Swindon, the ruling gradient being 1 in 660, but then he was faced with a difficulty. Swindon lay about 300 feet above sea level and Bath 100 feet. His answer was two gradients of 1 in 100 worked either by stationary steam engines, water power or a line on the atmospheric principle. In the event, in the interim between the line's planning and opening, locomotives had been improved to such an extent that they proved capable of climbing such a gradient.

Where a cutting or tunnel was necessary to keep the line flat, there was the need for an embankment to be built nearby to use the spoil. In the event of an embankment being required and no material dug within a convenient distance, side cutting was resorted to. This was simply digging a ditch parallel with the line. Brunel's choice of route between Paddington and Bristol meant that fewer earthworks were required than on other main lines: the London & Brighton required an average excavation of 145,000 cubic yards per mile, the London & Birmingham 115,000, but the GWR only 85,000. Furthermore, apart from the two inclines of 1 in 100, Brunel's ruling gradient was only 1 in 660 whereas the London & Birmingham was 1 in 330. The GWR main line, at 118 miles, was the longest in the country, exceeding the next longest, the London & Birmingham, by 6 miles.

Construction at the London end was relatively straightforward, the only important features being Sonning Cutting and the bridge over the Thames at Maidenhead. It was a different story at the other end of the line where four bridges were required over the Avon, along with Box Tunnel at 3,212 yards in length and eight tunnels between Bristol and Bath as well as lofty embankments and lengthy viaducts. East of Bath the Kennet & Avon Canal on a higher level was required to be diverted and an expensive retaining wall erected.

The length of the nine tunnels totalled 5,656 yards. They were cut by sinking vertical shafts along the line of the tunnel; then a bottom heading 7 feet wide and 8 feet high was excavated from either side of the shaft base and subsequently widened to form the finished tunnel. For visual effect, the portals were often higher than the rest of the tunnel. Brunel's tunnel mouths varied to suit their setting and have an aesthetic quality, while his country stations were designed to look like lodges on a great estate.

Constructional materials varied: bridges at the London end of the line were generally of brick, whereas those at the Bristol end were of Bath stone and pennant. Regarding the latter, their subsequent repair in brick has seriously detracted from Brunel's original quality.

Although the standard gauge of 4 feet 8½ inches was generally specified in Acts of Parliament, Brunel persuaded the chairman of the House of Lords committee to omit the gauge clause as a wider gauge might be of greater public advantage. Brunel said that the larger the wheel, the less friction on the axle and if the gauge was wider than standard, wheels could be placed outside the carriage or wagon body, thus considerably lowering the centre of gravity and making it much safer. The gauge of 7 feet was accepted by the GWR directors on 29 October 1835.

Brunel wasted no time after the Act was passed on 31 August 1835 and immediately set to work. The two committees acted quite independently and each was responsible for letting contracts in their area and for design – the Bristol Committee was not averse to expense on ornamental work such as the design of bridges and tunnel mouths, the west portals of Box, Middle Hill and Twerton tunnels being particularly fine.

2

Construction to Bristol: 1836–1841

The first contract at the London end was that for the eight-arch viaduct across the Brent Valley; work on this began in February 1836. The original intention was to share the London & Birmingham Railway's terminus at Euston, but negotiations failed as the London & Birmingham refused to grant the GWR permanent use of land. This meant that an Act had to be sought for a line from Acton to a new terminus at Paddington.

If the line was to be opened on schedule there was not time to build an elaborate structure, just a temporary terminus was required. Bishop's Road Bridge formed the passenger station façade, the rest of the makeshift station being constructed of timber.

The first two locomotives arrived in November 1837, having travelled by sea from Liverpool to London Docks and then by canal to West Drayton. On 28 December 1837 1½ miles of track had been laid between Drayton and Langley and the 2-2-2 *Vulcan* made a trial trip. On 12 May 1838 G. H. Gibbs, a London director, travelled behind an engine travelling at 60 mph.

The 22½ miles of line between Paddington and Maidenhead opened on 31 May 1838, Gibbs entering in his diary:

This being the day appointed for the opening of our Railway, the Directors and the Company invited met at the Depot before 11. A very pretty sight it was. At 11.30 we entered the carriages of the first train, and proceeding at a moderate pace reached Maidenhead Station in 49 minutes, or at about 28 miles an hour. After visiting the works we returned to Salt Hill, where a cold luncheon for about 300 people was laid under a tent. After the usual complement of toasts we returned to the line and reached Paddington (19 miles) in 34 minutes, or 33½ miles an hour.

The Times of 2 June 1838 reported that T. R. Guppy, a Bristol director, walked along the carriage roofs from one end of the train to the other while it was proceeding at full speed. The line opened to the public on 4 June 1838, but Gibbs was disappointed as the track proved rough and the locomotives slow and unreliable. On the first day 1,479 passengers were carried, fares totalling £226.

Eton College, afraid of the influence the railway might have on its pupils, had a clause inserted in the 1835 Act preventing the construction of a station, without the consent of the provost and fellows, within 3 miles of the school. The GWR easily circumvented this clause by merely stopping trains at Slough to pick up or deposit passengers and not actually having a station, passengers purchasing railway tickets at the Crown Inn. The provost and fellows applied to the Court of Chancery to halt this evasion of the Act, but their application was dismissed with costs. Curiously, within a month of their defeat, the college chartered a special train to convey its pupils to London for Queen Victoria's Coronation on 28 June. A station was opened at Slough in June 1840.

The next section, Maidenhead to Twyford, involved a bridge over the Thames. Brunel used two very flat brick arches of 128 feet span and many were convinced that when the supporting centring was removed, they would collapse. One night in the autumn of 1839 a violent storm blew down the centrings but left the arches quite secure. The line to Twyford opened on 1 July 1839, only first- and second-class coaches being provided. Goods traffic began in September 1839 and it is interesting that 'persons in the lower stations of life' were required to travel with the freight.

The section from Twyford to Reading involved a vast cutting about 2 miles in length. Ranger, the first contractor, was tardy and was dismissed and eventually the work had to be completed by the GWR. In February 1839, 1,220 men, 196 horses and 2 locomotives were at work creating the cutting.

Reading station was the first of Brunel's one-sided stations erected in situations where the town was on one side of the railway. Up and Down platforms set a short distance apart were both on the town side of the line. Logically the Up station was at the Up end and the Down at the other end. This design had the advantage that passengers and luggage did not require to cross the rails and non-stop trains could run clear of the platforms. In due course similar stations were erected at Taunton, Exeter and Gloucester.

On 12 March 1840 the 2-2-2 *Fire Fly*, the first GWR engine designed by its locomotive superintendent Daniel Gooch, reached a maximum speed of 58 mph on a return trial trip from Reading. On 30 March 1840 the line to Reading was opened to the public.

Opening to Steventon was delayed due to the particularly wet weather of the autumn and winter of 1839. Ballasting for one section proved a problem as the ground purchased for providing ballast was under water, so emergency supplies were obtained by dredging the river. The GWR opened to Steventon on 1 June 1840, a service of coaches and wagons linking with Oxford. Steventon, terminus of the London Division of the GWR, was the location of the house that Brunel designed for the superintendent of the line and later altered to accommodate the offices and board meetings, being conveniently located approximately midway between Bristol and London. On 20 July 1840 the line was extended to Faringdon Road (renamed Challow in 1864) from where road coaches ran to Cirencester, Gloucester and Cheltenham.

Meanwhile work had been proceeding at the Bristol end of the line. Due to the proximity of a bridge over the Avon, Temple Meads station had to be built on arches 15 feet above ground level. Likewise at Bath, bridges at each end of the station required it to be supported on arches.

Most of the contracts were let in 1836 and when the British Association met at Bristol that year, as publicity for the railway, the GWR directors invited members to view railway construction, so a flotilla of sixty boats set off from Bristol towards Bath. The party landed at Twerton to view work on the two tunnels.

As we saw earlier, the contractor Ranger proved unsatisfactory, lacking capital and energy, so the GWR had to seize his plant and complete the line itself. John Sharp worked as Ranger's foreman in charge of 600 men. His weekly pay was £1 4s 0d rising to £2 10s 0d, which placed him on a par with Brunel's young engineers who drew an annual starting salary of £150. When Sharp saw that Ranger was failing, he set up on his own as a subcontractor.

The foundation of the 1½-mile-long Saltford embankment was obtained from spoil heaps of the nearby Globe Colliery; this embankment also included burnt clay, which formed excellent binding material.

In May 1840 the GWR fell out with the parish of Newton St Loe as the company had blocked a lane and under its Act was therefore liable to a fine of £20 a day, the parish claiming a total of £2,300. The trouble arose because the GWR needed to divert the turnpike road and to do this required laying earth across a lane. At one time there was an exciting battle when, for several days, one party cut a channel through and the other filled it up. Eventually the GWR agreed to tail off the slope in a satisfactory manner and the parish agreed that the injunction against the company be dissolved.

Navvies were well paid and their work made them thirsty; these two facts could cause trouble. For example, on 5 July 1837 the Twerton vestry petitioned Bath magistrates for thirteen special constables 'in consequence of fighting and drunkenness on the Rail Road'. County rivalry raised its head in April 1838 when 300 navvies, mostly from Gloucestershire, attacked those from Devonshire and West Somerset. The trouble lasted for several days and was not suppressed until the military arrived on the scene.

By the end of 1839 the work most in arrears was that on the skew bridge immediately west of Bath station. Although planned to be constructed of iron, for more rapid completion laminated timber was used, the only Brunel example of this type. The timber was steam-bent to the desired curvature and secured by bolts and iron plates. Laminated timber arches normally had a life limited to twenty-five years because they were too flexible, this causing the laminations to separate and allow the ingress of water and thus decay. This bridge lasted thirty-eight years, and its longevity was only exceeded by Valentine's arch carrying the East Anglian Railway over the River Wissey.

The GWR respected the environment, the *Bath Chronicle* of 28 May 1840 reporting, 'Trees have been spared wherever practicable, and the masonry of the work has been executed so as to harmonise with neighbouring buildings and other objects.'

The 2-2-2 *Fireball* hauled the first train from Bristol to Bath on 31 August 1840. A design fault discovered on some of the coaches caused a wheel to grate on the underpart of a carriage. No less than 5,880 passengers were carried on the first day and £476 collected in fares, which compared most favourably with only £226 for the opening of the Paddington–Maidenhead line. Surprisingly, receipts at Bath exceeded those at Bristol.

It took some time for passengers to adapt themselves to obeying railway bye-laws. Two first-class passengers were fined in September 1840 for smoking cigars on Bath station. The fines of forty shillings each were divided equally between Bristol Infirmary and Bristol General Hospital. The behaviour of railway servants was not above criticism as in January 1841 a railway police inspector discovered the policeman in Bristol No. 3 Tunnel asleep beside a fire he had made. For this neglect of duty he was taken before Keynsham magistrates and committed to gaol for a month's hard labour.

Other GWR officials deserved a bouquet. In its issue of 13 October 1840 the *Bath & Cheltenham Gazette* reported:

Travelling by Railway to Bristol a day or two back, I put my head out of the carriage window to catch a sight of a train to Bath which had passed in the twinkling, before away went my hat to the no small, but good-natured merriment of my fellow travellers. This happened about Saltford. When the train stopped at Keynsham, I apprised an officer of my loss. He said I should have my hat again, and directed me to give certain notice at the office Bristol. On my return thither in the evening, my hat was obligingly restored to me. The exceeding civility I experienced from the Company's servants has led me to wish to indulge grateful pleasure, in thus publicly recording a circumstance, as also that others might profit by my want of caution.

The *Bath & Cheltenham Gazette* of 8 September 1840 attempted to compare the number of people travelling between Bath and Bristol by road and rail: 4,560 was the maximum number of passengers who could be carried by coach weekly; 19,618 was the number of passengers carried by rail in the first week.

To counteract railway competition from an approximately hourly train service, coach proprietors ran a road service every half an hour, but most coaches were soon taken off the road, some drivers put in charge of feeder buses to railway stations.

While the section west of Faringdon Road was being built, the Railway Regulation Act of 1840 was passed, requiring all new lines to be inspected by the Board of Trade. This extension to Hay Lane, officially named 'Wootton Bassett Road', was opened on 17 December 1840. Interestingly, no station was provided at Swindon, which was yet to be the site of the GWR works. With the opening to Hay Lane, Bath and Bristol coaches ran from there, but the Cheltenham and Gloucester traffic still continued to use Faringdon Road due to the poor state of roads between Hay Lane and Cirencester.

The works from Hay Lane to Chippenham were delayed by wet weather that caused the embankments to slip. In one place Brunel was forced to adopt the expensive method of driving piles through the embankment into the solid ground below and chaining the opposite piles together.

Sir Frederick Smith inspected the line from Hay Lane to Chippenham in mid-May 1841 and found it insufficiently completed for public traffic, but passed it in a later inspection that same month, the line being opened on 31 May 1841.

Today it is not always appreciated how startling the first sight of a train could be. The Reverend Charles Young took his parish clerk, William Hinton, to see one of the first trains descend Dauntsey Bank. Young wrote:

> The novelty of the sight, the strangeness of the sounds, the marvellous velocity with which the engine, tender, carriages and trucks disappeared, the dense columns of sulphurous smoke, were altogether too much for the reason of my simple dominie [Hinton], and he fell prostrate on the bank-side as if he had been smitten by a thunderbolt! When he had recovered this feet, his brain still reeled, his tongue clove to the roof of his mouth, and he stood aghast, unutterable amazement stamped upon his face. It must have been quite five minutes before he could speak, and when he did it was in the tone of a Jeremiah. 'Well, sir, that was a sight to have seen; but one I never care to see again! How much longer shall knowledge be allowed to go on increasing?'

The opening seriously affected settlements not on the railway route. Before the line was inaugurated thirty to forty coaches ran through Marlborough daily, but the advent of the GWR reduced this number to five. The £2,000 paid annually to horse keepers and helpers and then spent within Marlborough was no longer received. From the spring of 1840 only one Bath coach proceeded all the way by road from Bath to London without using the railway. The *Bath & Cheltenham Gazette* of 28 April 1840 recorded that innkeepers between Bath and Reading were 'starving' and that the value of tavern property within that area had been reduced within the last two to three years by 60 to 80 per cent.

The Chippenham to Bath section of the GWR included Box Tunnel, which at 1 mile 1,452 yards was 800 yards longer than any other cut prior to the 1840s. It was driven using eight shafts, the first and last being enlarged into cuttings.

Work started early in 1836 to ascertain the nature of the ground required for tunnelling. Shafts were sunk under the supervision of Charles Richardson, later responsible for making the Severn Tunnel. Two contractors won the task of boring the tunnel: George Burge of Herne Bay for the three-quarters of the tunnel, which passed through clay, blue marl and inferior oolite – material with which he had previous experience. At Box, Burge employed 1,200 men and 100 horses. The remaining half mile of tunnel was cut by Brewer of Box and Lewis of Bath, who had skills for working with great oolite.

It is believed that Burge used the 'English method' of tunnel construction. A pilot heading was driven along what became the tunnel arch; bars were then inserted, supported at one end by brick lining and at the other on timber props. Miners would then widen and deepen the excavation, which was supported by timber. Larch bars were preferred, as they gave an audible creak if the load proved excessive and collapse imminent, thus giving tunnellers more time to insert extra props. At no point were unlined excavations more than around 8 feet ahead of the bricklayers. Approximately 5,500 bricks were required for every foot advanced. A ton of gunpowder and a ton of candles, the latter made at Box, were used every week. Horse gins raised spoil and lowered material. The workmen lodged in neighbouring villages and because work continued night and day no bed was ever cold.

F. S. Williams in wrote *Our Iron Roads*:

On one occasion some of the directors of the Great Western Railway were inspecting the works at the Box tunnel, and several of them resolved to descend a shaft with Mr Brunel and one or two of the other engineers, who mentioned the incident to the writer. Accordingly all but one ensconced themselves in the tub provided for the purpose – he declined to accompany them. His friends rallied him for his want of courage, and one slyly suggested, 'Did your wife forbid you before you started?' A quiet nod in response intimated that the right nail had been struck, and the revelation was received with a merry laugh. But as the pilgrims found themselves slipping about a greasy, muddy tub, jolting and shaking as the horses stopped – by whose aid they were lowered – and how at length they were suspended some hundred and fifty feet from the bottom, till the blastings that had been prepared roared and reverberated through the 'long-drawn caverns', more than one of the party who had laughed before, wished that they had received a similar prohibition to that of their friend above, and that they had manifested an equal amount of marital docility.

Although cutting Box Tunnel led to some loss of life, the hundred deaths mentioned in some accounts is probably exaggerated as between September 1839 and November 1840, when about half the tunnel had been excavated, the GWR reported ten deaths, while outside these dates local newspapers reported only a handful of fatalities.

Curiously there was no public ceremony for the opening of the line between Chippenham and Bath on 30 June 1841, which completed the Paddington–Bristol line, only a beflagged train which carried the directors. It left Paddington at 8.00 a.m. and arrived at Bristol at noon before proceeding over the Bristol & Exeter Railway to Bridgwater, reached at 1.30 p.m.

The opinion was held, even by some doctors, that no passenger could possibly survive two journeys through Box Tunnel, so a significant number of passengers left the train at the station before the tunnel and covered the distance to the next station by road before continuing onwards by train. For the benefit of those who wished to avoid the tunnel, the eighteen-room Railway Hotel was established at Corsham, but apart from the very early days its size proved a white elephant. In an attempt to overcome tunnel phobia, the directors proposed installing lights, but Brunel sagely observed that it was quite unnecessary as the tunnel was no darker than the rest of the line at night.

Locomotives

When the GWR ordered its first engines, a locomotive superintendent had yet to be appointed, so responsibility fell on Brunel and unfortunately his expertise in the locomotive field proved to be low. He required builders to provide machines offering a standard velocity of 30 mph without requiring the piston to travel at a greater rate than 280 feet per minute, and the weight of the engine in working order not to exceed 10½ tons, or if over 8 tons, to be carried on six wheels.

This weight limitation was extremely low and less than most standard gauge engines on other lines, while to comply with the piston speed the wheels had to be large. Large wheels were heavier, so to keep the weight down boilers were kept small and thus had little or no reserve.

Meanwhile, Daniel Gooch was appointed locomotive superintendent on 18 August 1837, a few days before his twenty-first birthday. Previously he had been employed at the Vulcan Foundry, near Warrington, and by Robert Stephenson

& Co., Newcastle-on-Tyne. Gooch was far from impressed by the engines ordered, which were generally considered freaks, especially the 2-2-2 *Ajax*, which had all its wheels, including the 10-foot-diameter driving wheels, built up from solid plates instead of spokes. Another curiosity was *Thunderer*, articulated to overcome the weight problem, with the cylinders and driving wheels of 0-4-0 layout in front of the boiler and firebox, which were carried on six wheels. It also had a water space dividing the firebox into two, the fire being fed through two doors. One fire tended to die down when the other was burning fiercely. *Thunderer* was withdrawn after a mileage of only 9,882.

The rather unpleasantly named 2-2-2 *Snake* and *Viper* had their driving wheels turned by toothed gearing, a method which proved unsatisfactory, and Gooch in his report of January 1839 said that they were most unreliable and could only be used for ballasting. The gearing was removed the following year. Most of the remainder of these useless early engines were either withdrawn after working just over a year or converted to tank engines.

Fortunately for the GWR it had acquired two orthodox, reliable 2-2-2 engines almost by accident. They had been built, unhampered by Brunel's restrictions, by Robert Stephenson & Co. for the 5-foot-6-inch-gauge New Orleans Railway in the USA, but due to that railway's financial difficulties had been left in the maker's hands. After being converted to 7-foot gauge, they were purchased by the GWR. *North Star* arrived at Maidenhead on a barge on 28 November 1837, almost six months prior to the railway's arrival, and on 31 May 1838 worked the directors' special train.

Initially *North Star* failed to draw more than 16 tons at 40 mph, but Brunel and Gooch discovered that by increasing the size of its blast pipe and discharging exhaust steam up the centre of the chimney, power was increased and coke consumption decreased. Modifications made before Christmas 1838 allowed her to haul 40 tons at 40 mph burning less than one-third of the former quantity of coke. It proved the company's most reliable engine, remaining in service until December 1870 when it was preserved. Unfortunately it was broken up in 1906 though a full-sized reproduction, including a few original parts, was made for the Railway Centenary Celebration at Darlington in 1925.

Sister engine *Morning Star* was delivered on 24 January 1839 and these engines were so satisfactory that a further ten were ordered. All gave good service to the company over lives varying between twenty-three and thirty-three years, and covering an average of approximately 350,000 miles.

Apart from *North Star,* the six Tayleur engines purchased from the Vulcan Foundry were used and on 4 June 1838, when the line opened to Maidenhead, Gooch recorded in his diary,

> I had to begin in a measure to rebuild one half of the stock I had to work with. For many weeks my nights were spent in a carriage in the engine-house at Paddington, as repairs had to be done to the engines at night to get them to do their work next day. The *North Star* being the most powerful one, and in other respects the best, was my chief reliance, but she was often getting into trouble from other causes.

Coaches

Initially there were four classes of four-wheel coaches. These included a posting carriage, which was a clerestory saloon with a central table and cushioned seats all round except at the two central doors. Between the body and underframe were eight rubber air cushions. These fine coaches were little used, the last one being withdrawn in 1856. The other vehicle with outside wheels was a carriage truck for conveying both empty and occupied carriages, normally horse-drawn.

The four-wheel first-class coaches had three compartments, each seating eight passengers, the enclosed bodies hanging over the wheels. Herepath's *Railway Magazine* of March 1838 describes the early GWR first-class coaches:

> We, the other day, paid a visit to Paddington, to see some of the Company's carriages, of whose splendour we had heard so much that we thought the Directors had sunk all regard the proprietors in reckless extravagance. We, however, found nothing to justify our anticipations. The carriages are made very comfortable, but nothing more.

The second-class carriages with the same size body had four compartments, each seating twelve passengers. They were roofed, but had no glass in the openings. Some of these coaches had a wheelbase approximately the same as the rail gauge, which led to very rough riding. Regarding second-class rolling stock Herepath reported, 'We think these carriages preferable to the second class on the Grand Junction, and that the springs in each class are better adapted to the work they will have to do than any we have yet seen.'

Even before the line was opened, Brunel had decided to standardise using six-wheel passenger coaches. These offered a much more comfortable ride and most of the four-wheelers were withdrawn in July 1838. These new first-class coaches appeared like four stagecoaches joined together. They held eight passengers in each compartment. Some of these compartments were subdivided by a central partition with a door, thus offering greater privacy.

The six-wheel second-class coaches were divided into six compartments, each seating twelve passengers on planks 15 inches wide. Having no glass in the windows, they were well ventilated. Unlike the first-class coaches, they had brakes, the guard sitting with the passengers. As the wheels protruded through the floor they were protected by boxes reminiscent of a paddle-steamer and, as they partly coincided with doorways, could cause a passenger to make an undignified exit, made even more painful at some stations where pillars supporting the platform canopy were placed close to the platform edge.

Third-class passengers initially travelled in open wagons, made more luxurious by a hole drilled in the floor to let the rainwater out but unfortunately letting a draught in. Although this seems rather crude, remember that those passengers had hitherto been used to travelling on the outside of stagecoaches. These third-class coaches proved dangerous in an accident as passengers could so easily be thrown out.

When the Bristol to Bath section was opened in August 1840, the *Bath Chronicle* praised the rolling stock:

The carriages are of splendid construction: those of the first class being fitted up with an attention to luxurious comfort which we are told, coach-builders are not in the general habit of putting even into gentlemen's carriages. The second class carriages also afford very excellent accommodation. There is a total absence of the unpleasant jerkings and 'bumpings' which are felt by passengers on other lines and which, indeed, were experienced on the Great Western between Maidenhead and Paddington, until removed by an alteration in the principle of laying down the rails.

Permanent Way

Lines where George Stephenson was engineer used a permanent way consisting of rails carried in iron chairs fixed to stone blocks. Brunel believed riding could be improved by using a different design and advised utilising relatively light rails secured to longitudinal timbers. To hold these beams to gauge, every 15 feet the Up and Down roads were linked by a transom. These transoms in turn were fixed to the line's foundation by vertical piles 12 feet in length. This gave a very rigid track. These piles held the track down securely so that packing could be placed below the longitudinal timbers supporting the rails. However, some of the packing was defective, which meant that the piles actually supported the timbers instead of holding them down and this prevented them from contacting the ground. This led to a switchback road, with rails supported by piles and then dipping down in between.

The engineer Nicholas Wood was asked by the directors to report on the situation and he recommended that the piles be abolished. The directors adopted his suggestion of simply sawing off the piles from the transoms. They also seriously considered dismissing Brunel from his post for making such an expensive error of judgement.

West of Maidenhead the permanent way was modified: the weight of bridge rails – so called due to their inverted U-shape section – was increased from 43 lb/yard to 62 lb/yard and used more substantial longitudinal timbers. From 1843 the road between Paddington and Maidenhead was relaid with even heavier rails, 75 lb/yard, and this proved even better.

The longitudinal sleepers proved superior to the cross variety as in the event of a derailment, which was far from infrequent in the early days, they would keep rolling stock more or less in line. David Joy, locomotive superintendent of the Oxford, Worcester & Wolverhampton Railway, related that a horsebox jumped the rails at 60 mph, but after a mile then re-railed itself at a set of points.

All timber used on the permanent way was kyanised, that is, preserved by being saturated in a solution of bichloride of mercury, a process discovered by Dr Kyan. It was not in use for many years and soon creosote was adopted.

Staff

The original GWR staff began work in June 1838. Apart from engine drivers and firemen, who were appointed by Brunel, clerks, police, conductors, guards and porters were all appointed by the board of directors, or a committee thereof, after a personal interview. Appointments continued to be thus made until 1865.

The police were all sworn constables and actually appointed by 'two or more Justices of the Peace acting within their Jurisdiction' on the nomination of any three GWR directors. They were modelled on the contemporary Metropolitan Police Force and wore a similar uniform. The rules of February 1841 stated:

The duties of the Police may be stated generally to consist in the preservation of order in all the stations and on the line of the railway. They are to give and receive signals; to keep the line free from casual or wilful obstructions; to assist in case of accidents; to caution strangers of danger on the railway; to remove intruders of all descriptions; to superintend and manage the crosses or switches; to give notice of arrivals or departures; to direct persons into the entrance to the stations or sheds; to watch movements of embankments or cuttings; to inspect the rails and solidity of the timber; to guard and watch the company's premises; and to convey the earliest information on every subject to their appointed station or superior officer.

Several current grades of railwaymen, apart from signalmen and the railway police, are descended from them. The best policemen were chosen to manage the switches and received higher pay than 'common constables', in addition to a bonus of £3 or £5 annually for managing their switches correctly. In 1841 Brunel said that the number of police on the GWR averaged 1½ per mile. Although staff were predominantly male, on 25 May 1838 the directors appointed Mary Counsell 'Female Attendant at Paddington'.

In May 1838 the directors decided on the uniform. It was resolved

That the Coats and Waistcoats be made of dark rifle green edged with scarlet of the patterns now chosen.
That the Trowsers be made of dark Oxford mixture of the pattern also chosen.
That the Buttons be gilt and of the size now exhibited as a Pattern.
That the Inspector of Police be distinguished by a red stripe of

an inch and a quarter on the Trowsers.

That sub-Inspectors be marked by an edging on the Trowsers of the same width as the edging of the Coat.

That the Policemen have G.W.R. with a number marked on the stand-up collar in scarlet cloth.

That the Hats of the Policemen be precisely similar to those of the Metropolitan Police.

That the conductor be required to wear a small Badge on the button hole of his Coat with Buttons of G.W.R., not having any Livery.

That Guards have a Frock Coat and Waistcoat with G.W.R. on the fall of the collar.

Trowsers of Oxford Mixture plain.

The boys to have a common close Jacket with Trowsers.

The Porters to have sleeved Jackets with G.W.R. painted on Glazed Hats and a badge with G.W.R. and a number on the arm.

In September 1838 it was decided that porters should wear 'green plush' or corduroy. All men, even porters, wore top hats, those of the police being of beaver with a leather crown and leather sidestays.

Personalities

Isambard Kingdom Brunel was born in Portsmouth, but was educated in Paris and learned more skills from the watchmaker Louis Breguet and machine tool maker Henry Maudslay. He then worked with his father, Marc, on the Thames Tunnel. He crammed a lot of work into each day and this, along with his love of cigars, led to his death at the age of fifty-three. Apart from being engineer to many railway companies, he designed the first steam-powered ships to cross the Atlantic; the docks and suspension bridge at Bristol; and guns and hospitals for the Crimean War.

Daniel Gooch, later knighted, was a skilful locomotive engineer, while in later years, from November 1865 until October 1889, he was the GWR's brilliant chairman. He resigned as locomotive superintendent in 1864 in order to concentrate on laying the first transatlantic cable, this effort earning him a baronetcy. He became Conservative MP for Cricklade, the constituency that included Swindon. He took a great interest in the Severn Tunnel, which he saw through to completion.

The First Accident on the GWR

The first accident on the GWR happened on 25 October 1840. It was still dark and Brunel was waiting on the platform at Faringdon Road station, then the temporary terminus, for an engine to take him to London. Then, to his horror, he saw a Down goods approaching unusually fast. Despite the shouts of Brunel and others on the platform, coupled with the efforts of the guard in the open wagon next to the locomotive containing four third-class passengers (in the early days this class travelled by goods train), the train sped through the station and burst through the closed doors of the engine shed. The driver, seen motionless on the footplate of the 2-2-2 *Fire King*, was killed, and four passengers and the guard were injured. It transpired that the driver was asleep, suggesting that he must have been on duty for many hours to doze on such an uncomfortable place as a footplate.

The GWR was the first railway company to install the electric telegraph. Even before the first section of line was opened, the directors, acting on the advice of Brunel, made an agreement with W. F. Cooke for the trial of his and Professor C. Wheatstone's telegraph between Paddington and West Drayton. The system was certainly in operation by 6 April 1839. It reached Slough in 1843 and was made famous by its speedy announcement to London of the birth of Queen Victoria's second son on 6 August 1844. A few months later it became even more well known when it was the means of arresting a murderer.

On New Year's Day 1845 John Tawell had travelled to Slough with a packet of cyanide of potash in his pocket for the purpose of poisoning a discarded mistress living nearby. He successfully administered the poison in a glass of stout but, to his horror, his victim gave a piercing scream before expiring, thus alarming the neighbours.

He sped to Slough station, caught an evening train and arrived safely at Paddington where he boarded a sixpenny bus to the Bank. After visiting a couple of coffee houses, doubtless with a view to providing an alibi if necessary, he walked to his lodging in Scott's Yard, Cannon Street. Much to his surprise and horror, the next morning he was arrested and in due course tried and hanged at Aylesbury.

Apparently Tawell's train had scarcely left Slough when news of the murder was brought to the station by his ex-mistress's neighbours and his appearance described. A message was handed in at the Slough telegraph office informing the police of the murder and that 'a man in the garb of a Quaker', wearing a long, brown greatcoat was in a specified first-class compartment.

The telegraphic code did not include the letter 'Q' so the clerk, using his intelligence, spelled the word 'Kwaker' and his equally bright colleague at Paddington understood what he meant.

The train was duly met by a plain-clothes sergeant in the GWR police force who spotted the 'Kwaker' from the description given. The telegram was thought to have been insufficient grounds to arrest Tawell, but the sergeant shadowed him home before returning to Paddington. In due course a police officer arrived at Paddington from Slough and, with the sergeant, the arrest was made.

Sir Francis Head wrote in *Stokers and Pokers*, published in 1849:

A few months afterwards, we happened to be travelling by rail from Paddington to Slough in a carriage filled with people all strangers to one another. Like English travellers they were all mute. For nearly fifteen miles no one had uttered a single word, until a short-bodied, short-necked, short-nosed, exceedingly respectable-looking man in the corner, fixing his eyes on the apparently fleeting posts and wires of the electric telegraph, significantly nodded to us as he muttered aloud – 'Them's the cords that hung John Tawell.'

The GWR had the honour of operating the first royal train. The *Illustrated London News* reported on Queen Victoria's first railway journey, which took place on 13 June 1840: 'Queen Victoria abundantly attended by fashionably dressed ladies, took the special train from Slough to Paddington Station on the Great Western Railway line, the whole journey having taken a mere 25 minutes.'

Travelling in a specially built coach, she was driven by Daniel Gooch, with Brunel also on the footplate of the 2-2-2 *Phlegethon*. She enjoyed the experience and on 23 July returned from

Paddington to Slough with Prince Albert, the Princess Royal and the eight-month-old Prince of Wales.

On Christmas Eve 1841, an accident occurred on the GWR which had far-reaching effects on all British railway companies.

The 4.30 a.m. Down goods train from Paddington consisted of Leo Class 2-4-0 *Hecla*, two open-wagon type third-class coaches and a station truck conveying parcels for various stations, followed by seventeen goods wagons.

In the centre of Sonning Cutting it ran into a slip, caused by excessive rain, which had covered the track to a depth of 4 feet. The sudden stop caused the momentum of the goods wagons to crush the passenger wagons against the tender, smashing one coach and seriously damaging the other. Of the thirty-eight passengers, eight were killed outright and seventeen seriously injured.

The report said:

The third class carriages have seats 18 inches high, but the sides and ends are only two feet above the floor, so that a person standing up, either when the train is unexpectedly put in motion or stopped is, if near the side or end, in great danger of being thrown out of the carriage and those sitting near the sides are also in danger of falling; besides which, the exposure to the cutting winds of the winter must be very injurious to the traveller, who, if proceeding from London to Bristol, often remains exposed for ten or twelve hours, a great part of which is in the night-time.

The Board of Trade investigated the conditions of third-class passengers on various railways and the result was Gladstone's

Railway Act of 1844. As it happened, on 3 December 1841 the GWR directors had ordered passenger-carrying vehicles with higher sides and as an interim measure all those in use were boarded up to a height of 4½ feet above the floor.

3

Expansion:
1841–1874

Quickly following the publication of the GWR prospectus, public meetings were held in various places not served by the GWR proposing links with that railway. Although set up as nominally independent companies, they were associated with the GWR, having the same gauge, often sharing the same engineer and being worked by the GWR.

The Cheltenham & Great Western Union Railway (CGWUR) was one such broad gauge line planned to link Cheltenham and Gloucester with the GWR at Swindon. After paying each of the line's opponents – the Thames & Severn Canal and Squire Gordon of Kemble – £7,500 each as 'compensation for damage to be sustained', the Act was passed on 21 June 1836.

Unfortunately for the CGWUR investors were reluctant to risk money in the scheme, which involved a costly Sapperton Tunnel just over a mile in length beneath the Cotswold Hills. Lack of finance prevented the line being constructed as an entity, so initially the section between Swindon and Cirencester was concentrated on. Problems were encountered at Purton when an overbridge failed, fortunately sounds of its cracking giving sufficient warning, but 'a man with his cart and horses [...] had scarcely passed over the crown of the bridge before it fell'. A nearby clay embankment kept slipping in wet weather and delayed the railway's opening. As all the slips were on the east side of the double-track line, it was decided to lay just the permanent way on the Down side and use it for two-way working until the slips were cured.

The CGWUR opened to Cirencester on 31 May 1841 and the town, instead of being at the end of a branch off the Cheltenham line, possessed the company's main station. Connection with Gloucester and Cheltenham was by road.

The embankment continued to slip and early in December 1841 a worried traveller from Cheltenham wrote to the Board of Trade:

> I returned by the railway, and as far as Swindon all was very well, notwithstanding the wet, but from Swindon to Cirencester I was horrified at seeing the road I was passing over, and nothing shall tempt me to do it again. One line of rails has slipped for a mile or two completely away and the trains travel on the other line, which appears just hanging by a thread, and this on a precipice of 40 to 50 feet.

Brunel attempted to cure the trouble by driving a row of piles a minimum of 10 inches in diameter into the embankment, but such was the force of the slip that it sheared them. The resident engineer, Charles Richardson, then excavated 6-foot square holes, 12 feet deep, set 6 feet apart and filled them with stone. His plan proved successful – the rough stones caused sufficient friction to resist the slip.

Richard Boxall, a former pupil of the architect Augustus Pugin, was appointed as the engineer responsible for Sapperton Tunnel.

It was to be made in two sections with an open cutting at the summit level between them.

The first section of the CGWUR, the length from Gloucester to Cheltenham, was opened by the Birmingham & Gloucester Railway on 4 November 1840, the two companies sharing this portion. In 1842 the CGWUR obtained an Act for the authorisation of the sale or lease of its line to either the GWR, the Birmingham & Gloucester or the Bristol & Gloucester Railway. This Act also granted powers to raise an additional capital of £750,000 as Brunel had underestimated its building costs.

Transfer of the CGWUR to the GWR took place on 1 July 1843 and so for just £230,000 the GWR acquired a partly finished line on which shareholders had spent over £600,000. This story was repeated many times in the life of the GWR, that company taking over many smaller companies for less than cost price.

The GWR set to work to complete the CGWUR as it had agreed to have the Standish to Gloucester section, which it was to share with the broad gauge Bristol & Gloucester Railway, ready by April 1844 and powers for being able to repurchase half of the Gloucester to Cheltenham section from the Birmingham & Gloucester depended on the line from Swindon to Gloucester being opened by 21 June 1845.

The route down the Golden Valley from the west portal of Sapperton Tunnel to Stroud was notable for its nine timber viaducts. The line was opened on 12 May 1845, but the Birmingham & Gloucester withheld the use of Gloucester station for accommodating the GWR traffic in retaliation for alleged 'spiteful acts'. This dog-in-the-manger attitude was hardly unexpected as the GWR had prevented the Midland Railway, the new owner of the Birmingham to Bristol line, from laying an independent standard gauge line beside the broad gauge from Gloucester to Standish. The Gloucester station problem was solved by the GWR working its trains from Swindon into a platform that had been used by the Bristol & Gloucester Railway, and which had been added to the north side of the Birmingham & Gloucester terminus.

Following the partial opening of the South Wales Railway on 19 June 1850, the CGWUR became part of the main route from London to South Wales.

The GWR probably made a serious error of judgement in 1845 when it failed to offer the Birmingham & Gloucester a sufficiently high price. Two days later, two of the Birmingham directors chanced to travel from Birmingham to Euston in the same compartment as John Ellis, deputy chairman of the Midland Railway, and he promised to make a better offer if their meeting with the GWR at Paddington proved unsatisfactory. The GWR refused to countenance increasing its offer, so the Birmingham & Gloucester and Bristol & Gloucester became part of the Midland Railway's empire.

Steventon, 10 miles distant, was not an ideal station for Oxford, so on 11 April 1843 the Oxford Railway obtained an Act authorising a branch from Didcot. It was duly built and when Major-General Pasley came to examine the completed line on behalf of the Board of Trade, his only criticism was the insecure state of the bridge carrying the Oxford to Abingdon road, now the A423. Pasley stated the curious reason for haste in building this bridge:

Mr Brunel explained to me that the haste with which this arch was built was caused by the conduct of an individual in possession of part of the ground over which the embankment was carried, who after the site of the bridge had been decided on, erected what he called a 'house', which I saw but should never have guessed the use of, being a small hut of timber framework covered with *brown paper,* with a fireplace in it, for the purpose of claiming compensation from the Railway Company for having diminished the value of his property; and the work was delayed as this person's unexpected claim could not be settled until near the period of the entire completion of all other parts of the railway.

The line opened on 12 June 1844.

Problems overcome, the year 1844 brought forth a great number of broad gauge lines in association with the GWR: the South Wales Railway; Cornwall Railway; Wilts, Somerset & Weymouth Railway and the Oxford, Worcester & Wolverhampton Railway. The GWR itself promoted lines by means of subsidiary companies: the Berks & Hants; Oxford & Rugby and Monmouth & Hereford. Most of these lines obtained their Acts in 1845, while in an 1846 session of Parliament the West Cornwall Railway, the Wycombe Railway and the Great Western & Uxbridge Railway were promoted locally.

In 1848 the GWR achieved an Act for a line from Slough to Windsor with many provisions to protect Eton College: screens or vegetation to offer privacy to the bathing place; masters to have free access to the station to find any scholar; police to patrol the line to prevent access to scholars (men continued to be employed on this duty until October 1886); no intermediate station to be erected 'or passengers or goods taken up' (the GWR directors had learnt their lesson!) without the written consent of the provost.

By 1850 the GWR's temporary London station at Bishop's Road was proving inadequate, so early the following year the directors proposed the construction of a new 'passenger departure shed' to the east of the temporary station and a new 'merchandise building' north of the existing building, the latter to be used as a four-platform 'arrival shed'. By February 1853 the directors believed that the best course would be to erect an entirely new station east of Bishop's Road Bridge.

This new station was designed and constructed under Brunel's supervision and with the assistance of Matthew Digby Wyatt. The *Illustrated London News* of July 1854 commented, 'The principle adopted by them was to avoid any recurrence to existing style and to make the experiment of designing everything in accordance with the structural purpose, or nature of the materials employed – iron and cement.'

Three departure platforms and two arrivals were provided with five carriage-storage sidings between; in later years, these roads proved invaluable for offering space for further platforms to be laid. The two inner platforms were used as auxiliaries, access being via a hydraulically powered drawbridge, thus avoiding passengers having to trudge up and down the steps of a conventional bridge. When both departure platform roads were clear, the drawbridge was lifted from its storage space below the platform and raised approximately 1 foot, enabling passengers to cross from one platform to the other on the level. The narrow subway linking the arrival and departure sides was for station staff only. As had happened at the Bishop's Road station, the various roads were linked by space-saving turntables and traversers.

The four turntables on the siding at the Bishop's Road end of the main departure platform at the new Paddington station were for loading private carriages in which the owners were to travel, but the method of sitting in your own carriage soon died and by 1867 these turntables had been removed. Similar tables for discharging carriages were provided on the arrival side. A sector table released locomotives of incoming trains.

The hydraulic system at Paddington was installed by Armstrong, Whitworth & Co., Paddington being the first to be so equipped on such a large scale. This form of power was used for moving the sector table, larger turntables, passenger drawbridges and carriage traversers in addition to lifting and traction power via capstans in the goods depot.

The chief architectural feature of the new Paddington station was the awe-inspiring train shed, influenced by the Great Exhibition of 1851, but it was also the first large British station to have a metal roof. In *The Life of Isambard Kingdom Brunel* his son, I. Brunel, describes it:

The interior of the principal part of the station is 700 feet long and 238 feet wide, divided in its width by two rows of columns into three spans of 69 feet 6 inches, 102 feet 6 inches and 68 feet, and crossed at two points by transepts 50 feet wide, which give space for large traversing frames. The roof is very light, consisting of wrought iron arched ribs, covered partly with corrugated iron and partly with the Paxton glass roofing, which Mr Brunel here adopted to a considerable extent. The columns which carry the roof are very strongly bolted down to large masses of concrete, to enable them to resist sideways pressure.

The station may be considered to hold its own in comparison with the gigantic structures which have since been built, as well as with older stations. The appearance of size it presents is due far more to the proportions of the design than to actual largeness of dimension.

The pans of the roof give a very convenient subdivision for a large terminal station, dispensing with numerous supporting columns and at the same time avoiding heavy and expensive trusses. The graceful forms of the Paddington station – the absence of incongruous ornament and useless buildings – may be appealed to as a striking instance of Mr Brunel's taste in architecture and of his practice of combining beauty of design with economy of construction.

As Queen Victoria used the GWR frequently en route to Windsor, a suite of royal waiting rooms was provided for her at Paddington, with the convenience of direct access from the carriage approach to the station platform.

The station cost £650,000 and covered 8 acres. Unlike the other major London termini, because it is set in a cutting, Paddington has no imposing exterior façade. The departure side was brought into use on 16 January 1854 and the Up side on 29 May 1854, and demolition of Bishop's Road station was soon finished.

On 10 January 1863 the Metropolitan Railway opened a new Bishop's Road station with a timber overall roof, a connection being made with the Paddington arrival platform by means of a corridor and steps. It gave rise to an interesting curiosity. In June 1866 the morning broad gauge train from Windsor, which ran over the Metropolitan rails to the City, slipped coaches for Paddington, the vehicles freewheeling into the GWR terminus where they were due three minutes after the main train had arrived at Bishop's Road. This working continued for three years.

The Battle of the Gauges

The broad gauge was preferable to standard gauge as it offered larger and more comfortable coaches, as well as faster and more punctual expresses, which conveyed second- as well as first-class passengers. Greater width meant greater stability, which meant that the broad gauge was safer in the event of an accident.

A splendid example of this was shown on 3 January 1852. At Chippenham the stationmaster dispatched an Up goods. Fifteen minutes after the goods had left, the mail arrived and after spending five minutes at Chippenham went on its way. As twenty minutes was considered sufficient time for the goods to get 'far in advance', the stationmaster did not caution the driver (at this period trains were separated by time interval, rather than the more positive distance method used today).

About 7 miles beyond Chippenham, fog had caused rails on the 1 in 100 Dauntsey Bank to become slippery thus causing the heavy goods train to lose adhesion and almost come to a stop. That same fog also obscured the rear lamp on the guard's van and the mail crashed into it at 50 mph. The mail fireman and goods guard leapt out before the collision, but Driver Ellis on the mail remained at his post and received fatal injuries.

Fortunately, due to the splendid stability of the broad gauge, few passengers were hurt, some even remaining asleep throughout the event and only waking after the train had returned to Chippenham. Quite oblivious that they had been to Dauntsey and back, they complained of the lengthy time the train had spent at Chippenham!

When the GWR was in isolation, the fact that its gauge was incompatible with those of most other lines was of no consequence; problems only arose when stations were opened where two different gauges met. The first of these was Gloucester.

It was relatively easy for passengers from Bristol to Birmingham to change trains at Gloucester from the broad gauge Bristol

& Gloucester Railway to the standard gauge Birmingham & Gloucester, as they could simply step across the platform from one train to the other. However, it was a different story for those travelling in the reverse direction. It entailed trudging from the Birmingham & Gloucester platform, situated at the south part of the station complex, to the Bristol & Gloucester departure platform on the north side of the station and, furthermore, making this trek along platforms only 10 to 12 inches in width.

Matters were made more complicated due to the fact that no less than three different local times were used: the Birmingham & Gloucester used Birmingham time; the Bristol & Gloucester, Bristol time and the GWR, London time. Matters were even further complicated when Bristol & Gloucester trains departed, as they frequently did, from their arrival platform!

J. E. McConnell, locomotive engineer to the Birmingham & Gloucester, giving evidence before the Gauge Commission said, regarding passengers:

> We have tried to lessen this inconvenience ... passengers leave their carriage of either gauge and walk round under the shed to the other side where a 'broad' or 'narrow' train stands. The luggage is put into little barrows and conveyed round with them. Delays are, of course, inevitable, but passengers are under cover all the time. We must admit there is great inconvenience to invalids ... Delay is never less than fifteen minutes and often more if carriages and horses have to be transhipped; then the delay is as much as half an hour for an eight coach train.

Gooch had designed several methods of transferring goods between the two gauges, including wagons with wheels sliding on their axles and standard gauge trucks travelling on broad gauge transporter wagons, but he 'never had any faith in any of these plans working in practice'. The only answer was using an army of porters to transfer goods physically from a wagon of one gauge to that of another.

When the Parliamentary Gauge Committee visited Gloucester, J. D. Payne, goods manager of the Birmingham & Gloucester and later general manager of the South Staffordshire Railway, arranged for two trains already dealt with to be unloaded to add to the work, so that the chaos which the break of gauge caused would be the more impressive. Matters were not helped by the inadequate transfer shed which was far too small to handle the volume of traffic it was required to handle.

G. P. Neele wrote in *Railway Reminiscences*:

When members came to the scene, they were appalled by the clamour arising from the well-arranged confusion of shouting out addresses of consignments, the chucking of packages across from truck to truck, the enquiries for missing articles, the loading, unloading and reloading, which his clever device had brought into operation.

In the week ending 25 October 1845, 700 tons were transhipped at Gloucester, though the weekly average was 200–300 tons. Transfer took an average of fifty minutes for a 5-ton wagon and cost a maximum of 3*d* per ton. Nineteen extra porters had to be employed as a consequence of transhipment and the Birmingham & Bristol Railway estimated that the break of gauge cost the company £2,000 annually.

Broad gauge supporters fixed a poster at Gloucester:

Observe – Petition! Petition 50 miles an hour versus 25. Coaches before waggons – the blessing of the broad gauge for the Northern districts. Safety and speed before cramp and delay. Advancement before retreat. The petition will be ready in a day or two. Brunel for ever! Hurrah!

An Act of 1848 permitted the Midland Railway to lay an independent line from Gloucester to Standish and mix the gauge onwards to Bristol, the standard gauge reaching Bristol on 22 May 1854.

The problems experienced at Gloucester were repeated, generally on a smaller scale, at other junctions where differing gauges met.

The commission investigating the gauge problem acknowledged the superiority of the broad gauge but recommended its abolition due to the difficulty, including expense, of widening existing railways. Parliament failed to adopt the commission's recommendations and permitted further broad gauge railways to be constructed. This meant that in due course, the 250 route miles of broad gauge at the end of 1845 were more than doubled to 544 miles by 1860. Additionally there were approximately 78 miles of mixed gauge track capable of accepting trains of either gauge. However, no new broad gauge lines were laid after about 1874.

Locomotive Development

Gooch, the GWR's locomotive superintendent, prepared drawings for future engines based on the successful Star Class design: the 2-2-2 Firefly Class and its smaller version, the 2-2-2 Sun Class. The first railway engineer to adopt standardisation, on 4 April

1840, Gooch wrote to *Sun's* builders, R. & W. Hawthorn & Co., saying:

> I cannot pass the engine in her present state – she not being in conformity with our Drawings and Specifications and thereby totally defeating our main object in forwarding Drawings and Templates, viz., to get our engines so that one part of any engine will fit another.

To further standardisation, drawings were lithographed and sheet iron templates made for parts that needed to be interchangeable. Lithographs and templates were supplied to all locomotive builders who had GWR contracts.

The GWR's first goods engines were the Leo Class 2-4-0s and, like all GWR broad gauge engines, were named, but not numbered. The Hercules Class 0-6-0s were the first GWR engines of this wheel arrangement and the only broad gauge 0-6-0s with outside sandwich frames. Another instance of standardisation, their boilers were identical to those of the Firefly Class.

The first of Gooch's engines to be built entirely at Swindon was the aptly named 2-2-2, *Great Western*. Following running-in trials on 1 June 1846, she ran the 194 miles from Paddington to Exeter in 208 minutes, returned in 211 minutes with a 100-ton train on 13 June 1846 and covered the 77 miles from Paddington to Swindon in 78 minutes, thus averaging almost 60 mph. It was found that she had too much weight on her leading axle, so she was rebuilt as a 4-2-2.

105 standard engines were built between 1840 and 1842 comprising:

sixty-two 2-2-2 passenger engines with a single 7-foot driving wheel
twenty-one 2-2-2 passenger engines with a single 6-foot driving wheel
eighteen 2-4-0 goods engines with 5-foot coupled wheels
four 0-6-0 goods engines with 5-foot coupled wheels.

Engines had sandwich frames, that is ash or oak planking about 3 inches thick covered on each side with ½-inch iron plates bolted on, with triangular apertures cut out to lighten the structure.

In 1841 Brunel and Gooch introduced, in addition to the ordinary whistle, a deep-toned brake whistle to indicate the instant application of brakes.

Early engines burned coke as a smokeless fuel. Early GWR engines consumed 40.6–71.6 lb of coke per mile, but Gooch's standard engines were more economical – the Firefly Class *Mazeppa* hauling a thirteen-coach train weighing 100 tons from Paddington to Chippenham at an average speed of 31 mph and with a coke consumption of 32 lb/mile.

Initially coke ovens were established at West Drayton but were soon superseded by those at Bristol, which supplied the whole of the GWR. Rhondda Valley coal travelled from Cardiff to Bristol by sea. It was a legal requirement that locomotives consume their own smoke, which was why coke was used, but the batteries of coke ovens, being static, were not required to consume their own smoke!

Brunel tried anthracite in locomotive fireboxes but found that it burnt to a powder, which passed through the tubes to the smoke box from where, after a few miles, it had to be cleared. In 1841 Gooch experimented with peat, but it was found that consumption was so great it was uneconomical. The task of admitting air above the fire by means of a deflector plate and using a firebox arch allowed bituminous coal to be used and in 1857 coal replaced coke as a locomotive fuel.

Gooch solved the problem of heavy wear of locomotive tyres and their continual replacement by making them of steel instead of iron, expensive initially, but offering a life of 200,000 miles.

Gooch's most famous class were the Iron Duke 4-2-2s with flangeless 8-foot-diameter driving wheels. Designed in 1847 as an improved *Great Western,* they lasted until the end of the broad gauge in 1892, though actually from 1871 they were replaced by new engines carrying the same name. Tests in 1847 showed the class ran at an average speed of about 53 mph between Paddington and Swindon, hauling 55 tons and burning 35 lb of coke per mile. Tests in 1849 between Paddington and Bristol produced an average speed of 50 mph hauling 53 tons and with a coke consumption of 35 lb/mile. The highest maximum speed recorded was 78.2 mph down the 1 in 100 of Dauntsey Bank between Swindon and Chippenham.

Swindon Works

The GWR initially purchased locomotives and rolling stock from private builders, before realising that it would be more economical to construct them itself, but where to place the works? Land at London or Bristol would have been expensive, whereas agricultural land was cheaper. The closely associated Cheltenham & Great Western Union Railway was to branch off at Swindon and a site here would be approximately midway between the GWR's two termini and also at the junction of the flat and steeper sections of line.

Daniel Gooch, the GWR's locomotive superintendent, sent a letter to Brunel on 13 September 1840 recommending Swindon because:

1 It was at the junction with the Cheltenham line.
2 East of Swindon the line was virtually flat, whereas to the west were 1 in 100 gradients and banking engines could be kept at Swindon.
3 The railway crossed the Wilts & Berks Canal at Swindon giving communication with the Somerset coalfield. The canal and its reservoir at Coate could supply water in an emergency.

On 25 February 1841 the directors agreed to build a factory at Swindon intended just for repair, not for locomotive construction. The stone for constructing the works was obtained from Box Tunnel, though stone for subseque structures was extracted from Fox's Wood Quarry between Keynsham and Bristol. The buildings cunningly had walls consisting of arches, most of which were bricked up, but the design meant that if a new door was required, stones could be removed without the wall collapsing. In 1985 when the works closed, the radiator shop was an eighteenth-century barn of the farm on which the works was built. Double glazing was installed in the 1840s to keep sound out of the office buildings.

The works opened for regular operation on 2 January 1843, with over 423 men being employed. Brunel was convinced that they could erect locomotives at cheaper cost than purchasing them from contractors and the first Swindon-built engine, 2-2-2 *Great Western*, left the works in April 1846. Swindon built its first standard gauge engine in 1855 and transported it to Wolverhampton on a broad gauge wagon. By 1849 the works buildings had doubled in size to cover 14½ acres.

As there was insufficient housing available, the GWR directors built 300 cottages south of the line. Designed by Sir Matthew Digby Wyatt, architect of Paddington station, the streets led off from Emlyn Square, the western ones being appropriately named Bristol, Bath, Exeter and Taunton streets, while those to the east were London, Oxford, Reading and Faringdon streets. Bath Street was renamed Bathampton Street around 1902. Unlike other contemporary artisans' homes, they had a small garden at the front thus giving the street a spacious appearance. At the rear each had a yard containing a wash house and privy. The houses were built by J. & C. Rigby & Co. Although each house had a tap, the water was not always potable and an enterprising fellow was kept busy selling fresh spring water at a halfpenny a bucketful.

Under Wyatt's plans, the occupants had only the locomotive village slipper baths where cleanliness was rationed. If the clocked time of a bath was exceeded, the attendant, from the outside, pulled out the plug.

The GWR was a considerate employer and provided much more than housing. In 1842 G. H. Gibbs, a director, left £500 in his will towards building a school and church for the railway village. The latter, designed in Early English style by Gilbert Scott, cost £6,000, the balance being raised by public subscription as the company was unable to use share capital for that purpose, but until 1850 the GWR covered the vicar's annual stipend of £150. The grave and obelisk of Joseph Armstrong, locomotive, carriage and wagon superintendent, is prominent in the churchyard.

The mechanics' institute was built in Tudor style to provide facilities for mutual improvement classes, a library (no municipal library was established at Swindon until 1943) and a theatre.

In 1845 the GWR opened a school, initially for children of its own employees, but later admitting others. Fees were two pence a week for infants and four pence a week for juniors, but any family with four children at school could send others free. Children of non-GWR parents had to pay a shilling. In 1874 the GWR built a larger school in College Street and in 1881 handed over its 1,600 pupils to the care of the local authority school board.

The GWR Medical Fund provided doctors' surgeries and a dispensary and by 1948 the GWR Medical Fund Society Hospital dealt with a population of 40,000. The GWR even had its own hearse. So excellent was the GWR Medical Fund Society that when Lord Beveridge was planning the National Health Service the GWR scheme was studied in depth and many of its ideas used.

By its nature, working on a railway can be dangerous as there are many opportunities for mishaps. The GWR had a workshop at Swindon to make artificial limbs for its workers who lost their own in the company's service. It is believed that the first user of a GWR prosthetic limb was Harris, run over by a train in 1878 and requiring the amputation of both legs. He was a member of the GWR Medical Fund Society who ordered him 'a pair of legs with sockets'. By the 1930s approximately 4,000 limbs had been manufactured.

The GWR supplied coal and timber to its employees at advantageous prices; coal was delivered, but timber had to be collected. The entrance to the wood wharf was at ground level and the timber tipped down a chute from rail level about 20 feet above. In order to collect the purchase ticket, the attendant lowered a tin can on a piece of string to check whether it was for 'old timber', more expensive, or 'refuse'. In hard times, 'refuse' was ordered, but a penny or two dropped in the tin along with the 'refuse' ticket often resulted in good quality 'old timber' being supplied.

The GWR also supplied the local townsfolk with baths – both swimming and Turkish – and also a park given to the corporation in 1925. GWR employees had their own savings bank in Swindon which offered slightly higher interest than the main banks.

In the 1850s accommodation in the railway village was very short; in some instances ten or twelve people might share two rooms and when the night shift men rose the day men went to bed. The GWR attempted to overcome the problem by building a large three-storey building to accommodate over a hundred single men. Each occupant had his own room, the entrance and kitchen being common. The 'barracks', as it was called, proved a failure, as the young men preferred to lodge in the village where there were fewer restrictions. It was then converted into flats, each family with three rooms, with common washing facilities. This also proved unsuccessful as the families quarrelled. In 1869 peace reigned when it was converted into a Wesleyan Methodist church.

One of the features of Swindon works was the annual trip during the first week in July. This was set earlier than the closure of most factories in order that locomotives and coaches would not be taken from paying passengers at the height of the season a few weeks later. The majority of engines used on the trip trains were stock engines, that is locomotives recently ex-works, while the coaches came from the carriage store. The trip began in 1849 when 500 workmen travelled to Oxford on a special train.

When the works first opened, the hours were 6.00 a.m. to 6.00 p.m., which with meal breaks gave a 57½-hour week.

The unusually loud works hooter was one of the special features of the factory. Men walked in from a distance of 9 miles or more and in the nineteenth century, when personal and domestic timepieces were beyond the pocket of many, an audible warning was necessary in order that men did not arrive late and thus lose pay.

A large bell was used at first but a steam hooter had come into use by 1867, loud enough to be heard at Highworth and Cricklade 6 miles distant. It was blown for ten minutes at 5.20 a.m., three minutes at 5.50 a.m. and one minute at 6.00 a.m. In 1872 Lord Bolingbroke complained that it woke him prematurely from his seat at Lydiard Park 3½ miles to the north-west of the works.

The Local Government Board at first came down on the side of the GWR, but then revoked the hooter's sanction. It was only through the ingenuity of the Hon. F. W. Cadogan, at that time MP for the Cricklade Division which included Swindon, that a simple solution was found. Another hooter was fixed on the roof just a few yards from the banned one and, as the Hon. F. W. Cadogan observed, although the original hooter was not permitted to sound, no injunction had been granted against the second one, which, incidentally, was louder than the first. The beauty of the process was that it could be repeated indefinitely, a fact recognised by the authorities because the matter was allowed to drop.

A writer in 1935 said that the hooter had been heard at Bourton-on-the-Water 25 miles away. In the 1960s, when it was no longer a requirement for workers to be woken, people complained and the hooters were lowered 30 feet so the sound covered a smaller area. The final hooters were ships' sirens.

An example of the care the GWR took of its workforce was that it paid for the many footpaths from the various villages and hamlets to the works to be straightened in order to save its workers time and energy.

Coaches

Following the open goods-wagon type of third-class coach, the GWR designed very severe vehicles for this class of passenger, the walls of which were completely solid wood except for small Venetian vents at the top mostly set alternately with sliding shutters that could be open or closed according to the weather. The only view out was when a passenger stood up and peered through one of the shutters. These cosy coaches seated fifty-nine passengers in a space only 20 feet 9 inches by 8 feet 6 inches, the sixtieth seat occupied by the brakesman. As the door was only 18 inches wide, portly passengers perforce had to enter sideways. Until 1856 these coaches were used on parliamentary trains between Paddington and Bristol.

As we have seen, the state of third-class travellers being carried in open wagons was far from ideal, so the Board of Trade inquired into the conditions that these third-class passengers were subject to. On 1 November 1844 Parliament passed the Regulation of Railways Act requiring railway companies to run at least one train daily stopping at all stations, travelling at an overall average speed of not less than 12 mph and providing passengers an enclosed seat at a fare not exceeding a penny a mile. These trains were known as 'parliamentary trains'. Railway companies thus being no longer able to persuade passengers to use first- or second-class coaches by making third class uncomfortable, ran parliamentary trains at awkward times – such as at night. They were the butt of contemporary jokes.

On 14 March 1845 John Jonathan, a wire worker aged about fifty, travelled to Bath on the 10.10 a.m. third-class train from Temple Meads. On arrival at Bath, a porter found that Mr Jonathan was frozen stiff and unable to leave his open coach unaided, so assisted him to the platform where he expressed a wish for a pint of ale. After the train had departed, the porter, seeing him helpless on the platform, carried him down the stairs to street level and asked one of the urchins who frequented the station to take him to a tavern about 150 yards distant. Before crossing the street outside the station, John Jonathan collapsed and was carried to a chemist's shop while medical aid was sought. Unfortunately the efforts to save him were in vain and he died.

An inquest was held the following day when the jury viewed the very emaciated body. Mrs Jonathan revealed that her husband had suffered illnesses for fifteen years and had been affected with a severe cough on 1 March. As their finances were insufficient to allow both to travel by train, she saw him to Temple Meads station. In an effort to keep warm he wore two pairs of trousers, two waistcoats, two body coats and a woollen scarf. Mrs Jonathan then walked to Bath, arriving about 3.00 p.m. and found him deceased.

The jury brought in a verdict 'that the deceased died by the visitation of God, but his death was accelerated by the inclemency of the weather to which he was exposed in a third-class carriage of the Great Western Railway, the weather being unusually severe for March'. Ironically, a closed third-class carriage was included in the rake of coaches, but Jonathan's son said that his father (presumably ignorant of the Regulations of Railways Act of the previous year) was unaware of any coach for third-class passengers other than the open one.

The jury recommended that the GWR provide more closed accommodation for second- and third-class passengers, asking the directors that the promise, given at their last half-yearly meeting, to close those carriages be quickly carried out.

In return for providing parliamentary trains, the GWR was exempt from paying a passenger tax of 5 per cent on fares for parliamentary trains (this parliamentary fare distinction disappeared with the passing of the Cheap Trains Act in 1883, when all third-class fares were reduced to a penny a mile and most third-class fares were exempt from tax. The Finance Act of 1929 removed tax from all fares).

Some passengers travelling in open third-class coaches, or windowless ones of the second class, wore goggles of fine gauze to protect their eyes from cinders.

In deference to public wishes, from 6 June 1842 the GWR discontinued the practice of locking coach doors on the platform side, though it continued to lock them on the off side. Leaving doors unlocked led to wooden barriers being erected at stations to enable tickets to be checked at the termination, instead of the commencement, of a journey. This system meant that the GWR had to ban friends meeting or seeing passengers off, since tricksters, if asked for their tickets, could reply, 'Oh, we're not passengers, we've just come here to meet some friends.'

With the new system, non-travellers wishing to enter a platform had to be at the station well before the arrival or departure of a train in order to collect a pass written out and stamped by the clerk and then sent to the superintendent, who might be on duty some distance from the booking office.

In 1845 the rolling stock the GWR provided for third-class passengers were iron-sided coaches. They had small four-pane windows at intervals so that when standing one could see out. Unlike the earlier third-class coaches they were illuminated at night, one oil lamp sufficing for a coach 26 feet 8 inches in length. Luggage was carried on the roof. Until 1845 you could travel in your own carriage which was placed on a flat truck.

In July 1850 a first-class coach had body panels made of papier mâché instead of timber and until 1858 nearly all the panels of new coaches were made of this material.

In 1852 the GWR constructed the first eight-wheel coaches used on express passenger trains in Britain. At 38 feet in length, they were nicknamed 'Long Charleys'. The wheels were not arranged on bogies, but axles had limited side-play.

A luxury for second-class passengers in 1859 was the provision of hat cords. Contemporary gentlemen wore top hats which hit the ceiling of the low-roofed coaches, so provision was made for them to be held by the brim, when inverted, between two elastic cords fixed to the ceiling. At the same time, roof rails and tarpaulins were fitted to enable luggage to be carried on the roof. A drawback for footplate crews was that it greatly increased a train's air resistance.

In 1856 foot warmers were supplied to first-class passengers, this benefit being granted to the second class in 1870 and the third in 1873.

An Accident at Salisbury

A not dissimilar accident to that at Faringdon Road happened at Salisbury on 6 October 1856.

A train of thirty-five wagons filled with sheep, oxen and heifers arrived at Westbury and waited there for another goods and the 5.10 p.m. passenger train to pass. To enable the heavy train to climb the gradient of 1 in 70 to Warminster it was divided, the two locomotives at its head taking the first half to Warminster and then returning for the second portion. On the leading engine, *Virgo*, a Leo Class 2-4-0, was driver John Mays and fireman William Symonds, while the second engine, *Bergion*, a Premier Class 0-6-0, was driven by Samuel Nicholson and fired by William Isles.

The foreman of Westbury locomotive depot, knowing that Nicholson had never driven over the line only fully opened three months before, went over to the engine specially to warn him of the tricky gradients on the line, particularly those between Wilton and Salisbury. However John Mays, who had driven every one of the fortnightly cattle trains since opening, said, 'I know all about it; I'll take care.'

Driver Mays stopped at Wylye for water and took the opportunity of reminding Nicholson that stopping at Salisbury was difficult, as just before the terminus was a gradient of 1 in 99 down (we must remember that in 1856 the only brakes available on goods trains were those on the engine and the brake van).

Observers at Wilton said that the cattle train passed through 'at a fast speed' and heard the guard apply his brakes. William Bond, the signalman at the level crossing at the entrance to the GWR yard at Salisbury, seeing the train approaching rapidly, waved a red hand lamp but a train of that weight could not be halted quickly.

Whistling a warning, the leading engine crashed into the buffers of the terminus, carried away 9–10 feet of the platform and burst through the ladies' waiting room, crushing doors, walls and every other object in its path. The brick and stone outer façade of the station was demolished before the locomotives came to a halt.

Driver Mays on the leading engine was unhurt, but his fireman jumped off before the train reached the buffer stops, received a severe blow on his head and was carried to the infirmary. The driver and fireman on the second engine were less fortunate and lay dead between engine and tender. In addition, 108 sheep were either killed outright or slaughtered because of their injuries, the carcasses being auctioned in Salisbury market. Six dealers and drovers in the guard's van escaped with a severe shaking.

As it was feared that the mainly timber-built station might ignite, Stationmaster Duffet, rising to the occasion, obtained a hose and doused the locomotive fires and the portion of the platform that had caught alight. Because of the fire risk, the gas lights were turned off and the only available illumination was a few candles and lanterns.

Mays said that when he shut off steam at the usual place, he heard Nicholson's engine still working either in backwards or forwards gear. In fact, after the accident the leading engine was found with its brakes on and steam turned off while the second engine was in reverse – a well-known method of making an emergency stop.

During the night, Mr Tarr, the branch superintendent, arrived from Trowbridge and handed Mays into police custody. Three days later a jury returned a verdict of accidental death and he was released.

It was the jury's opinion that the GWR directors were censurable in sending out, at night, drivers without an accurate knowledge of the line over which they were to travel. It also recommended that the Salisbury distant signal be set further from the station. Mr Tarr undertook that it would be kept at red until there was no fear of danger.

Another accident on 5 August 1873 reveals more about the methods of working early railways.

As the 1.30 p.m. from Bristol was telegraphed as being twenty-eight minutes late at Warminster, the Salisbury stationmaster, not wishing to delay unnecessarily the 4.35 p.m. mixed train for Chippenham, which conveyed passenger coaches behind the goods wagons as far as Westbury, wired to Wilton for a crossing-order to permit the 4.35 p.m. to proceed to Wilton. His message read, 'The 4.35 Up mixed train ex-Salisbury will cross the 1.30 Down passenger train ex-Bristol at Wilton'. The order was written on the standard form and signed by the Salisbury stationmaster. As a check that the message had been received correctly, it was repeated by Wilton.

The ground switchman at Salisbury, having been shown the order before it was handed to the driver, exhibited the white flag indicating that 'line clear' had been received from Wilton. At this period, the reverse of the later practice took place in that the operator who *received* the signal pinned down the white, or 'line clear' key. The Salisbury switchman released the white disc and sent the 'train on line' signal, followed by one beat on the bell. No answer was given and the switchman was called away to alter points in the yard.

Meanwhile the 1.30 p.m. from Bristol had arrived at Wilton where the long-established rule that if the section ahead was blocked, signals should be kept at danger until the train had been brought nearly to a standstill was disregarded. No starting signals were in use at that period.

James Isaacs, the Wilton stationmaster who had the assistance of just one porter, had some official notices to discuss with the son of Inspector Joseph Liddiard who was travelling on the train and some passengers had asked questions concerning London & South Western Railway connections. As Isaacs had had a harassing time the previous day when a large Bank Holiday fête had been held in Wilton Park with Blondin, the tightrope walker, being the star attraction, in a moment of forgetfulness, the existence of the crossing-order slipped from his mind and he dispatched the train along the single line.

As it left, Isaacs suddenly realised his mistake, threw off his coat and made chase, but was unable to stop it. Unfortunately he forgot the practice of 'flashing' the distant signal in order to attract a driver's attention.

He rushed to the booking office and sent five beats on the bell – the danger signal – but, as mentioned above, the Salisbury switchman was out of his box, and even if he had heard could not have done anything to avert an accident.

The signalman in the nearby London & South Western box heard the bell and alerted the GWR man to the circumstance, but by that time the brake whistles of the two trains were sounding. The collision took place a mile west of the city where the present A30 crosses the railway.

The speed of the mixed train had been reduced to nearly a walking pace and that of the Down passenger to about 15 mph. The front brake van of the 1.30 was wrecked and pushed on the tank of the passenger engine resulting in the fatal injury of Guard Tucker and Driver Thomas Harvey who was on the 4-4-0ST *Homer* instead of his usual Sun Class 2-2-2ST.

Driver Atkins and his fireman on *Gladiator*, a Gooch Standard Goods 0-6-0, jumped off, the driver escaping with a broken leg, his fireman receiving less severe injuries. *Homer* was scrapped, but *Gladiator* was returned to service.

One of the outcomes of the inquiry was that all points at Salisbury were to be worked from the level crossing signal hut. Accordingly a small ground frame was provided outside the signalman's hut. Another recommendation was that trains should be more efficiently braked, but this was not implemented until the change of gauge.

The Bristol & Exeter Railway

Arguably the most important railway associated with the GWR was the Bristol & Exeter, (B&E), an extension of the GWR well into the West Country, though interestingly not one of its initial directors held a similar position on the GWR. Like the GWR, the B&E was opened in stages – to Bridgwater on 14 June 1841, finally reaching Exeter on 1 May 1844. Like many of the companies associated with the GWR, initially it was worked by the larger company to avoid the outlay on locomotives and rolling stock.

The advantage of being worked by a larger company was particularly favourable to a small railway such as a branch line. Although perhaps one locomotive and a couple of coaches would suffice for normal services, the number of passengers requiring to travel on market days and to flower shows would demand more coaches and it would be uneconomical for a small company to buy and maintain extra coaches only used occasionally. Similarly, although one engine could handle traffic, a second would be required when the first was undergoing maintenance or repair. A large company had the resources to deal with these problems.

Although initially the B&E was worked by the GWR, it decided it was large enough to provide its own locomotives and rolling stock so on 1 May 1849 took over working using twenty passenger and eight goods locomotives, plus one very interesting vehicle. This was a combined engine and carriage, designed and constructed by W. B. Adams at the Fairfield works, Bow. It had a vertical boiler above the four-wheel power section while the coach portion accommodated sixteen first- and thirty-two second-class passengers. Initially the B&E's engineer, C. H. Gregory, was in charge of the locomotive department.

The B&E engines were based on Gooch's GWR designs, the passenger engines being smaller versions of the 4-2-2 Iron Dukes and the 0-6-0 goods engines similar to those on the GWR.

James Pearson was appointed B&E locomotive superintendent and naturally wished to put his own stamp on the company.

He designed his own engines, the first being 2-2-2s. In 1853 he produced 4-2-4 express tank engines with 9 feet diameter driving wheels; one reached an authenticated speed of 81.8 mph down Wellington Bank. The B&E locomotive works at Bristol turned out its first engine in 1859. Until about 1860 B&E engines wore a green livery, but onwards were painted black. None were named.

The South Devon Railway

Just as the B&E was an extension of the GWR, so the South Devon Railway (SDR) was an extension of the B&E to Plymouth. Brunel's original plan had been for a flattish route following the coast, but as this involved expensive bridges and viaducts and because locomotives had become better at hill-climbing – an excellent example being the gradient of 1 in 37.7 of the Lickey Incline on the Birmingham & Gloucester Railway – Brunel decided to take a more direct route. This involved climbing for 2½ miles at 1 in 36/98 to Dainton, followed by a descent to Totnes and then the climb of 9 miles up Rattery Bank at 1 in 46/90.

Following the passing of the Act in 1844, Messrs Samuda contacted the directors. The firm had patented an atmospheric railway whereby instead of using locomotive power, a pipe ran between the running rails. Into this pipe a piston slung under a special carriage was fitted and when air was withdrawn, by means of stationary engines set at intervals along the line, from ahead of the piston, atmospheric pressure from behind would propel the special carriage and likewise the train to which it was attached.

Such a novelty appealed to Brunel and he was caught hook, line and sinker. When the SDR's directors sought his opinion, he was greatly in favour of adopting this system. Due to the cost of the pipe, he recommended single line and because a head-on collision using atmospheric working was well-nigh impossible, there would be no danger. Pumping stations were erected approximately every 3 miles along the line.

Using locomotives hired from the GWR, the line from Exeter to Teignmouth opened to passenger traffic on 30 May 1846 and working was extended to Newton Abbot on 30 December 1846 and Totnes on 20 July 1847.

Atmospheric traction was inaugurated on 13 September 1847 when passengers were carried between Exeter and Teignmouth. Brunel's biographer, I. Brunel, recorded in *The Life of Isambard Kingdom Brunel* that

> except when occasional mishaps caused delay, the new mode of traction was almost universally approved of. The motion of the train, relieved of the impulsive action of the locomotive, was singularly smooth and agreeable; and passengers were freed from the annoyance of coke dust and the sulphurous smell from the engine chimney.

Restarting a train from an intermediate station was not quite so prompt as using a conventional locomotive. As an atmospheric train approached a station, the piston left the pipe by means of a self-acting valve.

The biographer continued:

> An arrangement for starting the train rapidly from the station, without help of horses or locomotives, had been brought practically into operation. This consisted of a short auxiliary vacuum tube containing a piston which would be connected with the train by means of a tow-rope and thus draw it along till the piston of the piston-carriage

entered the main atmospheric tube. Some accidents at first occurred in
using this apparatus, but its defects were after a time removed.

The highest speed recorded for an atmospheric train was 68 mph
with a train of 28 tons and an average speed of 35 mph over 4
miles with a load of 100 tons.

Atmospheric working between Exeter and Newton Abbot
continued for eight months until problems grew too great. Leather
seals caused difficulties: the longitudinal seal at the top of the pipe
between the rails was difficult to keep supple as the natural oil was
sucked out by the pipe's inlet and outlet valves. Another problem
was that the pumping engines frequently failed.

The cost of installing atmospheric traction had been nine times
the estimate and working: it cost 3s 1d per mile compared with
just 1s 4d by steam locomotive. Of the initial £426,368, only
£50,000 was recovered from the sale of plant. The consequence
was that the SDR was left with 40 miles of single line, which
otherwise would have been made double, and steeper gradients
than if designed for locomotive working.

The GWR, which temporarily worked the line, had no suitable
engines for the gradients until Gooch designed two 4-4-0STs,
Corsair and *Brigand*, in 1849. A sledge brake was provided
between the coupled wheels. The SDR was able to start paying its
shareholders a dividend in 1851.

Charles Geach, ironmaster of Birmingham, was contracted
to supply engines similar to *Corsair* at a cheaper rate than the
GWR. When his contract expired in 1866, the SDR purchased
these engines and thereby reduced the average cost of a train mile
from 1s 6½d to 9¾d, so the contractor had been on to a good
thing.

Several branch lines were built from the SDR by subsidiary companies. The GWR took over the SDR on 1 February 1876.

The Cornwall Railway

The Cornwall Railway Bill received royal assent on 3 August 1846 to continue the SDR to Falmouth, its major engineering work being the Saltash Bridge over the River Tamar. The depression caused by the Railway Mania made it very difficult to raise funds so the project was temporarily shelved as many shareholders were unable to pay their calls. By 1854 no less than 29,299 of the 56,253 shares had been declared forfeit through non-payment.

The contract for the bridge was let in January 1853 and work completed in February 1859. Plymouth to Truro opened to passengers on 4 May 1859. In addition to the Saltash Bridge, the Cornwall Railway had no less than thirty-four timber viaducts, mostly set on masonry piers. These viaducts were cleverly designed so that any timber beams could be replaced easily without the need to close the line to traffic.

The Cornwall Railway never paid a dividend and the company was dissolved in 1889.

The West Cornwall Railway

The West Cornwall Act received royal assent on 3 August 1846, the same day as the Cornwall Railway. It authorised a line to continue from Truro on to Penzance. As with the Cornwall Railway, difficulties were experienced with shareholders not paying their calls. It opened as a standard gauge line from Redruth to Penzance on 11 March 1852, the missing link, Truro to Redruth, being opened on 25 August 1852.

Just as Brunel had brought trouble to the SDR, so he introduced problems to the West Cornwall Railway. Unfortunately he recommended the use of Barlow rails, also in use on the Oxford, Worcester & Wolverhampton Railway and the South Wales Railway. Barlow rails were in the form of an inverted 'V' with prongs to hold the rail secure in ballast without the use of timber. It was a case of 'cheap proving dear' as in practice they were unsatisfactory and had to be replaced by Vignoles flat-bottomed rail spiked directly to sleepers.

This rail also proved unsatisfactory as it cut into the sleepers. In 1862 double-headed rails were adopted using a special type of chair designed by Brunel which held the lower surface of the rail 1/32 in clear, thus avoiding any indentation and allowing the rail to be inverted for further use when the upper side was worn.

The Cornwall Railway was authorised to require the West Cornwall Railway to lay broad gauge. When it made this demand in 1864, the West Cornwall lacked sufficient capital to do this and so was forced to transfer its property to the Associated Companies (the GWR, B&E and SDR), though the West Cornwall Railway continued a nominal existence until 1948.

The Oxford, Worcester & Wolverhampton Railway

The Oxford, Worcester & Wolverhampton Railway (OWWR) Act of 1845 authorised a broad gauge line from the GWR at Oxford to the Grand Junction Railway at Wolverhampton. Brunel severely underestimated the cost and the GWR guaranteed the additional capital required. The line opened in 1853 as a mixed gauge line, though no regular broad gauge trains were ever run. The use of the standard gauge meant that trains were unable to run through to Paddington until 1861 when the line was mixed between Oxford and Paddington.

The 887-yard-long Mickleton Tunnel, later known as Campden Tunnel, caused the contractor trouble. Although started in 1846, in June 1851 the contractors, Messrs Williams and Marchant, ceased work. The OWWR took possession and handed the contract to Messrs Peto & Betts. The original contractor, Marchant, objected and kept his men on guard. Brunel then arrived with an army of navvies to take possession. As Marchant heard of this intention and expecting a fight, he asked two magistrates to attend:

> The magistrates were early on the ground, attended by a large body of police armed with cutlasses. Mr Brunel was there with his men, and Mr Marchant, the Contractor, also appeared at the head of a formidable body of navigators. A conflict was expected, but happily through the prompt action of the magistrates, who twice read the Riot Act to the men, they were dispersed.

The following day, a 2,000-strong army of Peto & Betts's men were assembled from various parts of the line and marched that night to the tunnel, arriving in the early hours of the following morning. Marchant and his hundred navvies, overawed by the 2,000-strong Brunel army, decided to come to an agreement. The Battle of Mickleton Tunnel was over and troops from Coventry, who had been sent for to back up the police, arrived to find that all was at peace.

The opening of the line between Wolvercot, Oxford and Evesham was announced for 7 May 1852, but when, a few days before, Captain Galton made the Board of Trade inspection he found that although the standard gauge was complete, several short sections were without mixed gauge. He also made other criticisms and the board ordered that opening should be deferred for a month.

When Captain Galton returned on 28 May and expressed a wish to travel the length of the line on the broad gauge, he was informed that the ballast below the broad gauge rail had been insufficiently packed to allow the passage of an engine. Captain Galton was then forced to order that the opening would 'be attended with danger to the public using the same, by reason of the incompleteness of the works and permanent way'.

He returned on 2 June, made his trip on the broad gauge and sanctioned opening. This occurred on 4 June 1853.

In order to carry out its statutory obligations the OWWR added broad gauge rail between Evesham and Dudley, but there were no broad gauge sidings. It also doubled parts of the line between Evesham and Wolvercot, but when Captain Galton made his inspection he found the new Up line between Evesham and Honeybourne just standard gauge but the Down mixed gauge. He believed this variety, double line on one gauge and single on the other, dangerous to the public and ordered the OWWR to postpone opening. Disobeying, the OWWR inaugurated its line, explaining that it had no intention of working on the broad gauge. Then, shortly after opening, the traffic manager submitted the timetable to the Board of Trade for its approval of the parliamentary train provision. Unfortunately for the OWWR, a sharp-eyed civil servant spotted that two trains crossed on the so-called single line between Evesham and Honeybourne.

The Board of Trade was tardy in taking legal action and it was not until March 1854 that it obtained an injunction restraining the OWWR from using the Up line between Evesham and Honeybourne until it had been sanctioned by the Board of Trade. Penalty for use was £20 a day. The Up line was then closed to passenger traffic and single line working from Evesham to Handborough resumed.

Month by month Captain Galton re-inspected the line and made the same comments. The OWWR kept claiming that the use of the line would be quite safe, that no broad gauge trains would ever be run and that the company had no cash to lay the extra rail.

The Board of Trade was determined to see that the terms of the Act of Parliament were complied with. Realising that it was beaten, the OWWR eventually found funds to lay the third rail.

In 1854 a spur was built from the London & North Western Railway's Bletchley to Oxford branch to offer the standard gauge OWWR trains through running to Euston.

By the end of 1854 the OWWR's finances were in a parlous state and it won for itself the nickname 'The Old Worse & Worse'. Its locomotive stock was in a deplorable state. Some was owned by the OWWR, some by a contractor and some by the London & North Western Railway. On 18 October 1855 the evening Down express arrived six hours late caused by no less than four engine failures. The 6.45 p.m. from Oxford to Wolverhampton was rostered to have been hauled from Worcester by No. 24, but her regulator had failed, so the driver of the 6.45 was compelled to continue on with No. 14, which had brought the train from Oxford and was really supposed to have finished its day's work at Worcester.

At Hartlebury the tyre of No. 14's near trailing wheel jammed against the firebox, so the stationmaster telegraphed to Kidderminster for a replacement engine. No. 25 was sent, but nearing Hartlebury its driver observed warning lights, reversed and 'lost his regulator'. As there was no other method of shutting off steam he proceeded to Worcester and reported.

Joy himself started off as soon as he could on No. 10, arrived at Hartlebury and was about to start when the gauge glass broke; when he attempted to close off steam from the gauge, one of the studs blew out. The result was that another engine had to be sent from Worcester and eventually took the train onwards at 3.00 a.m., six hours and eight minutes late.

David Joy had been appointed in May 1852 as locomotive superintendent to C. C. Williams who won the contract to work the OWWR until 1 February 1856. Unusually OWWR locomotives were initially lettered rather than numbered.

The 'Old Worse & Worse' nickname certainly expressed some truth, as David Joy wrote in his diary:

I was once on an engine (No. 23, Driver Joe Burt) with a bolted crank, known to be gone, and, on leaving Pershore with our train, I recognised the peculiar bump, which quietened down as it always did on getting into speed, but I told the driver the crank was gone, and so it proved on arriving at the running shed with the work done. On backing, the wheels opened and the engine dropped off the rails.

On another occasion he recorded a hair-raising experience:

We had another special, and took up to Oxford two engines and 22 carriages. I was on the leading engine, and they had sent down the line no notice of our coming. It was a lovely summer's evening. Suddenly slipping under the bridge the other side of Evesham at about 35 miles per hour, we saw the road lifted eight inches both sides, a longish sleeper under it. There was but time to whistle the men away, and to await the result. We went up, then down, like a horse over a gate.

71

In 1856 a new board of directors was elected and successfully managed to lower working expenses from 68 per cent of income in the first half of the year to 51 per cent in the second half, and only 43 per cent a year later. When the new board took over, only twenty-two of the forty-two locomotives were fit to run, but by 1857 the company had fifty-one, all in good working order.

In August 1858 the OWWR experienced a very serious accident. An excursion from Wolverhampton to Worcester carried 767 adults and 739 children in a train of thirty-seven coaches and two vans hauled by two engines. On the outward journey its weight caused a screw coupling to break on three occasions and on the second of these the side chains also snapped.

For the return trip two trains were provided. When the first stopped at Round Oak, the rebound of the buffers caused a coupling and side chains to fracture. The seventeen packed coaches ran down the gradient of 1 in 75 to strike the second train. Fourteen were killed and fifty seriously injured.

The train's guard claimed that he had applied the brake in his van, but it was believed that he was not occupying his van when the train ran back and the brake was certainly off at the time of impact.

At this period, drivers were unable to apply brakes on passenger trains, this function being carried out by one guard, or several, screwing down hand brakes, with the driver signalling to the guards by whistle.

This accident caused the OWWR to experiment with patent brakes, but they were not adopted.

The OWWR became friendly with the standard gauge Newport, Aberavon & Hereford Railway and plans were made for amalgamation and also the purchase of the Worcester & Hereford Railway. The three companies united in 1860 under the name of the West Midland Railway. With the completion of the 1,567-yard-long Colwall Tunnel and the 1,323-yard-long Ledbury Tunnel, the Worcester & Hereford opened on 13 September 1861 and two weeks later the completion of mixed gauge on the GWR between Reading and Paddington gave the GWR access to the OWWR and much of South Wales. The West Midland Railway amalgamated with the GWR in 1863.

The South Wales Railway

In 1844 the prospectus of the South Wales Railway (SWR) was issued. The line was to run from the Cheltenham & Great Western Railway at Standish, with a bridge across the Severn, and then through Newport, Cardiff and Swansea to Fishguard, thus attracting Irish traffic.

The route west of Newport caused no contention, but Monmouthshire folk believed the county would be better served if the line to the east went via Monmouth and Gloucester. The Admiralty opposed a bridge over the Severn, so in 1845 Parliament only sanctioned the line west of Chepstow.

Charles Russell, the GWR chairman, doubled as chairman of the SWR. The GWR took on a perpetual lease of the SWR. Construction began in 1846 at Chepstow, Newport, Neath and Swansea, but then financial difficulties caused by the Railway Mania set in and the directors decided to concentrate on the line east of Swansea. On 31 May 1848 the 1,200-foot-long timber viaduct across the River Usk at Newport, which was almost complete, ignited and was totally destroyed. In 1849 the effects of the Great Famine in Ireland showed that Irish traffic would not be profitable so the two connecting railways in Ireland, partly funded by the SWR, also curtailed their schemes.

Chepstow to Swansea opened on 18 June 1850 with the locomotives and rolling stock provided by the GWR having to be ferried over from Bristol, there being as yet no rail link. No goods traffic was handled for the first few weeks and no mineral traffic ran until 1853.

On 19 September 1851 the line opened from Gloucester to a temporary station, Chepstow East, close to the later junction of the Wye Valley Railway, horse-buses conveying passengers across the Wye to Chepstow station on the other side. The temporary station was necessary as Chepstow railway bridge was incomplete.

This bridge was an unusual structure as one end was on a cliff, while the other bank was low and required a viaduct of three spans. The 300-foot-long span across the Wye was unusual and provided a basis for the later Saltash Bridge. The river span consisted of girders supported by suspension chains hung from a horizontal 9-foot-diameter circular tube resting on piers approximately 50 feet above rail level. The tubes, very slightly arched to improve their appearance, prevented the chains dragging the piers inwards. A single line bridge opened on 19 July 1852 and the second on 18 April 1853. Before the opening of the railway, the journey from London to Swansea, partly by railway and partly by coach, took fifteen hours, but with the opening of the railway the journey took only five hours and the trip was carried out in much more comfort (the main river spans of Chepstow Bridge were replaced with steel trusses in 1962).

The line was extended from Swansea to Carmarthen on 11 October 1852, to Haverfordwest on 2 January 1854 and to Neyland on 15 April 1856 from where passengers and goods were ferried to Pembroke Dock. Neyland, in a sheltered position and having deep water, was made a port by Brunel. Ferries ran to Waterford and Cork. Cattle formed an important traffic, but the expected transatlantic liner service failed to materialise, even Brunel's ship *Great Eastern* only making a few trips. The SWR was amalgamated with the GWR on 1 August 1863.

The SWR was the first main line to be converted from broad to standard gauge, the work being carried out in 1866. A memorial for conversion, signed by 269 firms, had been received by the GWR directors. Most of the track consisted of bridge rail on longitudinal sleepers, kept to gauge by transoms. Narrowing the gauge consisted of disconnecting one end of a transom, sawing off around 2 feet 3½ inches, slewing the rail and its sleeper and refixing the transom. On double track it was the inner rails which were moved so as not to leave a gap between coach and platform.

For work on the actual conversion, the line was divided into lengths of about 4 miles, and each length had a depot set up with permanent way fittings, tools, a smith's shop, kitchen and also sleeping accommodation if none was available locally. The railway provided oatmeal for making a strengthening drink called 'skilly'. A pound of oatmeal was sweetened with half a pound of sugar. It possessed greater thirst-quenching properties than beer, cider, or spirits and gave the men more stamina.

To assist local platelayers, men were brought in from other parts of the system, assembled at Gloucester and taken by special train to their appointed length to begin at daybreak on 1 May.

The Up line was converted first, a limited service run both ways using the Down. On 12 May, when the Up line was completely standard gauge, all broad gauge stock was moved on the Down line to Swindon. As Swindon was unable to accommodate all these vehicles, most of the wagons were sent to the Down line between Newbury and Hungerford, which had been turned into a storage siding, all traffic between these stations using the Up line. Stock was gradually sent to Swindon to be broken up or converted to run on the standard gauge. Private owner wagons were returned to their owners, and if the owner's sidings were full trucks they were spread fanwise over the owner's property by successive slewings of the siding from which they were pushed. The SWR Down line was converted on 22 May when double line working was resumed.

The Cheltenham & Great Western Union Railway necessarily had to be converted too. This was also done one line at a time. The Didcot to Swindon section had been converted in February 1872.

The Wilts, Somerset & Weymouth Railway

Another line associated with the GWR was the Wilts, Somerset & Weymouth Railway (WSWR). It covered much of Wessex, running from junctions near Chippenham and Bath through Yeovil and Dorchester to Weymouth, with branches to Devizes, Salisbury, Radstock and Bridport.

A lengthy line through mainly agricultural country, it took a long time to complete; in fact the line through Bradford-on-Avon was not opened until 1857, although the station had been finished in 1848!

The WSWR Act was passed on 30 June 1845 and then, like so many other companies, suffered from the financial crisis following the Railway Mania as many shareholders were unable to pay the calls on their shares.

The WSWR was interested in the welfare of its navvies, the company offering to pay for one or more chaplains while a sick club was established for workmen. Another condition in a contract stated that the contractors agreed to not paying their workmen at beer shops or public houses. In July 1849 Brunel wrote a severe missive to contractors building the Radstock branch as he had discovered the 'truck' system was being used, whereby payment was made in goods, or tickets that could be exchanged for goods at truck shops. Supplies offered at truck shops were often bad, highly priced and light in weight.

The first section of line, which ran from Thingley Junction near Chippenham to Westbury, opened on 26 August 1848, but the line did not reach Weymouth until 15 January 1857. Following opening, the GWR took the opportunity of running excursion trains there in addition to the regular services. That Whitsun, 1,400 trippers enjoyed the 'sea breezes, ships and steamers' (*Dorset County Chronicle*).

The Lubbock Act of 1871 introducing four statutory Bank Holidays – Christmas, Easter, Whitsun and the first Monday in August – gave the Weymouth tourist trade a boost. Railways brought to Weymouth, and similar resorts, a different type of person to those who had come previously. The stagecoaches could only carry a maximum of 300 passengers to Weymouth each week, and only professional classes and gentry could afford the time and fares, but the coming of the railway offered cheap and speedy travel to the masses.

Weymouth welcomed the WSWR, as the opening of the London & Southampton Railway in May 1840 had resulted in the Channel Islands packets being diverted from Weymouth to Southampton on 26 May 1845 and it was hoped that the coming of the railway to Weymouth would signal their return.

The incomplete WSWR was sold to the GWR on 14 March 1850 and was converted to standard gauge during the long days of June

1874. The whole task of narrowing the 110 route miles, about 30 miles of which was double track, was amazingly completed in five days with 1,800 men.

The Berks & Hants Railway

The GWR promoted the Berks & Hants Railway as a subsidiary company. It was the outcome of an attempt by the London & South Western Railway to build a branch from Basingstoke to Newbury and Swindon, the GWR responding with plans for a branch from Pangbourne to Newbury. Parliament threw out both schemes, though the House of Lords' committee preferred that of the GWR. Charles Russell, the GWR chairman, wrote to his London & South Western contemporary, William Chapman, proposing a joint mixed gauge line from the Reading area to Basingstoke with a branch to Newbury, but the LSWR rejected this suggestion.

The GWR decided to extend the project and reach Hungerford and the Bill was passed in 1845. In the 1846 session of Parliament it was planned to extend westwards from Hungerford to Westbury to link with the Wilts, Somerset & Weymouth Railway. Branches were also to be made to Marlborough and Devizes. It was intended that this line, and part of the WSWR plus a new line, the Exeter Great Western from Yeovil to Exeter, would create a shorter route to Exeter.

At the same time, the LSWR promoted a rival line from Basingstoke to Salisbury and on to Exeter. As the Exeter Great Western was opposed by both the LSWR and the Bristol & Exeter, it failed to get through Parliament. Due to the difficulty of raising funds following the Railway Mania, the scheme was dropped.

Meanwhile work on the Berks & Hants proceeded and in August 1847 Brunel reported the works as 'all but completed' and that the temporary terminus at Hungerford would not hinder a future extension to Westbury. The passenger line to Hungerford opened on 21 December 1847, goods not being handled until a year later.

The Basingstoke line was delayed due to LSWR hostility, but in due course a broad gauge terminus was built at Basingstoke alongside that of the standard gauge LSWR and the branch opened on 1 November 1848.

The single-track broad gauge Berks & Hants Extension Railway received its Act in 1859 and opened between Hungerford and Devizes on 11 November 1859. Its name was interesting as unlike its parent company it did not enter Hampshire at all and only ran in Berkshire for 2 miles.

The Metropolitan Railway

As a significant number of GWR passengers, or potential passengers, had the City as their destination, a rather faster method was required than passing along busy, crowded streets from Paddington. The answer was the Metropolitan Railway, the world's first underground passenger-carrying line, but *The Times* of 30 November 1861 was not encouraging. It described the scheme as 'a subterranean railway suggestive of dark, noisome tunnels, buried many fathoms deep beyond the reach of light or life'. The line opened from Bishop's Road, Paddington, to Farringdon Street in the City on 10 January 1863. By then *The Times* was much more encouraging, stating the Metropolitan to be 'the greatest engineering triumph of its day ... ingenious contrivances for obtaining light and ventilation are particularly commended ... the novel introduction of gas into the carriages is calculated to dispel any unpleasant feelings which passengers, especially ladies, might entertain against riding for so long a distance through a tunnel.'

The *Illustrated London News* reported:

> It was calculated that more than 30,000 persons were carried over the line in the course of the day. Indeed, the desire to travel by this line on the opening day was more than the directors had provided for; and from nine o'clock in the morning till past midnight it was impossible to obtain a place in the up or Cityward line at any of the mid stations. In the evening the tide turned, and the crush at the Farringdon-street station was as great as at the doors of a theatre on the first night of some popular performer. Passengers were unanimous in favour of the smoothness and comfort of the line.

The Metropolitan Railway was constructed on the cut-and-cover method by the expedient of cutting a deep trench in a road, laying track in it and then reinstating the street by covering the trench with a roof.

A mixed gauge line, its Act empowered the GWR to subscribe £175,000 and an unusual feature was that the City of London subscribed £200,000 towards the million pounds required though normally public bodies did not invest in railway companies. Around this time a new meat market was being established at Smithfield and the GWR and Metropolitan Railway leased its basement for a goods station; in fact GWR condensing steam locomotives continued to work through to Smithfield until July 1962.

As early as November 1861 the GWR had agreed to work the line. As most of the line was in a tunnel, the line's chief engineer, Sir John Fowler, designed a locomotive with a fire to heat firebricks and these in turn would heat the boiler and retain the steam. The 2-4-0T was known as 'Fowler's Ghost'. It was tested on the GWR main line in 1861 and ran out of steam after 7½ miles. The GWR's locomotive engineer, Daniel Gooch, then designed a special locomotive, his last as it happened, which produced less smoke than normal. The answer was a 2-4-0 well tank engine fitted with condensing apparatus. They were the first condensing locomotives in the country and the only broad gauge engines built for the GWR with outside cylinders. Flaps, worked by rods from the footplate, sent exhaust steam up the chimney when working in the open or directed it into the tanks when in a tunnel. The water in the tanks became overheated and very often it was necessary to exhaust into air in the tunnel.

This happened all too frequently and on 7 October 1884 *The Times*, reporting a journey from King's Cross to Baker Street, likened it to 'a mild form of torture which no sane person would undergo if he could help it'. Despite all these fumes issuing from its locomotives curiously the Metropolitan banned smoking in its coaches, though this ruling was overturned in 1874 as a belated result of an amendment to the Railway Regulation Act of 1868, which required all railways to provide a smoking carriage on every train.

For carrying Metropolitan Railway passengers, the GWR provided forty-five eight-wheel broad gauge coaches. Six of these were the ten-year-old Long Charley composites, but the remainder were a new design. A new departure for the GWR was that all were illuminated by gas carried in rubber bags on the roof. The line was worked by block telegraph and four trains were run each hour.

Right from the start, the Metropolitan Railway was one of the first railway companies to provide cheap fares for workmen.

The GWR and the Metropolitan Railway soon began to quarrel and on 18 July 1863, hoping to force its own way, the GWR gave notice that it would cease working the line on 30 September. Unperturbed, the Metropolitan Railway said it would take over working on 1 October. The GWR replied stating it would withdraw on 10 August. Still unperturbed, on 11 August the Metropolitan Railway ran services with standard gauge stock borrowed from the Great Northern Railway (GNR).

Archibald Sturrock, locomotive superintendent of the GNR, had been the first manager of the GWR Swindon works. He quickly fitted some GNR locomotives with condensing apparatus.

The Metropolitan Railway's relations with the GWR improved in the autumn and the GWR initiated a service of through broad gauge trains between Windsor and Farringdon Street. The GWR agreed to work over the Metropolitan Railway exclusively on the standard gauge from 1 March 1869 which allowed the Metropolitan to lift its broad gauge rails. The GWR trains were extended to Aldersgate from 1 March 1866 and to Moorgate from 1 July 1866.

The Hammersmith & City Railway

The mixed gauge Hammersmith & City Railway opened from a junction with the GWR, at what is now Westbourne Park station, to Hammersmith on 13 June 1864. Built by the GWR and Metropolitan Railway it was set up as a separate company. The Hammersmith &

City Railway was worked by the GWR on the broad gauge until April 1865 when the Metropolitan Railway took over working, and the GWR broad gauge trains just worked to and from Kensington, Addison Road until 1869 when the broad gauge rails were lifted. The line had become the joint property of the Great Western and Metropolitan companies on 1 July 1867. Both owners operated services with their own stock.

The line was converted to electric working in 1906, the GWR erecting a power station at Park Royal for powering trains and also for lighting purposes in the Paddington area. Some trains were worked by electricity on 5 November and the entire service between Hammersmith and Addison Road and the City electrified on 1 January 1907 using joint stock. The multiple-unit cars were of Metropolitan design, numbered in that company's series and maintained by the Metropolitan.

Locomotives

Following the appearance of the Iron Duke Class engines in 1847 no new express broad gauge engines appeared apart from their renewals, which were virtually the same engines but fitted with a cab.

The GWR locomotive stock was swollen by the addition of B&E and SDR engines. B&E engines were given GWR numbers 2001 to 2095, while those of the SDR received numbers 2096 to 2180. Some of the names of the ex-SDR engines were the same as those of the GWR proper, so there were many cases of two GWR engines with the same names.

Some of the engines taken over were life-expired and were replaced in 1876 by Joseph Armstrong fitting ten Swindon-built standard gauge 0-6-0STs, with broad gauge axles. Proving

successful, more were built and in 1884 eight others were
withdrawn from standard gauge working and converted to the
broad gauge to alleviate the shortage of goods engines. In order
to make them better for use on passenger service, some had the
coupling rods between the driving and trailing wheels removed
thus turning them into free-running 0-4-2STs. Some standard
gauge 0-6-0s were also converted to run on the broad gauge and
given broad gauge tenders which looked odd against a narrow
standard gauge cab.

The first convertible passenger engines were Dean's 2-4-0Ts
and when the Cornishman was established to run non-stop
between Exeter and Plymouth, as these engines did not carry
sufficient water, three were converted to tender engines, the
first to run regularly west of Newton Abbot, as the SDR stock
had consisted entirely of tank engines.

As more passenger engines were required for the SDR and
Cornish lines, a convertible 0-4-2ST was built, but as they
had proved unsteady, the final engine in the class, No. 3560,
was given a trailing bogie with Mansell wooden wheel centres
normally only used on coaches. In an attempt to make it more
stable, short side and back tanks replaced the saddle tank.
Unfortunately this modification did not cure the problem and
following a derailment between Doublebois and Bodmin Road
in April 1895, their boilers were imaginatively turned back to
front and they became 4-4-0 tender engines.

In the 1880s the London & North Western Railway and the
North Eastern Railway were experimenting with compound
engines whereby the steam was used twice. In 1886 Dean built
a four-cylinder compound 2-4-0 No. 8 but it proved a dismal
failure.

E. L. Ahrons in *Locomotive and Train Working in the Latter Part of the Nineteenth Century*, recalls one such disastrous episode when having a footplate ride on No. 8:

One day the Hawthorn class 2-4-0 *Acheron* was coupled to the 3.00 p.m. Temple Meads to Paddington and seeing the weight of the heavy train, Driver Jones sent the usual SOS for piloting help. He was instructed to proceed to Bath, where he would find the new compound engine waiting to help him on to Swindon up the two banks of 1 in 100.

At Bath No. 8 was attached in front of *Acheron* to the great disgust of Driver Jones who scented trouble, but there were plenty of men to help him out, for in addition to the trial driver and fireman, the chargeman fitter and two other individuals were on No. 8's footplate. Jones's instructions were to give *Acheron* only sufficient steam to keep it going, and leave the work of pulling the train to No. 8.

For about 5 miles all went well, until we reached a point about 10 yards outside the western end of Box Tunnel, when two loud explosions were heard, and amid the roar of escaping steam we entered the tunnel. It was pitch dark, and a rain of fragments of cast iron mixed with large gun-metal nuts was projected against the roof of the tunnel, from which they rebounded like shrapnel on to the footplate. The position was distinctly uncomfortable; no one could tell what had happened, but the driver dare not shut off steam or the train would have 'stuck' on the 1 in 100 rise, for had this occurred, all the efforts of Mr Jones and the *Acheron* would have been useless.

As a matter of fact, No. 8 had smashed to bits three of her four pistons and cylinder covers, the fragments and nuts from which had broken the ports and been blown out of the chimney. Luckily no one was hurt, but one or two of us were hit on the shoulders by gun-metal nuts. The fourth piston – one of the high pressure ones – was fortunately intact, and by keeping steam on we just managed to crawl out of the Corsham end of the tunnel, the *Acheron* keeping the train moving.

At Chippenham we were pulled off by a goods engine that happened to be there, and after taking down the motion, we were ignominiously towed home to Swindon about supper time.

As the train emerged from Box Tunnel I happened to look back at the other engine, and to this day can recall to mind the pained expression depicted on the feature of *Acheron*'s driver, as he hung over the side of his cab. Mr Jones was, as a rule, a very taciturn individual, and on this occasion thought a good deal more than he said, but I was afterwards told that 'Jones on compound engines' was worth hearing if only on account of its extreme pungency of expression.

No. 8 was repaired and stronger pistons were put in, but the same thing happened again. For some reason it appeared that unequal expansion of the piston roads caused excessive strains in the piston heads.

In 1888 two large convertible 2-4-0s were built for working this heavy 3.00 p.m. Bristol to London train. They were the most powerful machines that the GWR had built to date. The last convertible appeared as late as August 1891, 2-2-2s to replace the Iron Dukes.

New engines appeared on the standard gauge. In 1866 Joseph Armstrong built the Sir Daniel Class 2-2-2 for express passenger working and it is interesting to record that when, by the end of the century passenger trains had become too heavy for them to handle, most of this class was reconstructed as o-6-os, thus extending their lives by about ten years.

For stopping trains the 111 Class 2-4-os were built in 1863, goods trains being handled by o-6-os. Passenger tank engines were either of the 2-4-oT or o-4-2T design. Interestingly, the former were constructed at Swindon and the latter at Wolverhampton. Several 2-4-oTs were fitted with condensing apparatus for working through the tunnels on the Metropolitan Railway. The Locomotive Department adopted the policy of using tank engines for long journeys thus saving the cost of providing a tender, having a greater adhesive weight available. At the end of a journey they were turned in order to run chimney-first.

Ahrons recalls that around 1884 no broad gauge pilot engine was stationed at Didcot, so if a broad gauge engine broke down between London and Swindon, a very rare occurrence, a standard gauge engine was used to tow it onwards.

Until Armstrong took charge in 1864, standard gauge engines were less powerful than those on the broad gauge, but from then on tractive effort was approximately the same, though the broad gauge boilers were considerably larger and thus held a greater reserve. The GWR was one of the last important railways in the country to provide footplate crews with shelter, William Dean providing them from 1878. Dean's 2-2-2s built as Iron Duke replacements, broke their front axles and were converted to 4-2-2s in order to spread the weight over more wheels.

2-4-os were built for secondary passenger services and six of these were fitted with the Westinghouse brake for working stock of those railways which used this type of brake rather than the vacuum pattern.

In 1886, a standard gauge compound was built similar to the one on the broad gauge and proved even more unsuccessful, mainly due to lack of accessibility for lubrication, and so was retired in 1887.

Coaches

By 1870 broad gauge passenger stock was divided into four classes: best express; second best; ordinary and excursion, the latter were designated 'never to be used in regular trains except in case of absolute necessity', which makes them sound as if they were something to be avoided. In subsequent years, gauge conversions allowed the worst stock to be withdrawn and the demand for more third-class accommodation was met by degrading old seconds. Many of the B&E and SDR coaches were condemned soon after the GWR took over these lines, while others were degraded, first to second, or second to third.

Until 1867 private contractors supplied rolling stock but then in 1869 Swindon carriage works was opened, initially only producing standard gauge stock but starting on broad gauge in 1876 building six- or eight-wheelers with Mansell wooden wheels, clerestory roofs and two lamps in each compartment. The eight-wheelers were not strictly bogie coaches as the wheels, in groups of four, did not turn on a central pin but used Dean's centreless, pendulum-suspended truck, of which the two end axles had side-play and the inside axles were rigid. They were lighter but less satisfactory than a true bogie.

Initially lighting was by oil lamps supplemented by passengers supplying candles in spiked candlesticks which could be thrust into the upholstery. In around 1874 gas lighting was introduced using crude burners.

The first GWR sleeping cars, six-wheelers, appeared in 1877 and worked between Paddington and Plymouth. Each was divided into two dormitories, seven beds for gentlemen and four for ladies. A central compartment held two small lavatories. The dormitory idea proved unpopular and the six-wheelers were replaced in 1881 with eight-wheelers with six double-berth compartments, three lavatories and a side corridor. They were far superior to anything on offer by the London & North Western Railway or the Great Northern Railway. They were the first coaches built at Swindon with standard gauge bodies on broad gauge frames. This practice became standard, although it meant losing two seats in every third-class compartment. The adoption of independent bogies in 1888 meant that convertible stock could be built with standard gauge frames as well as bodies, thus simplifying the process of conversion.

Towards the end of the broad gauge era, E. L. Ahrons in *Locomotive and Train Working in the Latter Part of the Nineteenth Century* recalled:

The remainder of the carriage stock, mostly six-wheeled, was employed on the local trains and branches in the west, and had to be seen to be properly appreciated. They were utterly unlike anything else on wheels. Many had the old-style of windows with the lower ends rounded, a few had oval windows, and some hard-featured ones were built with everything at rigid right-angles and square windows. Some of them were entirely of iron with flat roofs. Nearly all had the old-fashioned wheels with open spokes, many of which were of the double-elliptical pattern. They were not so much used north of Exeter, except on the Chard branch, but a few occasionally put in an appearance at Bristol, and Bridgwater yard generally had two or three of them in a siding to give the station an antique appearance. The weekly West of England excursions to and from London also frequently managed to collect a few, which were sandwiched between the eight-wheelers. Finally, some of them, with the insides removed, served as brake vans for the broad gauge 'Tip' and other goods trains.

Until 1868 standard gauge stock consisted of four-wheelers. Swindon turned out its first coach, a six-wheeler, in 1870 and over the next few years produced standard gauge stock for use on converted lines. Shops at Worcester and Saltney built four-wheelers until 1872 and 1874 respectively after which all new coaches were erected at Swindon. Eight-wheelers appeared in 1878 and the first corridor coaches in 1892.

Mansell wooden wheel centres were first tried in 1866 and adopted for new stock in 1868. By the end of 1874 over half of the stock of standard gauge coaches had Mansell wheels, but most of the broad gauge stock had iron-spoked wheels.

Richard Mansell, carriage superintendent of the South Eastern Railway, had patented a wheel which had an iron boss, around which was a disc composed of sixteen teak segments. This disc was forced on to the bevelled inner face of the tyre by hydraulic pressure. The great advantage of this wheel was that it ran more quietly than an iron-spoked wheel.

In 1872 the Midland Railway decided to carry third-class passengers on all its trains. The GWR stated that it would do likewise except – and then listed all trains, except the very slowest, running between Paddington and the West of England. Until 1882 the GWR continued to charge express fares between Paddington and Bristol, even for trains averaging less than 40 mph, but these special fares were abolished in 1882 when most trains carried third-class passengers. The first corridor train with lavatory accommodation for all classes was the 1.30 p.m. Paddington–Birkenhead which began on 7 March 1892; it was soon followed by others. In 1893 steam heating replaced foot warmers, while in 1899 electric lighting appeared, followed in 1905 by incandescent gas lighting which proved far superior to the crude burners hitherto used.

Brakes

The braking on early GWR trains was primitive, the only efficient brake being on the locomotive tender or by throwing the engine into reverse. Initially brakes were not applied to driving wheels because of the danger of the friction heating, and therefore loosening, their iron tyres.

First-class coaches were unbraked, while guards sat in the centre of second-class compartments to operate brakes that Brunel described in March 1841 as 'tolerably useless'. From 1844 covered third-class coaches also had brakes. When a driver wished to stop, particularly in an emergency, he sounded his brake whistle for the guard, or guards, to apply the brake.

In 1858 two braking systems were tried on the OWWR – one designed by Fay and the other by Newall – while the GWR experimented with Clark's chain brake in 1865 and later with Grove's modification. The GWR then used the cheapest pneumatic system, which was that developed in the USA by James Young Smith. When a driver wished to stop, an ejector on the locomotive exhausted air from a pipe running the length of the train and diaphragm cylinders beneath a coach applied the brake. The system was rather slow to act and was rendered quite useless if a pipe broke.

In 1876 this design was replaced by Sanders's automatic vacuum whereby the ejector was in use all the time a train was running, and to apply the brake vacuum was destroyed in the train pipe, atmospheric air pressure applying the brake. This system was far superior because if a pipe broke, say due to a coach becoming detached, the brake would be automatically applied.

Signalling

Until 1865 most of the GWR lines used disc-and-crossbar signals with their subsidiary fantail caution boards, but on 1 April 1865 semaphore signals were installed between Paddington and Kensal Green. From 1869 the gradual substitution of semaphores 'wherever practicable' occurred. Early semaphore signals at Swindon were worked by overhead wires, rather than being set at ground level.

The semaphores were constructed with a slot in the post for the arm, 'danger' being shown by the arm in a horizontal position, 'all right' by the arm being out of sight in the slot and 'caution' was indicated by the arm in the midway position. The latter was never really reliable as if it drooped too much it might be thought to indicate 'all right', or if too high could indicate 'danger'. The Abbots Ripton accident on the Great Northern Railway on 21 January 1876 was caused by snow blocking the slot and therefore causing a signal to show 'all right' when it was meant to show 'danger'.

The distinction of a distant signal having a notch cut in the end of the arm was adopted in 1876 and semaphores with the arm fixed on the outside of the post also appeared about this date. Few disc-and-crossbar signals remained after 1890.

Until November 1893 the normal position of signals, except at junctions and major stations, was 'all right'; they were only set at 'danger' where the block telegraph was in force should the section ahead be occupied, and elsewhere held for the appointed time following the passing of a train.

Until January 1895 a white light indicated 'all right' but from then onwards, this was substituted for green. On distant signals, in 1927 yellow began to replace red as the 'caution' indication.

Safety was improved when the first locking frame was installed in 1860 just outside Paddington. It was a mechanical device designed to prevent a signalman accidentally setting up a conflicting road. By 1875, 57 per cent of signal boxes on passenger lines had such frames and by 1882 the percentage was 83. In the 1870s facing point locks began to be installed. This was a safety device consisting of a lifting bar which made it impossible to move a point inadvertently when a train was passing over as the wheels prevented the bar from rising. The lock prevented a train from splitting the points. Facing points had been worked by capstans quite independent of a signal, apart from a low target on the capstan, until an accident on 29 June 1865 on the Wilts, Somerset & Weymouth Railway at Bruton when driver and fireman were killed when their ballast train was diverted into a siding, the policeman having forgotten to set the points to the main line after having shunted a carriage truck into a siding. This tragedy led to a simple form of lock that prevented a signal wire from being pulled unless the points were set correctly.

In 1863 most single-track lines were worked on the block system by single-needle telegraph and bell, but generally the only double-track block sections were those with long tunnels, or opening bridges, most double lines retaining the time interval system of keeping trains apart.

Disc block instruments were invented by the GWR's telegraph superintendent C. E. Spagnoletti and, although installed on the Metropolitan Railway in 1863, first appeared on the GWR between Bristol and New Passage the following year. By 1873 the Paddington–Bristol line was equipped with the block telegraph and by 1883 only 147 miles of GWR line were still worked on the time interval; this system was last used in August 1891.

Longer single lines were worked either by the block telegraph or train staff and ticket, while short single lines were worked by the train staff with or without ticket. Until 1865 the staff or ticket was carried by the guard, not the driver. The year 1891 saw the introduction of the electric train staff system and over the next few years it was extended to all the GWR's principal single lines.

As the block system was introduced, although many of the new signal boxes and signals were erected by contractors, particularly Saxby & Farmer, the bulk of the work was carried out by GWR engineers, the frames and signals designed by Thomas Blackhall and made at the GWR's Reading works, which produced its first locking frame in 1863.

W. G. Owen, the GWR's chief engineer, was responsible for signalling, but when he retired in 1885, Thomas Blackhall was appointed the GWR's first chief signal engineer and the company issued the notice:

All new signalling and locking gear will in future be constructed at Reading by Mr Blackhall. The Divisional Engineer will maintain all existing signals and lockings. No existing signals or locking to be made or altered except from tables supplied by Mr Blackhall and approved by the General Manager and Superintendent of the Line.

Between Blackhall's retirement in 1893 and the appointment of his son, A. T. Blackhall, to the post in 1897, the signalling works was under the control of William Dean. The boxes erected by the GWR were brick or stone structures with comparatively small windows and were replaced by the 1930s. Between 1896 and 1910 the works turned out an average of 150 signal boxes annually. In 1906 Reading signal works north-west of the station covered 8 acres and employed over 500 men.

Light Railways

The Regulation of Railways Act passed in 1868 enabled a light railway to be constructed under conditions laid down by the Board of Trade. A 'light railway', which term first appeared in the 1868 Act, was generally defined as a line allowing a maximum weight of 8 tons per axle with a speed limit of 25 mph and less rigorous requirements for signalling and station facilities, while level crossings could often be ungated. The aim was to allow a railway to be built at minimal cost in an area which was incapable of supporting a normal railway.

Light railways benefited from the Railway Construction Facilities Act, which had been passed in 1864, allowing the Board of Trade to authorise a railway rather than having to go through the expensive legal process of obtaining an Act, though the board could only do this if all landowners on the route agreed to sell the land required by the railway company.

One of the first of these lines was the Culm Valley Light Railway. Arthur Pain, who had been trained by R. P. Brereton, I. K. Brunel's chief assistant, was a keen proponent of light railways. His brother lived in the Culm Valley at Hemyock. He could foresee the benefit such a railway would bring to the district, which had industry, farming and the tourist potential of the Wellington monument only

3 miles from Hemyock, the great exploits of the duke still within living memory.

Pain estimated the cost of the line would be £3,000 per mile, which is only about a quarter of the cost of a normal branch line. He anticipated that landowners would keenly support the scheme due to the increased value it would bring to their property and trade. To encourage landowners to support the scheme, the route was designed to avoid hedge severance as much as possible and so minimise the inconvenience of owning small parcels of land. Showing foresight, Pain proposed that the line be standard gauge, rather than the Bristol & Exeter Railway's broad gauge.

Meetings were held and on 18 November 1872 it was announced that terms had been agreed with thirty of the principal landowners, but two had objected; therefore the railway had been obliged to apply for an Act of Parliament. Ironically on the evening of 16 November, the light railway's solicitors in London had received a letter from the two objectors saying that they had abandoned their opposition and were willing to sell their land. Unfortunately because by this date the directors had given notice to go to Parliament, they were unable to retract this decision.

The Culm Valley Light Railway Act was passed on 15 May 1873 and opened on 29 May 1876. The Bristol & Exeter, being a broad gauge company, did not own any suitable standard gauge engines for working the branch, so James Pearson, its locomotive superintendent, designed two 0-6-0Ts especially for the line. Numbered 114 and 115, they were constructed in the B&E locomotives works at Bristol. Each weighed 20 tons 8 cwt.

By the time the line opened, the GWR had taken over the B&E and renumbered the engines No. 1376 and No. 1377. In July 1876

1. Isambard Kingdom Brunel, born 9 April 1806, died 15 September 1859. (Author's collection)

2. Sir Daniel Gooch, born 24 August 1816, died 15 October 1889. (Author's collection)

3. 2-2-2 *North Star*, the first successful locomotive owned by the GWR. (Author's collection)

4. Waverley Class 4-4-0 *Antiquary*, built in 1855 and withdrawn in 1876. The class was mainly based at Swindon, working the heavier trains to South Wales and Bristol. Notice the hooded seat at the rear of the tender to hold the porter, looking back to ensure that all was well. (Author's collection)

5. Iron Duke Class 4-2-2 with a tender seat. Built in 1851, it was withdrawn in 1884. (Author's collection)

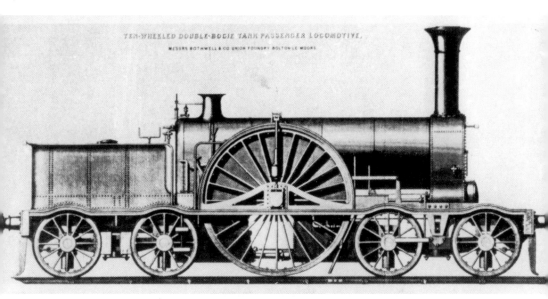

6. A Bristol & Exeter Railway 4-2-4T designed by Pearson with 9-foot-diameter driving wheels. The only brake blocks were on the wheels of the trailing bogie. They were the fastest locomotives of their time, the highest recorded speed being 81.8 mph. Built in 1853 the class was replaced or renewed in 1868–73. (Author's collection)

7. South Devon Railway 0-6-0T *Una*, built in 1862 and withdrawn in 1886. It was designed for goods working and had plenty of adhesion. (Author's collection)

8. GWR 2-4-0 No. 189 built by E. B. Wilson for the Oxford, Worcester & Wolverhampton Railway in 1853. It was withdrawn in March 1886. (Locomotive Publishing Company)

9. GWR 0-4-0ST No. 96 seen here *c.* 1930. Built by Sharp, Stewart for the Birkenhead Railway in 1856, it was not withdrawn until November 1935 after about seventy-nine years' service. Notice the lack of front buffers, the three-link coupling and the coal bunker beside the firebox. A coal stack is in the right background. (Author's collection)

10. The new Paddington station opened in 1854. Bishop's Road bridge can be seen in the background. (Author's collection)

11. No. 3028 was built as a 2-2-2 broad gauge convertible in 1891, altered to standard gauge in August 1892, rebuilt as a 4-2-2 in July 1894 and withdrawn in February 1909. (Author's collection)

12. Rover class 4-2-2 *Great Western* leaves Paddington with the very last broad gauge Cornishman, 20 May 1892. (Author's collection)

13. Comparison of broad and standard gauge locomotives both named *Rover.* The broad gauge 4-2-2 Iron Duke class built in 1871 was withdrawn in May 1892. On the right, No. 3019 required its boiler to be raised higher than on its broad gauge predecessor in order to clear the 7-foot 8 ½-inch-diameter driving wheels. Built as a 2-2-2, it became a 4-2-2 in 1894 and was withdrawn in 1908. (Author's collection)

14. Broad gauge engines at Swindon, May 1892, awaiting scrapping or conversion. St Mark's church can be seen in the centre-background. (Author's collection)

15. Conversion of a broad gauge coach with standard gauge body and underframe. Conversion simply required an exchange of bogies and the removal of widened footboards, the whole operation taking less than thirty minutes. Standard gauge bogies can be seen on the left. (Author's collection)

16. Up and Down disc and crossbar signals set to indicate 'danger'. (Author's collection)

17. When the crossbar was turned at right angles to the line, thus displaying the disc, this indicated 'all right'. A board, or fantail, signal indicating 'caution'. (Author's collection)

18. The atmospheric railway at Newton Abbot in 1848: the engine house is on the left and the station in the centre distance. (Author's collection)

19. The Saltash Bridge seen here in 1859, the year of its completion. (Author's collection)

20. The approach to Swindon from the west in the 1880s; notice the mixed gauge track. The line from Bristol is in the foreground and that from South Wales and Gloucester behind the signal box. Beyond the signal box are white posts carrying the signal wires. (Author's collection)

21. Swindon Junction, view Down *c.* 1890. Notice the mixed gauge tracks for the lines on the left. (Author's collection)

22. 481 Class 2-4-0 No. 489 built in November 1869, renewed in December 1887 and withdrawn in April 1919. In splendidly clean condition, it is hauling a horsebox, milk van and passenger coach. (C. L. Turner)

23. Metropolitan Class 2-4-0T No. 3570 at Old Oak Common *c.* 1921. Notice the condensing pipe from the smoke box to the water tank. The cab is well ventilated! In inclement weather the sheet on the spectacle plate could be drawn to the back of the cab. Built in April 1894, it was withdrawn in December 1938. (LGRP)

24. GWR crane tank No. 1299. Under construction by the South Devon Railway as a 2-4-0ST at Newton Abbot in 1875 at the time of amalgamation, it was completed at Swindon in 1878 as a standard gauge side tank. The crane was added in April 1881 and the engine was withdrawn in September 1936. (Author's collection)

25. Mr and Mrs Gladstone experience a ride in a contractor's wagon on the unfinished Metropolitan Railway at Edgware Road, 22 May 1862. (Author's collection)

26. An electric train to Hammersmith seen at the Paddington suburban station, Bishop's Road, in the 1930s. Notice the colour light signals on the right. (Author's collection)

27. The ungainly 2-6-0 Kruger No. 2610, formerly No. 99, at Swindon *c.* 1903. Built in June 1903, it was withdrawn in August 1906 having covered less than 50,000 miles. Its boiler was very advanced in conception but expansion caused problems. To the right is 2-6-2T No. 99. (Author's collection)

28. 4-4-0 No. 3711 *City of Birmingham* with an eleven-coach express picking up water on Lapworth troughs. Many GWR express trains were composed of a variety of coach styles. (LGRP)

29. The station site at Fishguard Harbour blasted from the cliff. Seen here shortly before the station opened on 30 August 1906. (Author's collection)

30. London, Brighton & South Coast Railway Marsh I1 Class 4-4-2T No. 597 at Paddington with the 3.40 p.m. Paddington–Brighton. This unusual service ran from 1 July 1906 until 30 June 1907. No. 597 was built at Brighton in November 1906 and withdrawn by British Railways in June 1951. (Author's collection)

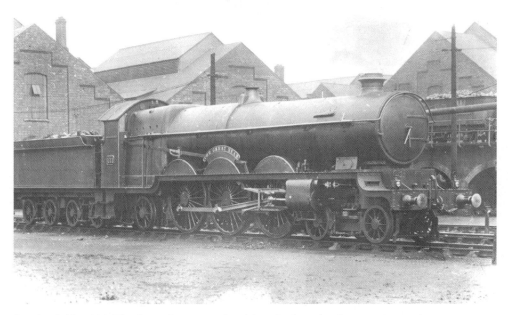

31. 4-6-2 No. 111 *The Great Bear*; note its eight-wheel tender. Locomotive coal wagons stand to the right on a viaduct giving access to a coal stage. (Author's collection)

32. Six inch naval guns and limbers entrained at Swindon, 25 October 1916, following construction. (Author's collection)

33. A lady volunteer drives a GWR parcels van at Paddington during the 1926 strike. Notice the barbed wire across the bonnet to deter attack and the tarpaulin to give a certain amount of protection against rain. (Author's collection)

34. Railways in South Wales favoured the 0-6-2T wheel arrangement. Here at Cardiff on 17 November 1923 just after a repaint is GWR No. 82, an ex-Rhymney Railway locomotive. Notice the flat-bottomed track. (Author's collection)

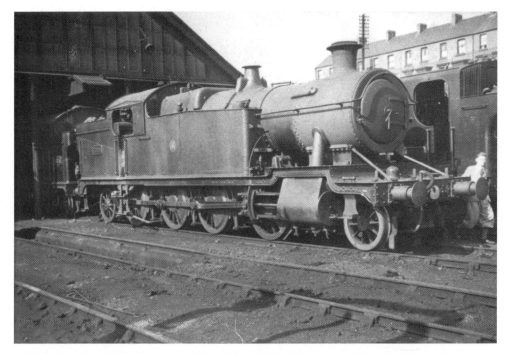

35. The massive 72XX Class 2-8-2T No. 7244. 57XX Class 0-6-0PT No. 9761 stands on the right. (Author's collection)

36. 4-6-0 No. 6014 *King Henry VII* at Swindon on 5 May 1935, eight weeks after being streamlined. The front end streamlining was later modified and all removed in January 1943. (Author's collection)

37. No. 5955 *Garth Hall*, *c.* August 1946. Renumbered 3950 in October 1946, it received its original number again when it was converted back to coal burning in October 1948. *Garth Hall* was the first GWR oil-burner; the oil tank is a prominent feature in the tender. (Author's collection)

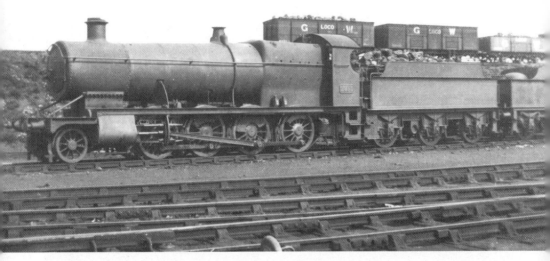

38. 28XX Class 2-8-0 No. 2813 at Bristol, St Philip's Marsh depot. Notice the steel locomotive coal wagons at a higher level on the road serving the coaling stage. (M. J. Tozer Collection)

39. Steam railmotor No. 75 at Swindon, 27 May 1925. Its vertical boiler is below the chimney seen towards the right-hand end of the vehicle. (Author's collection)

40. Diesel railcar W19W at Dymock with the 1.25 p.m. Ledbury–Gloucester Central, 16 May 1959. (R. E. Toop)

41. A GWR air services poster of 1933. (Author's collection)

42. 517 Class No. 1160 painted in chocolate-and-cream livery to match the auto coach. Notice the impracticably coloured cream cab and tool box. (Author's collection)

43. A Westland Wessex hired from Imperial Airways by the GWR in 1933 to work its air services. It bears the GWR coat of arms on its tail. (Author's collection)

44. Platforms 6 and 7 at Paddington following bomb damage on 22 March 1944. (Author's collection)

45. S160 Class 2-8-0 No. 1604, built by the American Locomotive Company and on loan to the GWR from January 1943 until September 1944. It is seen here outside 'A' shop, Swindon, after having been modified by the GWR. (Author's collection)

46. Gas turbine No. 18000 entering Bath Spa with a Bristol–Paddington express, 11 May 1951. (Revd Alan Newman)

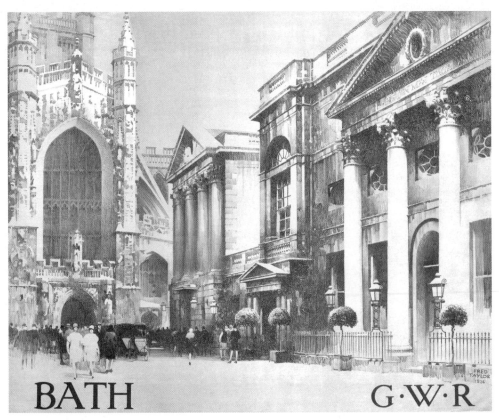

BATH

G·W·R

47. Advertising poster for railway travel to Bath showing Bath Abbey, the Roman Baths, and the Pump Room. (Amberley Archive)

48. 64XX Class 0-6-0PT No. 6435 and 4-6-0 No. 7029 *Clun Castle* en route to the Dart Valley Railway for preservation, October 1965. (W. H. Harbor)

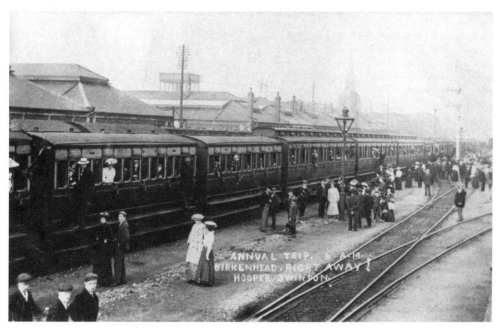

49. The trip train to Birkenhead is ready to leave from the works at 6.00 a.m. (Author's collection)

50. The GWR's first road motor, AF 37, a 16hp Milnes-Daimler. It inaugurated the Helston–Lizard service on 17 August 1903. It proved so successful that in October the GWR ordered twenty-five buses from Milnes-Daimler for a total cost of £19,541. (Author's collection)

51. GWR 20hp Milnes-Daimler AF 64 fleet No. 5, outside the Royal Hart Hotel, Beaconsfield, terminus of the route from Slough. The side board reads: 'Slough, Stoke Poges & Burnham Beeches'. (Author's collection)

52. Bus bodies under construction in the road motor shop at Swindon, 25 July 1907. (Author's collection)

53. Ransome's electric vans DX 1986/7/5 on 2½-ton Orwell chassis. The bodies were built by the GWR at Swindon. The vehicles had a speed of 9–14 mph. The electric motors can be seen by the front wheels. In this 1919 view the vans wear a crimson lake livery with a black tilt. (Author's collection)

54. A GWR-owned van, YH 7477, in Macfarlane, Lang & Co.'s livery. It delivered biscuits from a GWR railhead to local retailers. (Author's collection)

55. The SS *Great Western* at Weymouth on the Channel Islands service. The GWR had a tramway running through the streets to the quay on the far side of the vessel. (Author's collection)

56. An 1890 poster advertising Cardiff Races. (Author's collection)

one became derailed, so the GWR locomotive superintendent instructed that the coupling rods be shortened to convert it to an 0-4-2T arrangement. After this, all subsequent steam engines used on the branch were four-coupled designs.

Another GWR light railway was the Wrington Vale, situated south-west of Bristol. This had two ungated level crossings.

Some light railways were acquired by the GWR. One such was the Lambourn Valley Railway which ran north-west of Newbury. It used low-level platforms, so its coaches were provided with steps to enable passengers to climb inside. In 1900, while the Lambourn Valley was still an independent company, the GWR investigated the line and found that there was no hope of economising on staff as all its employees worked hard, turning their hand to various duties. At each of the small stations, a lad carried out all the tasks such as cleaning, parcel delivery and superintending the goods traffic. At Lambourn tickets were issued by two girls who also dealt with the correspondence. Mr Brain, the stationmaster, assisted in the yard, 'putting his shoulder to the horseboxes and trucks as required'. He also travelled to Newbury to bank the takings and, on at least one occasion, with the help of a lad pushed an empty wagon from a siding on to a train.

The light railway found it impossible to run the railway at a profit and the undertaking was sold to the GWR on 1 July 1905.

The Lampeter, Aberayon & New Quay Light Railway owned by the GWR opened on 1 June 1912 and was worked with steam railmotors and auto trains.

The Tanat Valley Light Railway, opened on 5 January 1904 south-west of Oswestry, was owned by the Cambrian Railways and became GWR property when the GWR took over the Cambrian.

The Burry Port & Gwendreath Valley Railway opened in July 1869, was reconstituted as a light railway and opened for passengers on 2 August 1909. It was incorporated into the GWR in 1922.

The Mawddwy Railway had a similar history. Opened on 1 October 1867, it closed to passengers on 17 April 1901 and entirely on 8 April 1908. It reopened as a light railway worked by the Cambrian Railways on 29 July 1911 and was then taken over by the GWR with grouping.

Shipping

On 13 July 1871 the GWR (Steam Vessels) Act was passed, allowing the company to own and work steamers between Weymouth and/or Portland to the Channel Islands, Cherbourg and St Malo, and from Milford Haven to Cork and Waterford.

The GWR was reluctant to take over the Channel Islands service opened by another company, partly due to the postponement of the gauge conversion. Most of the Channel Island potato traffic went to the Midlands and North of England, and the break of gauge prevented running through trains. The Weymouth line was converted in June 1874 and the following year potato traffic really took off.

A joint GWR/Western Railway of France Weymouth–Cherbourg service began on 1 August 1878, the journey from Paris to Paddington taking 20 hours 55 minutes. Passenger traffic was almost non-existent and the joint service ended on 30 June 1885.

Following the termination of the agreement with the Weymouth & Channel Islands Steam Packet Co., (from 1857 the GWR had provided trains which connected with the packet company's ships), the GWR's Channel Islands service began on 1 July 1889. This competed with the London & South Western Railway's service from Southampton.

On 1 February 1872 the GWR took over the New Milford–Waterford service.

Personalities

Joseph Armstrong was born in Canada where his father had emigrated, but returned to settle in Newburn-on-Tyne being educated at Bruce's School where Robert Stephenson had been a pupil. He started work under Robert Hawthorn who went on to found a locomotive-building firm. He became friendly with George Stephenson and Timothy Hackworth. In 1836 he became an engine driver on the Liverpool & Manchester Railway and then on the Hull & Selby Railway. On the latter he became foreman of the sheds and locomotive shops at Hull. He then became assistant locomotive superintendent and then superintendent on the Shrewsbury & Chester Railway. When the Shrewsbury & Birmingham opened in 1849 it was operated with the Shrewsbury & Chester as an entity and Armstrong was transferred to Wolverhampton. In 1854 the system to Chester was amalgamated with the GWR thus forming a standard gauge division. Armstrong became locomotive superintendent of this division of the GWR, responsible only to Daniel Gooch. During Armstrong's ten-year reign there he added many new designs.

In 1864 both Gooch and J. Gibson, the carriage and wagon superintendent, resigned and Armstrong became the very first locomotive, carriage and wagon superintendent at Swindon. He built very few new broad gauge locomotives but established a carriage and wagon works at Swindon and, from then onwards, most GWR rolling stock was built there. In his thirteen years at Swindon approximately 600 engines were constructed. By 1877 he was in charge of almost 13,000 employees and the strain began to affect him. He decided to have a holiday but on his journey to Scotland died at Matlock on 5 June 1877 aged sixty.

He had been president of the mechanics' institute for thirteen years and a local preacher in the Wesleyan Methodist church which in 1869 acquired the building that had formerly been a hostel for GWR employees. Following his death an RNLI lifeboat, *Joseph Armstrong*, based at Cadgwith in Cornwall was given by the people of Swindon in his memory.

Not to be confused with his father was Joseph Armstrong junior. Born at Wolverhampton in 1856 he had a short life. Educated at Tettenhall College he became a pupil at Swindon works under his father. Full of sound and original ideas, when William Dean became locomotive, carriage and wagon superintendent, Dean entrusted him with the design of the GWR vacuum brake, giving him G. J. Churchward as an assistant. This work successfully completed, Dean promoted Armstrong junior to the position of assistant divisional locomotive superintendent of the Swindon Division. In 1885 he was promoted to assistant divisional superintendent of the Northern Division and works manager at Wolverhampton. On 1 January 1888, while walking beside the railway at Wolverhampton, he was struck by a train and killed.

4

Expansion Continues: 1874–1900

Although the splendid terminus at Bristol Temple Meads was initially adequate, with the opening of the Bristol & Gloucester Railway and the B&E it was becoming inadequate to handle all the traffic. The B&E had opened its own terminus in 1845, but in the 1860s considerable expansion of the station was essential as two platforms were quite inadequate to deal with GWR trains to and from London, Westbury and New Passage and Midland Railway services to Birmingham. The *Bristol Times & Mirror* remarked:

It would be difficult to find in all England a more rambling, ill-arranged and melancholy-looking group of buildings than those for the Midland, Great Western and Bristol & Exeter lines. The Midland and Great Western station makes a massive show outside; but the outside is delusive, for the accommodation provided by way of offices is of the smallest. It is really a punishment for a man to have to squeeze himself in among the crowds that assemble every day at the starting of almost every train, in front of a single pigeon-hole that is used for the issue of tickets and for a lady, the difficulty of getting a ticket must be something dreadful. The Bristol & Exeter is certainly a trifle better in this respect than the others, but not much.

In 1865 the GWR, B&E and Midland Railway obtained an Act to build a new joint station, but because of disputes regarding the proportionate division of the cost another six years elapsed before the task was completed. The B&E terminus was demolished and a great curved train shed with a span of 125 feet was erected to cover the new platforms. Brunel's original train shed was sympathetically lengthened in similar style to the original, though the roof supports were metal, not wood, and had thin ties.

The enlarged station, opened on 1 January 1878, had a fine rising approach road to an architecturally pleasing main entrance, with offices and a 100-foot-high clock tower. Sir Matthew Digby Wyatt, an old friend of Brunel who had assisted with his 1854 Paddington station, was architect for the extension and his design blended with the original. Francis Fox of the B&E took his share in the scheme, the green and gold exterior canopy almost certainly of his design as it is virtually identical to the one he designed for Weston-super-Mare.

Each company had its own booking hall within the Great Hall and passengers for the respective companies entered by separate doors. The extended station had seven platforms but even before completion the station was inadequate, several minor accidents between 1871 and 1876 being attributed by Board of Trade inspectors directly, or indirectly, to the congested state of the new station.

Crossing the Severn

The Severn Estuary was a severe hindrance to trade between Bristol and South Wales. The beeline distance of 18 miles between Bristol and Newport required no less than 81 miles by rail. Matters were somewhat ameliorated by the Bristol & South Wales Union Railway (BSWUR).

New Passage Ferry across to Sudbrook was used until Cromwell's time when traffic was diverted to Old Passage Ferry 2 miles north, but in the stagecoach era New Passage was reopened only to be made redundant when the South Wales Railway was inaugurated.

The BSWUR obtained its Act on 27 July 1857 for building a broad gauge line from Bristol to New Passage Pier from where a ferry would link with Portskwett Pier across 2 miles of water. From that pier a short branch connected with the South Wales Railway.

On 14 September 1858 Brunel invited Charles Richardson to be resident engineer of the BSWUR. He explained:

I want a man acquainted with tunnelling and who will with a moderate amount of inspecting assistance, look after the tunnel with his *own eyes* – for I am beginning to be sick of Inspectors who see nothing – and resident engineers who reside at home. The country immediately north of Bristol I should think a delightful one to live in – beautiful country – good society near Bristol and Clifton etc. I can't vouch for any cricketing, but I should think it highly probable.

Richardson was offered an annual salary of £300 rising to £450, the beautiful countryside and cricket considered compensation for the low salary. Tunnelling experience was necessary to deal with the 1,246-yard Patchway Long Tunnel and the 62-yard Patchway Short Tunnel.

The building contract was carried out by Rowland Brotherhood of Chippenham. As he required locomotives for use in his various contracts, and moving these from one location to another was difficult, his son Peter designed an engine capable of travelling on either road or railway. One of these 11-ton machines travelled from Chippenham to the BSWUR at Patchway over ordinary roads at an average speed of 6 mph.

The two piers were of timber on a stone base and designed so that trains could run to the end of the piers. Stairs led passengers to pontoons of hulks moored alongside. Ferry steamers were able to land passengers at any state of the tide, despite rises of as much as 46 feet. Steam-operated lifts took merchandise and luggage to the correct level. New Passage Pier was 1,635 feet in length and Portskewett 708 feet.

They were designed by Charles Richardson, one of Brunel's pupils. While engaged in building the piers, he was led to consider the project of cutting a tunnel beneath the Severn. The BSWUR was ceremonially opened on 25 August 1863 and to the public on 8 September 1863. On Sunday 13 September 1863 over 1,500 passengers were carried from Bristol to New Passage in a train of twenty-one coaches.

The first railway to cross the Severn Estuary was the Severn Bridge Railway which linked the Severn & Wye Railway and the GWR at Lydney, with the Midland Railway at Berkeley Road. The line also enabled ships that had unloaded at Sharpness to coal there and thus avoid having to use a South Wales port.

At 4,162 feet it was the longest English railway bridge and in Britain, third only to those across the Tay and Forth. It consisted of a series of twenty-one iron bow-string girders, plus at its eastern end, a steam-operated swing span crossing the Gloucester & Berkeley Canal. An engine driver was required to be on duty on one of the day shifts to maintain the machinery, the signalman on the other shift assisting with cleaning and coaling. The bridge opened to traffic on 17 October 1879, exactly a century after the first iron bridge in the world was constructed, also across the Severn but at Ironbridge.

On 23 May 1881 John Williams, night watchman, a lad aged nineteen, at 1.45 a.m. discovered Portskewett Pier on fire. Telegrams were sent to summon the Chepstow fire brigade, which failed to respond. The Cardiff fire engine arrived at 6.00 a.m. and its pump handles were operated by navvies from the Severn Tunnel works. The Newport engine arrived shortly after. The glow alerted the watchman at New Passage Pier on the far bank of the Severn. He roused other employees and the paddle steam *Christopher Thomas* left. A fire engine and hose from Bristol was placed on the 7.15 a.m. train to New Passage and this engine afloat on the *Christopher Thomas,* and others on shore, eventually doused the flames.

As the ferry was inoperable without the use of Portskewett Pier, passenger trains were run from Bristol over the Midland Railway to Berkeley Road across the Severn Railway Bridge, and joined the South Wales line at Lydney. This alternative route was actually twenty-five minutes faster, but after temporary repairs had been carried out to the pier, the ferry was reopened on 16 June 1881 to avoid the GWR having to pay some of its profits to the Midland Railway.

The end of the Severn Bridge came on the night of 25 October 1960 when it was struck by an oil tanker, which destroyed two spans. Unfortunately under the Merchant Shipping Act the limited liability only allowed British Railways to receive £5,000, whereas the cost of replacing the missing spans was £294,000. In 1967 the bridge was dismantled.

Although the BSWUR and the Severn Bridge Railway were better than nothing, a more direct route from Bristol was required. The GWR had to consider the advantages and disadvantages of a bridge or tunnel. Bridge spans need support and at times a strong wind can be a problem, blowing a vehicle off the track. Tunnels need ventilation and require to be pumped dry. In 1872 the GWR obtained an Act to carry out Charles Richardson's Severn Tunnel plan.

The year following the passing of the Act, the GWR sank a shaft on the Welsh bank and drove a small heading below the Severn to test the strata and prove whether a tunnel was feasible, and if so this heading could be used as a drain for the full-sized tunnel.

After four and a half years of work, one shaft and about a mile of 7 feet square heading was completed. Then on 16 October 1879 when headings driven from both sides of the estuary were within 130 yards of each other, the Great Spring of fresh water broke in under the land portion.

This disaster resulted in Sir John Hawkshaw, the tunnel's consulting engineer, being appointed chief engineer. He said that he would only accept the post on condition that the contract was let to a man he could trust – Thomas Walker.

When Walker took over the contract on 18 December 1879 he worked ten-hour shifts. Blasting was done immediately before a meal break taken outside the tunnel, as dynamite fumes were dangerous – so dangerous that he changed to tonite as fumes from this were so slight that workmen could return in a minute

Men came on at 6.00 a.m., worked till 9.00 a.m., breakfasted until 10.00 a.m., worked till lunch at 1.00 p.m. and then worked 2.00 till 6.00 p.m. On Saturdays they worked for seven hours, but were paid for ten. The Saturday-night shift began at

2.00 p.m. and worked only till 10.00 p.m., making seven hours with one off for a meal.

Walker, in his book *The Severn Tunnel*, recorded an incidence:

One Saturday, after refusing to commence the shift, they went off to the nearest public-house, came back primed with drink, and gathered in front of the pay-office grumbling; but they never came to me or the foreman and stated any grievance or asked for an concession. They simply determined to make trouble and stop the works if they could. I was in the office at the time, so I went down into the middle of them, and said: 'Now what do you fellows want?' No answer. 'Now tell me what you want, and don't stop hanging about here.'

Then one of them said: 'We wants the eight-hour shifts.' I said: 'My good men, you will never get that if you stop here for a hundred years. There is a train at two o'clock, and if you don't make haste and get your money you will lose your train. You had better get your money as soon as you can, and go.'

The men looked sheepish, went to the pay office, and got their money, and the works were absolutely deserted for the following four days.

The next day, Sunday, Portskewett Pier caught on fire. Walker did not believe it was caused by the strikers. Walker continues:

It was a good thing for the works that this strike occurred when it did, for it cleared away a number of bad characters who had gathered on the works; and from this time to the completion of the contract there was hardly any trouble with the men, and I think there was a thoroughly good feeling between employer and employed.

Walker certainly looked after his men. In almost all parts of the tunnel, waterproof clothing was required. He provided this and also drying rooms at the shaft tops. He made life easier by providing ponies to haul the spoil skips, instead of them being pushed by hand. Although work was arduous pay was good, the average weekly earnings of a miner being £1 18s 0d and a miner's labourer £1 7s 6d, that is more than twice the average weekly agricultural wage at Chepstow of 13s 0d.

McKean rock drills were first used in the tunnel towards the end of January 1875. Like many men, the tunnellers preferred the old way, but after a few days they ceased complaining about the new drills. An additional advantage was that after powering the drills, the air assisted ventilation.

Walker built houses at Sudbrook for his men, a hall for church services, a day school for the children and also a hospital. The principal illness suffered by the men was pneumonia caused by heat and damp of the tunnel and then exposure to the normal atmosphere when they left the works.

The houses at Sudbrook were built of either stone, timber, or concrete – the latter a very early example of concrete houses. As on the east bank difficulty was experienced in obtaining land, wooden houses were built over the line of the tunnel, timber being lighter and less likely to cause settlement.

One night a brick chimney between two houses collapsed straight down into the ground. The next morning it was amazing to hear of all the trousers and waistcoats containing money and watches which had been hung on nails driven into that chimney!

Walker was up to date and used electricity from generators owned by the GWR to provide light through Swan & Brush bulbs for both surface and underground operations.

Returning to the story of the Great Spring, to cope with the problem a shield was lowered down the shaft to cover the spring's entry, but despite efforts water leaked in. Divers, including Lambert, were sent down. Lambert was sucked so strongly by the pumps that it required three men on the end of a rope to drag him away.

After seven months when the pumps had at last begun to overcome the water, one pump broke and the shaft refilled. Pump repairs took three months.

Walker decided that an iron door in a headwall had been left open by the panic-stricken men when the Great Spring first burst in and it was essential that it be closed.

To do this, a diver was required to walk 1,000 feet along the headway dragging the air hose after him; close the valve; pull up two tramway rails; close the door and shunt another valve. As one diver was insufficiently strong to draw 1,000 feet of hose, three divers were deployed:

One to stand at the foot of the shaft and feed the hose into the heading;
One to go 500 feet along the heading and feed the hose forward;
One (Lambert) to go 1,000 feet along the heading and undertake the listed tasks.

Lambert groped his way in total darkness past upturned skips, tools and rock but then, when within 100 feet of the door, failed to drag the hose after him.

Walker heard of Lieutenant Fleuss RN, the inventor of a pipeless diving apparatus consisting of a knapsack of compressed air making a diver independent of an air hose. Fleuss was exhibiting his equipment daily at the London Aquarium and he was invited to the Severn Tunnel to close the door.

Fleuss came, but had insufficient diving skill to traverse the heading.

Lambert donned the Fleuss apparatus and reached the door. He lifted one rail, but then had to return as his air supply needed replenishment.

Two days later, on 10 November 1880, he closed the valve, lifted the other rail and turned the valve the number of times he was told would close it.

The pumps were started and the water level slowly lowered. A month later when the heading was finally pumped clear, pump foreman James Richards walked up the heading and discovered the cause of the slowness – the valve had a left-hand crew and was in fact closed when Lambert reached it and turned it open! However, the Great Spring was at last contained.

Troubles were not yet over. On 18 January 1881 a great snowstorm blocked the railway and coal was unable to reach the pumps. Messrs Walker had to borrow all possible coal from the neighbourhood and also burn wood. It was three days before coal could be got through.

At the end of April 1881, saltwater burst through into the heading on the east bank. As at low water the bed of the pool from which the water came was only about 3 feet deep, the exact site of the hole was determined by the simple expedient of men holding hands and walking in a line through the pool. One man suddenly fell and was supported by those on either side.

A schooner was loaded with clay puddle and taken to the pool at high tide. When the water subsided the vessel was unloaded and the hole stopped with alternate layers of loose clay and clay in bags.

The headings from each side of the estuary linked at 10 p.m. on 26 September 1881. Work then started on the main tunnel.

On 10 October 1883 the night shift was entering the heading at around 6.00 p.m., had just reached the face and was clearing away material blown down by the day shift when, in the words of the ganger, 'the water broke in from the bottom of the face, rolling up at once like a great horse' and swept men and skips out of the heading and back into the finished tunnel. The Great Spring had been tapped again, and once more Lambert had to be sent for to close the door.

No tide had been known to rise as high as the location of the top of the shafts, but on 17 October 1883, a south-west storm coincided with one of the year's highest tides. Waves 5–6 feet high swept through the workmen's houses, extinguished fires in the pump and winding house and cascaded 100 feet down the shaft.

Not realising that the lift was inoperable, men ran to the cage to be hoisted. Four climbed an upright ladder against the shaft wall and one was knocked off and killed. Eighty-three of the men were able to retreat to higher workings.

Walker obtained a small boat, lowering it end-on down the shaft, but found it difficult to float. Eventually they made it dive and then bailed it out. The men were rescued the next morning.

On 27 October 1884 it was possible to walk from the open cutting on the east side to that on the west side, Sir Daniel Gooch recording in his diary:

I went this morning to the Severn Tunnel. Lord Bessborough met me there before lunch, and we inspected the surface work, and after lunch went below. It fortunately happened that the headings were just meeting, and by the time we had finished lunch the men had got a small hole through, making the tunnel open throughout. I was the first to creep through, and Lord Bessborough followed me. It was a very difficult piece of navigation, but by a little pulling in front and pushing behind we managed it, and the men gave us some hearty cheers.

On 22 October 1884 work of laying the permanent way began and on 5 September 1885 Sir Daniel Gooch, the GWR chairman, passed through the tunnel in a train recording in his diary:

I took a special train today through the Severn Tunnel. We had a large party, and all went off well. This tunnel is a big work, and has been a source of great anxiety to me. The large spring of water we cut on the Welsh side, a short distance from the Severn, had been a great cost and trouble. I hope, now the arch is finished, it will keep out any serious quantity of water. It will be some months yet before we can open to the public, as the permanent pumping and ventilating machinery has to be arranged and fixed.

The line opened to goods traffic on 1 September 1886, Gooch recording:

The first train that passed through was a goods leaving Bristol at 6.35 p.m. Fourteen trains were worked through during the night, and all was most satisfactory. This has been a long and very anxious and costly job. Our estimate for it was about £900,000. We have now spent over £1,600,000. The water is still a large expense to us, but it is under perfect control.

The tunnel was inspected by the Board of Trade on 17 November 1886. Local passenger trains used it from 1 December 1886 and reduced the Cardiff to Bristol time from 2½ to 1¼ hours. A contemporary Welsh paper reported:

> Without fuss or demonstration of any kind, the first passenger trains passed through the gigantic tube linking the shores of Monmouthshire and Gloucestershire. With a freedom from smell truly marvellous and an entire absence of reverberation, or oscillation, the submarine journey, if such it may be called, proved to be more like a run through a deep cutting, than through a tunnel 4½ miles long.

The first passenger train from Paddington to South Wales passed through the tunnel on 1 July 1887. The tunnel also created a new route from the west to the north via Abergavenny and Shrewsbury.

To compensate for the £1,806,248 cost of construction and loss of revenue by shortening the route between Paddington and South Wales by 15½ miles, a clause in the Act permitting its construction allowed the 7 miles from Pilning to Severn Tunnel Junction to be charged as 12 miles. Charles Richardson made a fortune from manufacturing bricks for lining the tunnel.

Experienced men working in the tunnel knew immediately from the movement of their open flame lamps when a train entered from either end. Although working in the tunnel had its disadvantages, fumes there prevented these men from catching colds. Sometimes the air was so polluted that footplate crews had to lie down to breathe the fresher air found at a lower level.

Heavy mineral trains stopped at Severn Tunnel Junction to pick up a pilot engine to assist in controlling the train. The point a quarter of a mile before the level portion was marked by a single white light, then a double white light indicated the train was 40 yards before the level stretch. A train was usually brought fairly carefully down the gradient of 1 in 90, but when the engines were opened up for the climb of 1 in 100 care had to be taken to ensure that the snatch when the coupling chain became taut did not fracture it. The working timetable stated that a guard, or guards, should try to control the speed down the incline by their brakes, but if it was necessary for engine brakes to be used the engine brakes must be gradually eased off before passing the single light in order that tight couplings should be maintained and steam must be put on steadily before reaching the double lights. Guards should keep their brakes on and not ease them off gradually until the train passed from the level to the ascent, when they should be eased off gradually.

On occasions when the tunnel was full of smoke, the lights might be invisible. To guard against such an event, some crews oiled the hinges of the coal bunker doors and opened them so that going downhill they hung forward and then when the gradient changed they swung back against the bunker and so gave an audible indication.

On the English side trains usually stopped at Pilning for the assisting engine to be transferred to the rear before entering the single bore Patchway Tunnel where the exhaust from two locomotives toiling up the gradient of 1 in 100 would have created unacceptable atmospheric conditions. The banker dropped off at Patchway station.

When a fireman had an assisting engine in front of him, sometimes he was tempted to take things easy and let the banking engine do the lion's share. When the fireman of the leading engine realised that advantage was being taken, it was standard practice to pull the smoke plate out of the firebox on the shovel and urinate on it before replacing. The obnoxious gas from the evaporated liquid made the engine behind accelerate to get away from the stench. An even better effect could be had by throwing rotten fish heads into the firebox.

The operation and maintenance of the drainage and ventilation of the tunnel was the responsibility of the locomotive works' manager at Swindon and included the pump for the Big Spring which might run at 15–20 million gallons daily. A resident engineer at Sudbrook oversaw the three pumping stations, the main one at Sudbrook dealing with the Big Spring and ventilating fan, with drainage pumps at Pilning and near the western portal of the tunnel. If the pumps stopped working the water level would be up to rail level in about twenty minutes.

The tunnel could cause a bottleneck as every coal train that passed through displaced three faster-moving passenger trains. If a passenger train received a pilot, it could work through to Badminton.

As the standard GWR brake vans with the open veranda became unpleasant with smoke and fumes in the tunnel when the brakes needed applying or releasing, a special Severn Tunnel brake van could be added to supplement the ordinary brake van for controlling heavier goods trains. These special vans had closed in verandas and drop-light doors. Gunpowder vans whether loaded or empty were banned from using the tunnel as were gas tank wagons. Dead steam engines were also prohibited from working through the tunnel. Goods trains were examined before entering the tunnel to ensure that no wagons were faulty.

The End of the Broad Gauge

Although the broad gauge had many advantages, with the expansion of the British railway system and the requirement to run through trains to destinations on standard gauge lines in order to avoid troublesome changes of trains for passengers, or transference of freight, the end of the broad gauge was inevitable. In 1885 James Grierson, the GWR's General Manager, reported that the broad gauge stock consisted of 170 locomotives of which 73 had been designed for conversion and a further 41 could be converted with new boilers. Of the 385 broad gauge passenger coaches, 200 were convertible, while only about a third of the goods stock was convertible.

The capital cost of conversion, including the removal of the third rail on mixed gauge sections, would cost £128,698 and this would be offset by the £146,979 value of the recovered material. The charge to revenue was estimated to be £413,250 for the conversion and replacement of stock, against an annual saving of £39,060 on maintenance and transfer expenses.

A serious depression in trade prevented an early decision and it was not until 26 February 1891 that, in view of the quadrupling between Taplow and Didcot, the decision was made that the broad gauge should be abolished in May 1892. The broad gauge, as opposed to mixed gauge, was found on the main and branch lines west of Exeter.

No traffic for Cornwall was sent from Exeter after 17 May 1892. On 18 May the first of eight trains carrying 3,400 permanent way men ran to the west. On 20 May the final broad gauge train from Paddington to Penzance was the 10.15 a.m. Cornishman. The very last broad gauge train to leave Paddington was the 5.00 p.m. to Plymouth. The last Up broad gauge train arrived at Paddington early on 21 May.

West of Swindon works, 13 miles of temporary sidings had been laid to accommodate the broad gauge stock. The actual work of conversion started at daybreak on 21 May and it was carried out so expeditiously that a standard gauge train was able to run that evening from Exeter to Plymouth. Standard gauge engines and coaches had previously been sent to stations in the west on broad gauge crocodile wagons.

The conversion of 177 miles in just two days was a very remarkable achievement. Regular standard gauge passenger services started on 23 May and goods the following day. Most of the now-redundant third rail on the mixed gauge was lifted by the end of 1892.

A bogie coach was changed from broad to standard gauge as a special effort in ten minutes before a party of directors, but could normally be done easily in twenty minutes. The operation was merely a matter of changing the bogies and altering the footboards and on one occasion twenty-five coaches were converted in only six and a quarter hours by means of specially constructed hydraulic lifts.

T. I. Allan, assistant manager of the GWR, said:

We had a party of directors from one of the northern lines down at Swindon recently, travelling in saloons on the broad gauge. While they were looking at the Works, the bodies of the carriages were lifted on to narrow gauge frames, and they were sent on without changing their carriages from the Great Western line, to, I think, the Midland at Gloucester.

Swindon works was efficient and by 14 January 1893 only 27 locomotives and 145 wagons awaited conversion. Convertible engines generally only needed shorter axles, but the convertible coaches were of three types:

1 Bodies designed so that a section could easily be removed to narrow the coach.
2 Standard gauge bodies on broad gauge underframes.
3 Standard gauge bodies on standard gauge underframes.

The last broad gauge engines in steam were South Devon Railway 0-6-0STs *Leopard* and *Stag* used as works shunters and not withdrawn until June 1893. Three broad gauge engines were preserved: *North Star, Lord of the Isles* and *Tiny*. Unfortunately the first two were cut up in 1906 and the vertical boiler 0-4-0T *Tiny* is the sole remainder.

The abolition of the broad gauge eased the work of quadrupling the main line east of Didcot and doubling the single line between Exeter and Plymouth, while at some stations, running could be expedited by using the space to either widen the platforms or lay extra track. In order not to halt traffic, the doubling of the line to Plymouth required new masonry viaducts to be built duplicating the original single-track timber viaducts, which explains the apparently useless piers hitherto supporting the timber that can still be seen today. Single-line tunnels were widened without stopping traffic by the method of having a wheeled frame through which trains ran, the tunnel widening taking place above and beside this frame. A better alternative to widening the 5 miles between Saltash and St Germans was constructing a new line which opened for goods on 22 March 1908 and passengers on 19 May 1908.

The abolition of the broad gauge was helpful in offering space for quadrupling the line to cope with the steadily increasing traffic.

This work took place between Paddington and Didcot 1875–1893, and Didcot to Challow in 1932. When this took place, generally a wing wall of an existing single arch overbridge was demolished and a standard gauge arch added.

In 1893 the Columbian Exhibition was held in Chicago and the GWR was invited to send the broad gauge locomotive *Lord of the Isles* which, although withdrawn in 1884, had been preserved. It travelled across the Atlantic with another broad gauge engine, *North Star*. *Lord of the Isles* was set up in the place of honour and a plaque read: 'The Greatest Locomotive in England'. Books and pamphlets publicising the GWR were distributed. The engines arrived back in January 1895.

Locomotives

Dean Goods 0-6-0s were long-lasting machines. The first appeared in 1883 and the last was withdrawn in 1955. Those with cylinders 17 inches by 26 inches were part of an early form of standardisation as classes of 2-4-0 tender engines, 2-4-0Ts and 0-6-0STs all had interchangeable driving wheels, cylinders and boilers and a similar valve motion. Apparently the advantages of interchangeability were outweighed by disadvantages in design, for Dean did not develop the scheme.

In 1887 twenty 0-4-2Ts were built with double frames. The design of the trailing axle boxes caused dangerous swaying, so they were replaced with a bogie having the Mansell wooden wheels normally only seen on coaches.

From its inauguration, the GWR had always worked its principal expresses by engines with single driving wheels, so in 1891 some 2-2-2s appeared on the standard gauge. The size of the

7-foot 8½-inch driving wheels restricted the diameter of the boiler to 4 feet 3 inches and to give an adequate heating surface its length had to be 11 feet 6 inches. Extra steam space was provided over the firebox by a raised casing – a traditional feature not hitherto used by Dean. Another innovation was having a very large dome on the back ring of the boiler instead of a moderate dome on the front ring.

Unfortunately the long boiler barrel made these engines heavy at the front end and consequently unsteady at speed. When No. 3021 became derailed in Box Tunnel on 16 September 1893 it was time to take action. The frames were lengthened at the front end and the front axle was replaced with a bogie, thus making the Achilles Class a 4-2-2 arrangement like the broad gauge engines they were replacing. Certainly, with hindsight, Dean showed little foresight as expresses were getting heavier as corridor trains were introduced and the single drivers lacked sufficient adhesion. Their life was short as the first was withdrawn in 1908 and the last in December 1915.

Concurrently with the 4-2-2s Dean built 4-4-0s with double frames and boilers similar to those of the Achilles Class. They had 7-foot-diameter driving wheels, but subsequent Dean 4-4-0s had either 6 feet 8 inches or 5 feet 8 inches.

Although the 4-4-0s were successful, it was apparent that an even more powerful engine was required and to provide this Dean built the first GWR 4-6-0 in 1896. No. 36 had double frames. An innovation was that the inner members of the double frames ended at the front of the firebox in order to allow the firebox to have a width of 5 feet 10 inches, which was the first wide firebox on a British main-line engine. The grate was flat at the front and rear with a steep slope in its centre and the brick arch was supported by arch tubes. This arrangement was only possible with small driving wheels, in this case 4 feet 6 inches. Its tractive effort was 24,993 lb compared with about 19,000 lb of a 4-4-0. It was nicknamed the Crocodile and could take thirty loaded wagons and two vans through the Severn Tunnel in eleven minutes compared with the eighteen minutes required by two 0-6-0s hauling thirty-five wagons and two vans. It was withdrawn in December 1905 with a mileage of only 171,428.

In 1899 the first of the Krugers's Class appeared and showed the influence of George Jackson Churchward, Dean's deputy. No. 2601 was a 4-6-0 while No. 2602 was a 2-6-0. The original boiler pressure on No. 2601 was 200 lb, when other GWR engines had a pressure of 160 lb. The 200 lb was soon found to be too great and reduced to 180 lb while later engines came out with only 165 lb. All ten Krugers had a very short life and were withdrawn by 1906. They were replaced by the 2-6-0 Aberdare Class which were the goods version of the Bulldog and Atbara 4-4-0s. Aberdares were originally used on coal trains between Aberdare and Swindon and some lasted into the British Railways era.

The City Class, largely designed by Dean's deputy, Churchward, were the best GWR 4-4-0s. They had a boiler pressure of 200 lb, 6-foot 8½-inch driving wheels, Belpaire fireboxes and large boilers with coned barrels. *City of Truro* is famous for its exploit of reaching a speed of 102.3 mph in 1904. Initially they monopolised the expresses to Cornwall, but within a few years were outclassed by 4-6-0s and were cascaded to short-distance express work. *City of Truro* was the last to be withdrawn in 1931, and fortunately preserved.

Although Dean did not resign until 1902, Churchward's influence on the design of GWR locomotives had been in evidence before that date.

In 1901 Churchward had set out a range of standard classes capable of handling future railway developments. A prototype for this scheme was No. 100. Initially unnamed, it received the designation *Dean* in June 1902 (Dean had retired on 31 May 1902), amended that December to *William Dean*. No. 100 was almost entirely different from any other previous GWR engine. In addition to having six-coupled wheels, it had inside frames and outside cylinders, whereas most of its predecessors had outside frames and inside cylinders. The cylinders had the longest stroke the GWR had ever used and piston valves were fitted. In 1903 it was given a Churchward 200-lb tapered boiler and became a member of the Saint Class.

George Jackson Churchward was appointed Locomotive, Carriage & Wagon Superintendent on 1 June 1902 and was responsible for providing the GWR with superb locomotives whose basic design was used until the end of the company forty-six years later. Although the GWR had only just changed to using four-coupled passenger engines, the weight of trains demanded something even more powerful so two-cylinder 4-6-0s No. 98 and No. 171 appeared in 1903.

No. 98 was the first true Churchward engine and had a tapered boiler from the beginning. Its front end and valve gear differed from No. 100 and became the GWR standard pattern. Its boiler pressure was 200 lb/square inch. The third engine No. 171 *Albion* had a boiler pressure of 225 lb which became standard. These became part of the Saint Class.

The de Glehn compounds in France were doing excellent work on the Chemin de Fer du Nord proving to be high-speed, economical machines, so Churchward took the highly unusual and original step of persuading his directors to purchase one – just

122

the locomotive; the GWR provided the tender. He wanted to be able to compare the French machine with his own No. 98 and No. 171. The first French engine to arrive was 4-4-2 No. 102. In order to make comparison fairer, Churchward converted No. 171 to the 4-4-2 wheel arrangement. Nineteen engines similar to No. 171 appeared, six as 4-6-0s and thirteen as Atlantics, all capable of being converted to either type. Two similar, but larger, French engines were purchased: No. 103 and No. 104.

The French engines and Churchward's 4-4-2 both worked in the same link so that performances could be compared. Little difference was found in the coal consumption and more oil was used on the more mechanically complicated French engine. The latter ran more smoothly because of its divided drive – the outside high-pressure cylinders driving the rear pair of wheels and the inside cylinders the front set. This smoother running resulted in much longer periods between major maintenance.

The French engines suggested that Churchward could improve his own machines. The swing link on the bogie was replaced by a side control spring while the four-cylinder compound suggested that Churchward should try four cylinders. The result was No. 40, similar to No. 171 but with four cylinders.

The first result of the trials was to adopt the six-coupled wheel arrangement as it offered greater adhesion when tackling the severe inclines between Newton Abbot and Plymouth. Superheaters were then added. No. 2901 emerged from Swindon in April 1906 and was the first engine in the country to be fitted with a Wilhelm Schmitt superheater and Churchward's modification, the Swindon superheater. It proved highly successful and almost all subsequent GWR locomotives, apart from shunting engines, were fitted with one. By 1913 use of the superheater saved approximately 15 per cent, or 60,000 tons, of coal annually.

Churchward's two-cylinder engines became the Saint Class and his four-cylinder engines the Star Class. They were simple engines, equally economical as a compound but cheaper to maintain and suited to burning Welsh coal. The Stars were intended for the GWR's longer non-stop runs and the two-cylinder Saints for less important expresses. The Star Class was the best British express engine design of its time and remained the basis of all the larger GWR express engines until the company ceased to exist in 1948.

Only a few years after the GWR had produced a new class of 2-2-2s, in February 1908 a really startling locomotive appeared from Swindon, a 4-6-2, the very first in Great Britain. This was No. 111 *The Great Bear* and, as the name suggested, she really was a super Star. It was believed that she was built for prestige rather than necessity, the Stars being quite capable of handling the traffic. She was built economically – the cylinders, motion driving wheels and bogie were standard with the Stars and the large boiler, although a one-off, was of simple construction. As a standard tender would have appeared too small with such a machine, a unique longer tender was provided, carried on two bogies with inside bearings. Although the size of *The Great Bear* appealed to boys and enthusiasts, Churchward himself disliked it. No. 111 was always shedded at Old Oak Common and, due to its weight and length, was restricted to the Paddington–Bristol run, though very occasionally it was spotted elsewhere. Apart from weight problems, the inside axle boxes of the pony truck tended to run hot due to the close proximity of the ash pan. Not infrequently it went outwards with an express, returning with a vacuum-fitted goods train. When the inner firebox required renewal in 1924 the decision was made to use the front part of its frames and turn it into a Castle and it emerged from the shops as No. 111 *Viscount Churchill*. *The Great Bear's* tender was used at various times by a member of the County, Saint and Star class.

Most contemporary railways, including the GWR, used 0-6-0s, either tender or tank, for goods and mineral work. As a requirement for an engine capable of hauling heavy loads became desirable, Churchward designed No. 97, the first 2-8-0 in the country. It was really a goods version of a Saint. Trials proving satisfactory, from 1905 more were built and many of the parts were interchangeable with Churchward's 4-6-0s. The GWR continued to build these 2-8-0s for the next thirty-nine years with only minor modifications. The first of the class was not withdrawn until 1958 when it had given almost fifty-five years' service and covered 1,319,831 miles.

Churchward's standard scheme included a modern 4-4-0 for use on lines over which a 4-6-0 was prohibited – such as the Shrewsbury to Hereford line – and for lighter expresses. They first appeared in 1904. Unlike previous 4-4-0s they had outside cylinders, but their relatively short wheelbase caused them to roll badly and so they earned the sobriquet 'Churchward's Rough Riders'. Until the restriction over Stonehouse Viaduct between Bristol and Gloucester was lifted in 1927, these were the heaviest engines the LMS would permit over its line and so they were seen on the GWR Bristol to Birmingham expresses. They also worked Paddington–Weymouth expresses. In 1928 they were replaced on the Bristol to Birmingham and London to Weymouth lines by Saints. The last County was withdrawn in 1933.

The 4-4-2 County Tank was the tank engine version and the class spent most of its time in the London area working fast services from Paddington to Reading and semi-fast services to High Wycombe and between Reading and Oxford. They were fitted with two-way water pick-up apparatus, which could cope whether the engine was travelling bunker- or chimney-first. With the need in the 1920s to combat road competition, the 61XX Class 2-6-2T was developed with a boiler pressure of 225 lb compared with the 195 lb of the County Tanks so the last 4-4-2T was withdrawn in 1935.

It was not until 1911 that the first 43XX 2-6-0 appeared. It was rumoured that Churchward had seen the Midland & South Western Junction Railway's 2-6-0s at work on Swindon's other line, was most impressed and wanted some like it. The Churchward 2-6-0 proved a highly versatile engine, a maid of all work, capable of travelling over most lines and handling goods or passenger trains, even expresses. Minor modifications were made over the years. Experience showed that in areas with severe curves, flange wear on the leading coupled wheels became serious. This was obviated by transferring more weight to the front end by the expedient of moving the buffer beam forward 1 foot and placing a heavy casting behind it. The pony truck therefore gave a greater side thrust to the main frames and bore a greater share of the flange wear. The modified engines were renumbered in the 83XX and 93XX series so that they could be more readily identified. Their extra weight precluded them from some routes.

The 43XX could travel at up to 80 mph and there is the story that a freight train headed by a 2-6-0 overtook the Cheltenham Flyer on which Chief Mechanical Engineer Charles Collett, Churchward's successor, was a passenger. At that time Collett was considering the design of the 4-6-0 King, and this incident settled the point of a reduced driving wheel diameter for them!

In 1919 Churchward brought out a mixed traffic 2-8-0 with a Standard No. 1 boiler but with an extra-long smoke box. This boiler proved too small for such a large machine so a large and impressive boiler, Standard No. 7, was provided. To ease running round curves, thin flanges were fitted to the wheels of the two inner coupled axles, which was general practice for GWR eight-coupled engines. When new they were scarcely seen by most people as they were employed almost exclusively on night express freight trains. When the Hall Class appeared, these took over some of the express freight duties and the 47XX Class became more widely distributed. Particularly on summer Saturdays, they appeared on express passenger trains.

A class which was built over a great number of years was the 31XX 2-6-2T. The prototype appeared in 1903, with two-way water pick-up apparatus being fitted. The final members of the class appeared in the British Railways era of 1949. Various minor modifications were made over the years, for example from 1909 struts were added between the front of the smoke box and the buffer beam to relieve the strain on the frames, particularly when banking. Between 1919 and 1922 bunkers were extended increasing the coal capacity by almost a ton.

Those based at Gloucester were used principally for Sapperton Bank duties and those in Devon and at Severn Tunnel Junction were also employed mainly on banking. Those in the London area were mainly used on passenger trains.

The first member of the 2-6-2T 44XX Class appeared in 1904 being a miniature 31XX. With coupled wheels of only 4 feet 1½ inches they were endowed with terrific acceleration and revolutionised hilly branch lines. From about 1912 the bunker tops were extended to increase the coal capacity and front-end struts were fitted. From 1924 the backs were extended by 9 inches to increase coal capacity even further to 3 tons 11 cwt, that is about a ton more than the first engine.

Most of the class was stationed in Devon and Cornwall, though one or two were allocated to Tondu and Porthcawl. In 1935 five were sent to Wellington (Salop) for working the Much Wenlop branch. They were most famous for working the Princetown branch with its steep gradients and sharp curves. The latter problem was eased when in 1931 No. 4402 was fitted with a wheel-flange lubrication system powered by a Westinghouse pump and air reservoir from an ex-ROD (Railway Operating Department) 2-8-0. This modification, far from curing the trouble, was found to cause slipping as the fine mist of oil, as well as being sprayed on the flanges, was blown on the tyres and caused violent sliding. The gravity-feed wheel-flange lubrication system on No. 4407 caused a similar problem.

Nos 4402 and 4410 were then fitted with an apparatus which used steam under pressure to spray coolant on the rails in front of the pony truck on the ascent to Princetown. Two reservoirs alongside the smoke box had to be filled each morning. The apparatus was cunningly designed to feed only the outer rail on a curve and cut off completely on straight track. Lubricators were also fitted to the rear driving wheel flanges to reduce friction on the descent.

The other GWR 2-6-2T was the 45XX Class which appeared in 1906 being like a 44XX with 4-foot 7½-inch coupled wheels allowing a speed in excess of 60 mph. The first of the class were the last engines to be built at the Wolverhampton works. Like the 44XX, engines were given extended rear bunkers, to hold 3 tons 14 cwt, and front end struts.

Until 1923 they were mainly confined to the Newport area,

South Devon and Cornwall. Following this date they became widely spread over the extended GWR system.

In 1905 Churchward considered constructing a tank version of his 28XX Class. It would have been a 2-8-2T but the wheelbase was probably considered too long and it was modified to a 2-8-0T – a rare type hardly found elsewhere in the world. The first of the class No. 4201 appeared in 1910. To overcome the wheelbase problem, the second and third pairs of coupled wheels had thin flanges and the trailing coupling rod bushes had spherical seatings at the forked ends to allow for a certain amount of flexibility. Subsequent engines, built 1912 or later, had extended bunkers. About 1919 the back was extended by about 6 inches to further increase the bunker capacity to 4 tons 2 cwt.

The class was designed for the short heavy hauls of coal in South Wales between pit and port or factory.

Churchward improved the locomotive numbering system by allocating figures so that the first two indicated the class; for example 4300 to 4399 were 43XX 2-6-0s and the class continued, with 53XX, 63XX etc.

A completely new concept was the steam railmotor introduced by Churchward. At the start of the twentieth century electric tramways were being set up in many towns and these offered serious competition to urban railways, as tramways had more frequent stops and were generally located closer to a passenger's home.

A tramway pioneer sought powers to build a network of light railways in the Gloucester-Cheltenham-Stroud-Nailsworth district, a busy industrial area. When the application was refused on the grounds of competition with the GWR and Midland Railway, he applied to construct electric tramways in the same area.

The GWR's answer was to open halts at level crossings and operate service with a steam equivalent of a single-deck electric tram. The steam railmotor, as it was called, had a vertical boiler within a coach body and, to avoid undue line occupation at a terminus, could be driven from either end.

The idea of a GWR railmotor was put forward by its General Manager, Sir Joseph Wilkinson, when he read a paragraph in *The Globe* of 18 October 1901 regarding a self-propelled railcar being tried on the Nord Railway in France. He wrote for details, as the GWR chairman and some of the other directors were anxious that the GWR should be first in the British field.

A frame was laid down at Swindon in January 1902 and a letter of 18 March 1902 from Dean to Wilkinson read, 'Have the construction of a light locomotive for burning oil fuel well advanced and hope to have it running in three months.' This 'light locomotive' was intended for railmotor working and shunting.

On 29 May 1902 Dean wrote, 'Expect engine to be ready for experimental running in three weeks', but in the event he was unable to get the engine to work.

On 11 October 1902, Churchward, who had succeeded Dean, wrote to Wilkinson, 'Preliminary designs for a combined carriage and motor have been prepared and will go into it again and submit best designs for Mr Inglis' [chief engineer] approval as to weight etc.'

Wilkinson wrote to Churchward on 13 March 1903, 'It is now some eighteen months since I begged your department to try and help us, but no assistance has yet arrived.'

A design drawn by Charles Collett, assistant works manager, was sent to Wilkinson on 21 April with the promise of plans for a petrol-driven vehicle to be sent the following day, though this latter project fell by the wayside. On 29 April the directors authorised the construction of three motor cars – two for running in service and one held as a spare.

Cost to the GWR:

	£
3 motor cars at £2,000 each	6,000
6 stopping places at £500 each	3,000
Stabling for cars	1,000
	Total £10,000

Annual Expenses

	£
Interest on Capital	400
Running costs – wages, fuel, water	1,400
Wages of two guards	150
Car maintenance	300
	Total £2,250

In 1903 the London & South Western Railway and London, Brighton & South Coast Railway Joint Committee had built railmotor No. 2. The GWR, being in the process of designing its own railmotors, sought permission to borrow it. On 7 May 1903 Sir Joseph Wilkinson said, 'The London & South Western have consented to lend the Motor Car from 6.00 p.m. on Saturday when it will be transferred to Kensington Addison Road, until

9.00 a.m. Monday when they desire it to be returned at the same place'.

The car was hauled from Nine Elms to Swindon on the evening of Saturday 9 May and from Swindon to Chalford on the morning of the 10th, Sisterton, the LSWR's locomotive superintendent's assistant, accompanying the vehicle.

The *Stroud Journal* of 15 May 1903 reported:

News of the proposed trial trip reached Stroud on Saturday, and all down the line groups of interested spectators had gathered to have a view of the new departure. The motor ran from Swindon, and the car was well-filled with passengers, including officials from Swindon works and most of the district traffic and permanent way inspectors. Contrary to expectations it did not arrive until nearly twelve o'clock, although a considerable number of people had assembled as early as ten o'clock, and waited with some impatience. It was understood, however, from intelligence which filtered down the line by means of passing goods trains, that the motor was stopping at several crossings, and this proved to have been the case. The engine was at the rear when it steamed into Stroud. A general stampede of people ensued from the Up to the Down line, but the car hardly stopped for a minute on its way to Stonehouse, where it returned later in the afternoon. The officials (including J. C. Inglis, General Manager and G. J. Churchward, Locomotive Superintendent) partook of luncheon served in the waiting room at Stonehouse.

The borrowed railmotor was not suitable for the Stroud Valley, being designed for the 1¼-mile-long branch from Fratton to East Southsea where it eventually began work on 31 May 1903. Between

Brimscombe and Chalford, with a load of thirty passengers speed did not exceed 8 mph on the 1 in 70 gradient and 27 mph on the level. On two 7-mile runs from Chalford to Stonehouse steam pressure dropped from 150 lb per square inch to 80 and 60 lb respectively. Uphill it fell to 100 and 80, even less being recorded between stopping places, and the car had to wait to raise steam.

Churchward took particulars of acceleration, running speeds and the time occupied in stopping and was confident that the GWR car would be of ample power and steaming capacity for the work. Supporters of the tramway scheme were among the interested spectators.

As late as 11 September 1903 the idea of having no fireman was in vogue, with Inglis, who had been appointed General Manager on Wilkinson's death earlier that year, writing:

If there is difficulty in getting the driver of the steam car to fire as well – so as to save a fireman – consider whether the driver should be required to get his steam up before, starting with coal, and to keep up steam during his running, to turn on a petroleum (crude) spray over the fire. Maybe in this way one man could drive such a locomotive satisfactorily.

The *Stroud Journal* of 16 October 1903 reported:

The new motor car service on the Great Western Railway between Chalford and Stonehouse Stations commenced on Monday [12 October], and throughout the day the cars were well patronised, those in the morning and evening being crowded.

On Friday [9 October] a large number of press representatives and others, who were accompanied by Mr J. C. Inglis, general manager of the line, Mr C. Aldington, Mr W. Dawson (assistant superintendent), Mr G. J. Churchward (locomotive superintendent), Mr Marillier (carriage construction superintendent), and Mr Waister (locomotive and carriage running superintendent), made a trial trip on the car. Everything worked satisfactorily. The trip was made in good time with a full load, and the vehicle was well under control, even when stopping at crossings on the steep gradients.

The new cars, which were designed and built at Swindon Works under the direction of Mr G. J. Churchward, are handsome vehicles, 57 feet long, 8 feet 6¾ inches wide, and 8 feet 2 inches in height, inside measurement. The under frames, which are of steel, are carried on suspension hung bogies.

The total wheelbase of each of the vehicles is 45 feet 6 inches, that of the motor bogie being 8 feet and the carriage bogie 8 feet 6 inches. The cars can be driven from either end. Each car is divided into the following compartments:- Passenger, 39 feet long; motor, 12 feet 9 inches long, and vestibule 4 feet long. The structural framing is of Baltic and Canadian oak, the upper part of the outside being panelled with Honduras mahogany, and the lower part cased with narrow match boarding. Electrical communication is provided for the convenience of the conductor and driver, and hand and vacuum brakes, which can be operated from either end of the vehicles, are fitted to each bogie.

In the passenger compartment all finishing work is in polished oak, and the roof is painted white, relieved with blue lining. This compartment will accommodate 52 passengers, 16 in cross-seats in the centre and 36 in longitudinal seats towards each end. The seats and seat backs are composed of woven wire covered with plaited rattan cane. The longitudinal seats are arranged in sets of three, each seating three passengers. The divisions of these seats, also seat-ends of the cross-seats, are of polished oak, and support arm rests. There are eight large windows, fitted with spring blinds, at each side of the compartment, with two ventilator lights above each, which may be opened and closed by the passengers. Two brass rails, supported by pendants fixed to the roof, run from end to end of the compartment, to which are attached leather hand-loops for the assistance of passengers. The vestibule, which is at the end of the cars, is provided with steps, by means of which passengers can enter and alight at all level crossings. Hinged flaps will cover the steps to allow passengers to enter or leave the cars at station platforms, and collapsible swing gates are fitted to prevent passengers leaving or entering the cars while in motion. Sliding doors of polished oak, with glass panels, allow of communication between the vestibule and passenger compartments. The cars are lighted by gas lamps, 14 candlepower each. The gas is stored in cylinders attached to the under frame. There are six duplex burners in the passenger compartment, one in the vestibule, and two in the motor compartment.

Steam for the engines is supplied by a vertical tubular boiler [fire-tubes], 4 feet 6 inches in diameter and 9 feet 6 inches in height, situated in a compartment at one end of the car. The engines are placed underneath the vehicle, and the cylinders drive on the trailing wheels of the bogie, which are coupled to the leading pair of wheels. The wheels are 3 feet 8 inches in diameter, and, with the boiler working at 180 lb pressure, the tractive force equals 8,483 lb. Water for the boiler is carried in a tank fixed under the car. The capacity is 450 gallons.

The public is already aware of the stations at which the cars will stop, and the time-tables are also published by the company. The cars will run at every hour from Chalford, and at the half-hour from Stonehouse, and the single journey will occupy about 23 minutes. There will be no service on Sundays. Tickets will be issued to passengers in the train itself on the tramway principle and the second car will be held in reserve, which will be available whenever necessary.

During the week the service of cars has worked well, although for a short time on Tuesday there was a slight hindrance, which was easily remedied. On Monday 2,500 passengers were carried, and the traffic has been well-sustained.

Number of persons travelling by the car: Tuesday 1,700; Wednesday 1,200. The amount of money taken for the three days was respectively £20, £17 and £11.

On the Saturday nearly 5,000 passengers were carried, the two cars running coupled together. On Thursdays and Saturdays the motors ran to and from Gloucester. A unique feature of the GWR scheme, not at first adopted by the North Eastern Railway and the LSWR/LBSCR which were the first rail motor users, was that the cars did not stop only at stations but also at four level crossings, the object being to enable them to pick up and drop passengers close to their homes in a similar way to an electric tramcar.

The railmotors became so popular that in 1905 the GWR was forced to provide a bus service between Chalford and Stroud as the demand exceeded the railmotors' capacity, but only lasted three months until further cars became available to augment the train service. Trailers were not the answer as the power unit was not strong enough to cope with the extra load on gradients, and difficulties were experienced in keeping time. As a result over the years the motors were converted into trailers by the engines being removed to give additional passenger accommodation and were alternately pushed and pulled by auto tank engines of the 0-4-2T or 0-6-0PT variety. The 0-4-2Ts were speedy and occasionally timed at nearly 80 mph between Stonehouse and Gloucester.

Churchward's standardisation was a great scheme as standard parts could be used on a wide range of different locomotives and in addition to speeding up repairs and reducing costs a smaller range of spares needed to be held at works or depot. It was particularly useful having standard boilers as one could be quickly replaced and the engine did not have to wait for its own special boiler to be repaired before returning to service. Churchward concentrated all locomotive building at Swindon so construction at Wolverhampton ceased in 1908.

From about 1881 Dean introduced a lighter shade of green for locomotives and used orange chrome for lining. The front of splashers was Indian red as were the outside frames, and the wheels were green. This was later changed to purple-brown. In 1889, in addition to the garter crest on the engine, the monogram of the entwined letters GWR appeared on the tender.

In 1897, the year of Queen Victoria's Jubilee, double lining appeared on the two engines used for the royal train, rather than just the boiler. Black was used for the footplate, smoke box, chimney wheel tyres and undergear, tank tops and fittings on the tender. Frames, splashers, wheels, springs, sandboxes and brake gear were purple-brown, buffer beams, buffer casing and inside frames China red. The chimney top was copper while the dome, safety valve cover, whistles, splasher beading, cabside beading, driving axle box and number and nameplates were polished brass. Handrails, smokebox door fittings, buffer heads, couplings and hooks were of polished steel.

In around 1900 a considerable amount of time and money was spent on the elaborate finish of locomotives, companies and their employees taking great pride in their presentation to the public. However, in the following decade many railway companies adopted a simpler style. In Churchward's time brass dome covers were either painted over, or replaced with, steel pressings. He wanted to abolish the copper cap to the chimney, but this was retained except during the First World War when, for economy, new chimneys were plain, and frames painted black instead of Indian red. Instead of tenders having three panels and a monogram, there was a single panel with the words 'Great Western' in capitals and the company's crest. In around 1904 some engines were just painted a plain grey, but this may have been because the traffic department required the locomotives urgently before they could be painted normally. From 1907 the practice of painting the locomotive number on the front buffer beam of tender locomotives and on the front and back of tank engines was adopted.

As the public demanded faster trains, one method of providing these was to omit some of the stops required for water. This could only be done if engines could pick up water at speed. The GWR laid its first water troughs between the tracks at Ludlow in 1896 and, finding the experiment successful, opened many more in 1898. They were set at intervals varying between 40 and 70 miles apart. The troughs themselves varied in length, most being about 560 yards in length.

The troughs were 18 inches wide and 6 inches deep and kept full by a regulating valve connected to a storage tank by pipes. When approaching a water trough, a fireman unlocked the handle on the tender and lowered the scoop. A float indicator on the tender registered the quantity of water taken in and the fireman, watching the indicator, attempted to lift the scoop before the tender overfilled. He was not always successful and the wise traveller, if in a coach near the front of a train, kept well away from windows when near water troughs. The author recalls on several occasions seeing passengers receive a soaking.

When ice formed in freezing weather, if it was relatively thin the scoop could break its surface, but if more than an eighth of an inch thick the water troughs were closed and a train would have to call at a station to take on water. When scooping water there was inevitably a certain amount of splashing; in freezing weather ice could build on the sleepers and cause a derailment. Water troughs were therefore closed if there was an inch of ice on the sleepers. Water troughs strained the surrounding track and required an overhaul approximately every ten years.

Tank engines were fitted with water pick-up apparatus, cunningly designed so that they could pick up whether going backwards or forwards. It was then discovered that the pressure of water being forced into their relatively slender tanks tended to split them, so the apparatus was removed.

In areas where water was hard, lime (calcium carbonate and magnesium hydrate) would build up in the boilers, reducing their efficiency. Temporary hardness, which is hardness that can be removed by boiling, was nullified by the addition of lime while the presence of sulphates causing permanent hardness is nullified by adding carbonate of soda. The GWR treated over 1½ million gallons of water daily.

Rolling Stock

At the end of the nineteenth century freight stock was painted grey with the letters 'G.W.R.' in white and the wagon number. In italic script was the legend: 'To carry *x* tons' and the tare. In 1894 the GWR experimented with cast-iron plates giving the lettering and wagon number. Initially these appeared on permanent way vehicles and Crocodile wagons, but 1899–1903 they appeared on vans and open wagons. Goods brake vans bore the name of the home station on a plate, while the guard's name was written in italic script level with the number. Cattle wagons bore the mysterious letters 'L', 'M' and 'S'. This was not a prediction of a company to be set up in the 1923 grouping but simply that in order to avoid cattle being bumped around, a moveable partition could make the vehicle large, medium or small depending on the number of its occupants. The plates indicated to where the partition should be moved.

Cattle trucks had slots in the lower planks to allow any effluent to seep away. Unfortunately this seeped on to the brake handle below, which the unfortunate shunter had to touch when he had to apply the brake. His conditions were improved when in later years there was no slot in the body side immediately above the brake handle.

In 1908 GWR freight stock received a startling change. The company's initials, instead of being a discreet small 'GWR', became 'GW' in letters 25 inches high. Numbers of the stock remained the same size, as did the italic script showing load, tare and any other information.

Ahrons, in *Locomotive & Train Working in the Latter Part of the Nineteenth Century*, gives details of crows on the GWR:

I became somewhat interested in the railway crow, and made enquiries of engine drivers with whom I was firing. They said that the crow was after the grease and oil that is always to be found on the line, and implied that a crow would sell his soul for railway grease. Moreover, I was also informed that he is such a wily bird that he knows all about the trains, even to the extent of timetable alterations – hence the impossibility of hitting him with a smoke box front. I am not so sure that crow has as good a time on the railway today as he had formerly, since wagon axle boxes, which used to be filled from the top with what was to him that great delicacy yellow grease, are now often provided with totally-enclosed oil wells with sponge pads. Crows were also to be seen hopping about under the wheels of stationary wagons in sidings, and in this connection an incident may be recalled which bears out the views of the engine drivers quoted above.

A number of empty wagons for the West had accumulated in the sidings at Didcot, and after a few days, an engine and van were sent for to clear them out to Swindon. The train of empties started out but was pulled up by the signalman at Challow, who reported sparks coming from several hot axles. An examination was made of the train, which resulted in the discovery that on several wagons, on which the axle box lids were loose and easily lifted, the crows had eaten out the yellow grease. The marks of their feet were plainly visible and the lids of several axle boxes were in an upright position. I hasten to add that I do not give this incident as the reason for the abandonment of the old grease axle boxes in favour of the closed oil-well type.

Swindon Works

New foundries were built in 1873 and two years later 2,000 men were employed, with another 500 added three years later. In 1888 the gas works was extended and automatic stoking machinery installed. At the time it was the largest gas plant in Europe and supplied gas to the railway village in addition to the works. Due economy was effected by discontinuing street lighting on the three nights either side of the full moon. The gas works closed about 1959.

In preparation for storing broad gauge stock at the final conversion, in 1891 sidings were constructed at a cost of £8,500 on a 10-acre site immediately west of Rodbourne Road; between 1901 and 1903, this area was used later for building the enormous erecting shop 'A'.

G. A. Sekon wrote in the *Railway Magazine* of October 1901:

Its vastness appals one ... Mere figures convey no idea of its size to the ordinary minds; within this shop could be comfortably accommodated two parallel streets of lower middle-class villas, each street of modern regulation width of 40 feet, with four rows of 30 houses each, with the usual forecourts and back gardens. Now you have it – a roof big enough to cover 120 suburban residences, gardens, road and all!

In 1892 it was claimed that the works was the largest establishment in the world for the manufacture and repair of railway engines, carriages and wagons, 10,000 men being employed. It produced one new engine a week, one new coach every day and one new wagon every working hour.

Distribution of staff at Swindon works 1892

Locomotive Department		Total
Locomotive factory	5,000	
Rolling mills	300	
Running shed	300	5,600

Carriage Department		Total
Carriage works	1,800	
Saw mill	400	2,200
Wagon works	1,600	
Office staff	300	
Railway owned stores, Platelayers' dept, etc	350	
		10,050

A laundry was opened in November 1892 for washing railway-owned articles arriving in baskets from all over the GWR system. In 1930 towels were the most common item washed, providing 2,800,000 out of the 3,000,000 annual articles. Annually the laundry used 10 tons of GWR soap powder manufactured in the GWR grease and soap works in Whitehouse Road.

By 1908 no less than 24,564 workers and their families travelled on the trip trains. They left in the early morning in twenty-two trains before most of the ordinary traffic had started. Weymouth, or 'Swindon-by-the-Sea', was the most popular destination, 6,171 going there. Other specials ran to London; Weston-super-Mare; Winchester; South Wales and the East and North of England. Two trains ran to Southsea via the Midland & South Western Junction Railway, these consisting of London & South Western Railway stock hauled by a T9 4-4-0. To ease congestion at Swindon station, trip trains were dispatched from various parts of the works, portable steps being used. In 1913 the trip was extended to a whole week.

As insufficient water for works' use was available locally, supplies had to be brought in old tenders from Kemble. With the enlargement of Swindon works, this method became inadequate and in 1903 gangs of men excavated a trench for 13 miles alongside the Down line between Swindon and Kemble and laid a 15-inch-diameter main. It held approximately 2,350 tons of water travelling at a speed of 10½ mph. As there was an obvious danger should the main burst on an embankment and wash it away, pressure alarms were fitted, and if an alarm was given no train was allowed to pass along the line until it had been visibly inspected.

In February 1891 the directors offered privilege tickets to GWR employees at a quarter of the full ordinary fare, and half this price for their children under twelve. This proved a great advantage to those visiting friends and relatives in other settlements on the system, especially as railwaymen tended to be moved about and were often separated from other family members.

A great social event was the annual Children's Fête held in the GWR Park. Showmen arrived on Friday and set up their amusements on the Saturday morning. At 1.30 p.m. the gates opened and for an entrance fee of three pence per adult and two pence a child, the fun could be enjoyed. Each child received a half-pound slab of fruit cake and a free ticket for a roundabout ride. By 1891 about 20,000 attended and a firework display was given in the evening. That year 2 tons 16 cwt of 5-lb cakes were made and the trimming shop foreman devised a cake-cutting machine with four cross blades and one longitudinal blade in a press worked by a lever. The machine had a canvas belt feed that carried a cake to the cutter and then fed the sliced cake to tables where ladies packaged it. The machine reduced the packing time to four hours. That day 680 gallons of tea were brewed and taken in huge urns to marquees. Old locomotive tenders supplied drinking water which came from Kemble. Oatmeal water was available free to children.

Ahrons, in *Locomotive & Train Working in the Latter Part of the Nineteenth Century*, tells of another celebration in the GWR Park:

In the year 1877 Her late Majesty Queen Victoria had a Jubilee, and as the Great Western Railway is nothing if not exceedingly loyal, it was forthwith decided to commemorate the event in suitable fashion. The participation of Swindon took the form of a fête and tea in New Swindon park. Great as were the rejoicings, greater still was the quantity of tea to be provided for perhaps 15,000 people, and the locomotive department was called upon to solve the problem. Finally, after much cogitation, some genius, whose name ought to be immortalised with that of George Stephenson, suggested that the tea should be boiled in the tenders of a number of locomotives set apart for the purpose. I believe the original idea was to empty cases of tea into the tenders filled with cold water and then turn live steam from the engine loose into the mixture. The drawback was that the resultant tea might have left something to be desired as a cheering beverage, and moreover if someone had turned the wrong handle and started the injectors to work, the cones of the latter would have become blocked with tea leaves, so that the fête have to be temporarily stopped while a new engine was sent for. However, a modification of the original idea was actually adopted. There were a number of older tenders which were regularly used as water tanks, and travelled between Swindon and Kemble Junction, where the water was obtained.

The first thing was to have the tenders cleaned out. They were in a pretty bad state too, for the man who got inside to do the job came out in about ten seconds with the remark that if tea was to be made in those tanks he would turn over a new leaf and drink beer for the rest of his natural existence. However, they were finally got into a fair state of internal order, so that the resulting beverage in the end had only a moderate 'twang'. Taps were fixed in the sides of the tenders and on the festive day three or four tenders were placed in the siding at Rodbourne Lane Crossing, the nearest point to the park, with a goods engine duly connected to them by means of a steam pipe. Steam was then blown into the tenders, one by one, and the revellers filled their tea urns from the taps. Never had Swindon imbibed so much tea in the course of its existence, and I am glad to be able to add that the doctors, in spite of the 'twang', had no more cases than usual to deal with during the following week. The whole scheme was a veritable locomotive triumph for the cause of temperance – the man who cleaned the tenders alone excepted.

The Engineering Department

Steel rails first appeared on the GWR in 1867, initially installed where use was exceptionally heavy, but three years later W. G. Owen, the GWR's chief engineer, recommended to the directors that, for economy in maintenance, their use should be extended where the life of iron rails was short. Heeding this advice, by 1878 about four-fifths of its main lines had been relaid in steel.

Just over half the track was on bridge rail laid on longitudinal sleepers, most of the remainder being double-headed rail on cross sleepers, drivers commenting that an engine was 'two coaches better' when running on cross sleepers. Bridge rail was found principally on broad gauge, or ex-broad gauge track, while double-headed rail was found on standard gauge lines. Although it was intended that, with double-headed rails, when the upper surface rail was worn they could be inverted, it was found in practice that where they rested on chairs, indentations were made and this caused noisy and sometimes uncomfortable running. Cross-sleeper track was cheaper to maintain and renew, and better for fast running. Use of bull-head rail was extended in the 1880s and adopted as standard in 1894.

Catering

Swindon and other refreshment rooms and the Great Western Royal Hotel, Paddington, were let to others to manage, but when in 1863 the Great Western acquired the South Wales Railway it also obtained the South Wales Hotel at Neyland. The GWR took over its operation and in 1878 the Tregenna Castle Hotel, St Ives, was leased by the GWR, which in around 1891 founded a catering department with staff managed from an office at Plymouth. When the lease of the Paddington Hotel ended in 1896 the GWR decided to run it and move the headquarters of the Hotels & Refreshment Room Department there. In 1898 the Wyncliff Hotel at Fishguard became the fourth GWR hotel. When the first GWR restaurant cars appeared in 1896, and until 1898, catering for them was carried out by Messrs Browning of the Paddington refreshment rooms.

What the GWR directors thought was a smart move in the company's early days proved to be a bad mistake. They had signed a contract with Messrs J. & C. Rigby for that firm to construct Swindon station for nothing and lease it to the GWR for a penny a year in return for the GWR undertaking to stop all passenger trains at Swindon for ten minutes, the idea being that Messrs Rigby would recoup their costs from catering profits.

This was fine in early days, but proved a bad mistake when passengers wanted and expected a faster train service. Within a week of signing the lease Messrs Rigby had sold the lease for seven years at a premium of £6,000 and an annual rent of £1,100. Then in August 1848 Rigby's sold the lease for £20,000 and in 1875 its owners sold it for £45,000. Following two more changes of ownership the GWR purchased the lease for £100,000 and abolished the frustrating ten-minute compulsory stop. On 1 October 1895 hundreds of works employees watched the 10.15 a.m. Paddington–Penzance and the 10.45 a.m. Paddington–South Wales pass through Swindon non-stop for the first time.

Before the abolition of the compulsory stop the GWR was not always punctilious in the time spent at Swindon and sometimes trains left after a call of only seven minutes. F. S. Williams wrote in *Our Iron Roads*:

On 7 August 1891 a Mr Lowenfield joined the 3.00 p.m. train at Paddington, with a first class ticket to Teignmouth. The time of the arrival of the train at Swindon was 4.27, and it was booked to leave again, of course, at 4.37. Since he was not due to reach Teignmouth till 7.42, Mr Lowenfield, somewhat rashly perhaps, elected to take an early dinner during the Swindon stop. It may be that he demolished the peculiar fare, which Swindon dignified with the name of dinner in eight minutes. If so, the Great Western was too fast for him, for the train only waited seven minutes, and when a presumably replete Mr Lowenfield stepped on to the platform it had gone.

Mr Lowenfield, of course, was furious. There was no further connection to Teignmouth for another four hours, and even on an August evening, there are perhaps few who would enjoy Swindon for that length of time. He accordingly decided to take the next train to Bristol, and ordered by telegraph a special train to be ready to convey him thence to Teignmouth.

This special cost him £37 17s 0d which he paid with a cheque that the next morning he asked his bank to stop,. The GWR brought an action against him for the cost of the special and he responded with a counter-claim for damages, on the ground that the railway had failed to carry him to Teignmouth and had broken its contract by not stopping at Swindon for the stipulated ten minutes.

The judge agreed that Lowenfield was entitled to damages for the premature start, which he assessed at two pounds and that he was also entitled to a refund of the first class fare between Bristol and Teignmouth and to the reimbursement of three shillings spent on telegrams to an anxious family. The judge did not agree that the suffering which would have been caused to Lowenfield was such that he was justified in ordering a special. The GWR was therefore granted the recovery of the cost of the special and also the full costs of the action.

A portion of Swindon station was destroyed in a fire on 26 March 1898. At around 2.30 a.m. men working in the yard noticed what they believed was a chimney fire in the Up station building. Every fireplace was examined and seemed in order, when flames were spotted emerging from the roof. The Swindon Fire Brigade arrived at 3.50 a.m. and the GWR's own fire engine came ten minutes later. The conflagration was under control at 5.55 a.m.

What caused the fire? The chimney was Z-shaped and, although it had been swept a fortnight before, its shape encouraged lodgement of soot, but more important was that a timber beam ran across the chimney and matters were not aided by the fact that a lead gas pipe ran down the flue!

The Norton Fitzwarren Accident of 11 November 1890

About half past midnight on 11 November 1890, Signalman George Rice was dealing with the thirty-eight-wagon 6.45 p.m. ex-Bristol goods, which was shunting in the sidings. Interestingly, although a standard gauge train headed by Standard Goods 0-6-0 No. 1100, it was assisted by a broad gauge pilot locomotive. As only one engine was required for shunting, until the goods was ready to continue, the broad gauge locomotive was sent a short distance along the Barnstaple branch to be out of the way.

Shunting completed, the Down goods was crossed to the Up line to allow the 9.55 p.m. ex-Bristol fast Down goods to overtake. When he reached the Up line where his train was to wait, Driver Charles Noble correctly changed the colour of the headlight from green (then the normal colour of a headlight) to red as a warning to an oncoming train.

When the Down goods had passed, in anticipation of the signalman giving him the road, Noble changed the light back to green. However he was not allowed to continue because Signalman Rice had completely forgotten about the Down goods. Unfortunately Rice had accepted a special train conveying passengers and mail from a South African Cape line travelling from Plymouth to Paddington. This was the second of two trains; the first, carrying just mail, had passed Norton Fitzwarren at midnight.

The second special consisted of only two eight-wheel coaches and a van and was hauled by 4-4-0ST No. 2051 with Driver John Scott and Fireman John Thomas on the footplate, both from Exeter.

With such a light load, No. 2051 came hurtling towards Norton Fitzwarren at 60 mph, Driver Scott having no warning of the obstructing goods train because its lights were green and not red. Moments before the crash the goods fireman yelled to his driver, 'Here's a train a comin' on our line and he's never going to stop!'

Despite the 60 mph impact, the broad gauge locomotive and train remained upright and in line, although the standard gauge goods train debris made a 30-foot-high pile. The crew of No. 2051 were badly, but not fatally, injured. Unfortunately ten of the fifty passengers were killed and nine seriously injured. A large proportion of those killed were miners returning to the North of England from the South African gold mines, many of them bearing large sums.

Signalman Rice was to blame for the accident. Aged sixty-three, the poor man had not been well since being knocked down by a light engine the previous January when his ribs and skull were injured. At the time of the accident he had worked in the signal box for twenty years, had been on duty for five to six hours and had felt 'bad in the head' for the whole of that evening.

Some good came of the accident. In order to prevent a repetition, Rule 55 was adopted by all railways in Great Britain. It ordered that when a train halted at a signal, the driver was to blow his whistle and if the signalman did not lower his board after three minutes in clear weather, or immediately in fog or falling snow, then he must send a fireman, guard, or shunter to the signal box to inform the signalman of the train's presence and not to leave until a collar had been placed over the relevant signal lever to prevent a conflicting movement being made. Additionally, the person sent was to sign the train register.

As the end of the broad gauge was in sight, No. 2051 was scrapped, but Standard Goods No. 1100 was repaired and returned to service. She was sold to the Government in 1916 and sent to Serbia to haul military trains for the Railway Operating Division. She never returned.

Personalities

William Dean, born in 1840, was educated at the Haberdashers' Company's School. In 1855 he entered the GWR works at Wolverhampton as an apprentice under Joseph Armstrong, later becoming his chief assistant. When Armstrong moved to Swindon in 1864, Dean was appointed manager of Wolverhampton works in charge of 850 men. In 1888 Dean was appointed chief assistant superintendent. On Armstrong's death in 1877 Dean succeeded him.

Dean designed good, strong, reliable engines such as his 0-6-0s which lasted well into the British Railways era, 4-2-2s and Duke Class 4-4-0s. His work with coaches was significant in introducing corridors, lavatories, electric lights and heating. Towards the end of his career, his mental powers began to fail and he gave increasing freedom to his chief assistant, G. J. Churchward, who was able to experiment and develop his new domeless Belpaire boiler on the Dean engines, so that when Dean retired in May 1902 and Churchward himself took over the transition was seamless. He retired to Folkestone where the GWR had purchased a house for him and died there in 1905 aged sixty-five.

Dean held the rank of major in the volunteer regiment at Swindon and was a JP for Wiltshire.

George Jackson Churchward was born at Stoke Gabriel, Devon, in 1857 and aged sixteen was articled to the locomotive superintendent of the South Devon Railway. When the GWR took over the company in 1876 Churchward was transferred to

Swindon, working in the drawing office. In 1882 he was appointed manager of the carriage and wagon works and manager in 1885. He rose to assistant locomotive works manager in 1895 and manager the following year being then appointed chief assistant to Dean. When Dean retired in May 1902 he took over responsibility. Churchward developed a wide range of standard components which could be developed into a wide range of locomotives. From the French he adopted high steam pressure of 225 lb and from the USA long-travel valves, tapered boiler and cylindrical smoke box. He retired in December 1921 but continued to visit the works almost daily. When crossing the line he was killed when struck by one of his engines, No. 4085 *Berkeley Castle*, on 19 December 1933. He was seventy-six.

Development: 1900 – The British Railways Era

There was a lot of truth in the saying the 'GWR' stood for 'Great Way Round' as quite a few of its routes were far from beelines. For instance, the route to the west was via Bristol, as was that to South Wales; the Paddington–Birmingham line was also indirect.

The GWR already owned lines which could become a direct route from Reading to Taunton: the Berks & Hants Extension Railway to Devizes; the Wilts, Somerset & Weymouth Railway from Devizes to Castle Cary and Langport to Taunton, which just needed the first and last lines doubling; building a cut-off from Patney and Chirton to Westbury; and building a new 15-mile-long line between Castle Cary and Langport. Such a route would save 20 miles over the route via Swindon and Bristol.

The chief engineering features were five- and ten-arch viaducts and the 1,056-yard-long Somerton Tunnel and a 105-foot-long girder bridge over the River Parrett. The new line opened to goods on 2 April 1906, it being the practice to just run freight trains over a new line initially in order to allow the embankments to be compacted and any settling adjusted before passenger trains were run.

It had been planned that express passenger trains to the west would use the new route on 2 July 1906, but on the first of that month, a portion of Box Tunnel caved in, so West of England expresses were diverted via Castle Cary a day earlier than planned. As it happened, the new line was the only route available to the west on 1 July, for the London & South Western line was blocked at Salisbury by a crash caused by the Up boat express from Plymouth travelling at too great a speed round a tight curve at Salisbury.

Subsequently the line has seen improvements. Speed restrictions of 30 mph were in force through Westbury and Frome. The slowing down and then accelerating wasted fuel as well as time. Messrs Logan & Hemingway started work on the two cut-offs and they were opened in March 1933, saving each train using the cut-off five minutes and the GWR at least a ton of coal a day, quite apart from wear and tear.

Quadrupling the line from Cogload Junction to Norton Fitzwarren eased the Taunton bottleneck and a flyover at Cogload Junction avoided delays caused by the flat crossing.

When the Severn Tunnel was opened to passenger trains in 1886, expresses from Paddington to South Wales had to curve southwards at Wootton Bassett, pass through Bath and Bristol before bearing northwards to reach the tunnel. Trains therefore travelled an unnecessary mileage and a direct link was need through the southern end of the Cotswold Hills between Wootton Bassett and Filton, north of Bristol.

Coupled with the criticism of indirectness was the fact that many people in South Wales were highly dissatisfied with the service offered by the GWR, and threatened to build an entirely new railway from Cardiff to Andover from where trains could run onwards to London over London & South Western Railway tracks.

The GWR countered this threat to its South Wales traffic by proposing the Bristol & South Wales Direct Railway. This 30-mile-long line had several advantages. It shortened the distance from South Wales to Paddington by 10 miles; avoided two steep inclines, thus enabling locomotives to haul twice the load; shortened the distance between Bristol and London by a mile and additionally offered an alternative route to that via Bath and reduced the number of trains on the crowded Bristol to Bathampton section over which traffic had increased since the opening of the Severn Tunnel.

No opposition was encountered at the parliamentary committee stage and the Act was passed in 1896, the contract being let to S. Pearson the following year. When the first sod was cut by the Dowager Duchess of Beaufort, appropriately at Old Sodbury on 29 November 1897, the GWR invited to lunch all parish priests and the owners, or farmers, of the land through which the line was to run.

More than 4,000 men were engaged in its construction. The line was laid out for speedy running, with no gradient steeper than 1 in 300 and no curve sharper than a mile radius and, considering that the line had to cross the Cotswolds, this was a fine achievement. Four of the stations had quadruple track enabling non-stop trains to bypass the platforms and, if necessary, overtake slower ones. Most of the embankments were wide enough to allow for quadrupling.

Messrs Pearson experienced problems with Sodbury Tunnel; at 4,444 yards in length, its length was second only to the Severn Tunnel on the GWR system. When planned, it had been estimated to be a dry tunnel, but one spring proved so intractable that a drainage tunnel had to be constructed beneath the trackbed in order to carry away the excess water. This resulted in Messrs Pearson, far from gaining a profit for six years' hard work, making a loss of £312,000. An attempt to gain redress from the GWR failed, as did expensive legal proceedings, resulting in Pearson refusing to work for the GWR again.

It was anticipated that on 1 April 1903 would be the opening date for through goods trains, but the treacherous nature of the cutting at the Badminton entrance of Sodbury Tunnel and the slipping of the great embankment at Winterbourne required trenching, draining and strengthening of its earth slopes, so the first goods train was delayed until 1 May 1903, the first passenger trains running two months later on 1 July, children at most schools along the line being given a holiday.

The villagers of Badminton welcomed the railway as it was the means of bringing them a piped water supply. The GWR had arranged with the West Gloucestershire Waterworks Company to supply water for the line's contractors, and the mains, when laid, also served the village.

In return for permission to run its line through 3½ miles of the Duke of Beaufort's estate, the GWR agreed to give the duke and his successors the right to stop any train at Badminton station. In 1963 British Railways made an unsuccessful attempt in Parliament to end this perquisite. With the exception of Badminton all stations on the line were closed to passenger traffic when the local service between Bristol and Swindon was withdrawn in April 1961, but five expresses continued to call at Badminton until 3 June 1968 when BR succeeded in having its obligation abolished.

The line passes through Beaufort Hunt country and before hounds were taken to meets by road, a kennel van was stabled at Badminton station. Engine drivers' working timetables carried in bold print on the cover:

> Every care should be taken to avoid running over Packs of Hounds which, during the Hunting season, may cross the line. All servants of the Railway are hereby enjoined to use every care consistent with a due regard being paid to the proper working of the Line and Trains.

The GWR wanted a route from Bristol to Birmingham. It had running powers over the Midland Railway from Bristol to Standish from where it had its own line to Cheltenham. All that was required was a link between Cheltenham and Honeybourne, which the GWR was able to reach by a branch from Stratford-upon-Avon. A line north reached Bearley where it joined the Birmingham, North Warwickshire & Stratford-upon-Avon Railway. The latter had found it impossible to raise capital for construction and so made overtures to the GWR and, by an Act of 9 August 1899, abandoned entry into Birmingham and satisfied itself with a line from the GWR at Tyseley to the Stratford branch at Bearley. Because the GWR was engaged in so much construction elsewhere, particularly on the shortened line to the west, it was not until 5 September 1905 that C. J. Wills & Sons started work on the Birmingham and Stratford-upon-Avon contract. The line opened to goods on 9 December 1907 and passenger trains, including one from Wolverhampton to Bristol, began on 1 July 1908.

The other new main line required for the route was the 20¾-mile gap between Cheltenham and Honeybourne. The contractors,

Messrs Walter Scott & Middleton, started work towards the end of 1902. A year later an accident occurred at Stanway Viaduct where gangs of thirty to forty men had been working day and night towards its completion. On 13 November 1903 three out of the ten completed arches collapsed, killing two men initially with two more dying later. Frederick Gibbins met his death by a crane falling on him. A pork butcher by trade, he had been unsuccessful in business and was making ends meet by undertaking general labouring work.

The arches fell in reverse order to their construction. When No. 10 fell the adjoining arches, having lost their support, followed, No. 9 falling ten minutes after and No. 8 twenty minutes later. No. 7 fell the next day and by that time the contractors had managed to secure the other arches by binding together the whole of the finished arches with steel chains. The disaster was caused by the five centreings being removed before the hydraulic lime mortar joining the brickwork had set.

The line opened in sections, and work was completed throughout on 1 August 1906, three months ahead of schedule. It had given employment to 1,200 men. The line developed its anticipated potential in providing a direct GWR route from Birmingham to Bristol and the West of England, and also to South Wales. Quite apart from these trains, the line generated a fair amount of local traffic, particularly during the fruit season.

The last of the shortcuts was that from Paddington to Birmingham. The GWR route via Didcot and Oxford took passengers too far west. Apart from the need for a shorter route to rival London & North Western Railway competition to and from Birmingham, American passenger traffic using Birkenhead had developed and a more direct route was essential. Powers for building the first section of the line from Old Oak Common to High Wycombe received parliamentary approval in 1897. Then a joint committee was formed with the Great Central Railway to double and improve the GWR's existing single line from High Wycombe to Princes Risborough and extend it to Ashenden Junction. From there the Aynho & Ashendon railway was authorised by an Act of 11 July 1905 to link with the original GWR route.

These 17½ miles of line through Bicester to Aynho Junction south of Banbury reduced the Paddington to Birmingham distance by 18½ miles and made it 2 miles shorter than the rival London & North Western Railway. The contractors Messrs Scott & Middleton did not start work until the joint line was fully opened on 2 April 1906. Designed for fast running, it had easy gradients and gentle curves of not less than 2 miles' radius. The line from Ashenden Junction to Aynho Junction opened to goods traffic on 4 April 1910 and to passengers on 1 July 1910. Flying junctions were at both ends of the new section and helped to avoid conflicting movements.

Another shortened route was the Avonmouth to Filton line opened on 9 May 1910. Apart from providing a more direct route, it avoided the steeply graded Clifton Down line.

It was not only the main lines that received an improvement, sometimes this happened to a branch line. An example of this was the Bristol & North Somerset Railway's Camerton branch, opened from Hallatrow, on the Bristol to Radstock line, to Camerton on 1 March 1882. The principal purpose of the line was to carry coal from Camerton Colliery, but unfortunately this involved a climb with loaded wagons up a gradient of 1 in 47 made more difficult by the fact that the line was sharply curved. Mineral trains were restricted to fifteen loaded wagons.

57. A poster advertising Paddington–Birmingham expresses. The engine is 4-6-0 No. 4073 *Caerphilly Castle*. (Author's collection)

58. A 2-2-2 *c.* 1841 heads an Up train at Twerton, west of Bath. In the first wagon a shepherd accompanies his flock, while the second vehicle is a double-deck pig wagon. The driver and fireman appear relaxed. (Author's collection)

59. The pumping station and atmospheric railway at Dawlish in 1847, view Down. The disc signal indicates 'danger'. (Author's collection)

60. The broad gauge 4-2-2 *Great Western*. (Author's collection)

61. 4-2-2 No. 3069 *Earl of Chester* passes Hayes with an Up Birmingham express. Notice that the distant signal arms are red as are the coaches, which suggests a date of *c.* 1908. (Author's collection)

62. 4-4-0 No. 3701 *Stanley Baldwin* leaves Paddington *c.* 1910. (Author's collection)

63. No. 171 *Albion* as a 4-4-2 works the Cornish Riviera Express. Notice that this postcard is designed to be sent at Christmas. (Author's collection)

64. The French-built 4-4-2 No. 104 *Alliance*. (Author's collection)

65. 2-6-2T No. 3120 *c.* 1908. (Author's collection)

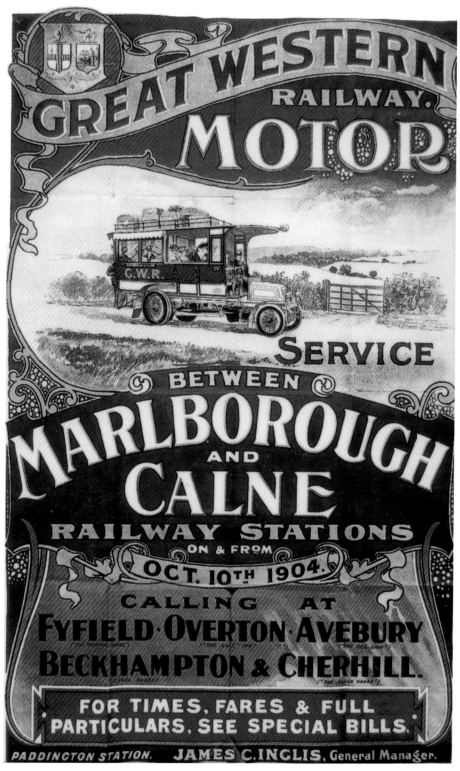

66. Poster advertising the opening of the GWR's Marlborough–Calne bus route, 10 October 1904. (Author's collection)

67. 4-6-0 No. 4013 *Knight of St Patrick* heads a hospital train during the First World War. The picture was sent as a Christmas card and posted on 24 December 1915. (Author's collection)

CORNISH RIVIERA EXPRESS.
GREAT WESTERN RAILWAY.

68. 4-6-2 No. 111 *The Great Bear* heading the Cornish Riviera Express near Teignmouth. The artist has taken considerable licence as this locomotive was limited to working trains between Paddington and Bristol! (Author's collection)

GREAT WESTERN RAILWAY
"FREEDOM FROM ACCIDENT"
COMPETITION

Certificate of Merit

Awarded to *W. J. Talbot*

General Manager

Date *January 1934*

President of G.W.R Social & Educational Union

Editor of G.W.R. Magazine

69. Freedom from Accident certificate awarded to W. J. Talbot. It is signed by the general manager, Sir James Milne. (Author's collection)

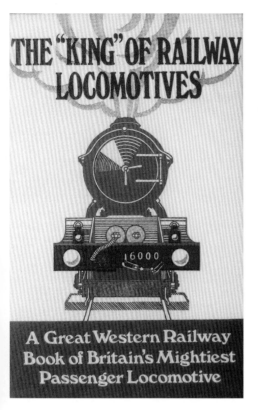

Previous page bottom:
70. Old Oak Common locomotive depot in the early 1900s. Nearest engines left to right: 4-6-0 No. 2916 *St Benedict*, 4-4-0 No. 3391 *Wolseley*, 4-6-0 No. 4003 *Lode Star* and a 3001 class 4-2-2. A turntable is in the foreground. (Author's collection)

This page and next: 71, 72, 73, 74, 75, 76 & 77. Covers of books the GWR published for 'Boys of all Ages'.

CHELTENHAM FLYER

J.B.Jones.

A NEW RAILWAY BOOK
FOR BOYS OF ALL AGES
FULLY ILLUSTRATED
PRICE ONE SHILLING

BRUNEL and After

The
Romance of the
GREAT
WESTERN
RAILWAY
PRICE ONE SHILLING

"CAERPHILLY CASTLE"

A GREAT WESTERN
RAILWAY BOOK

"THE 10.30 LIMITED"

A GREAT WESTERN
RAILWAY BOOK

78. The cover of *GWR Engines*, published in 1947, price 2s 6d.

79. GWR poster advertising the delights of South Wales. (Author's collection)

GWR

JIG-SAW PUZZLE

SIZE OF PICTURE 16" x 12"

DOMINE DIRIGE NOS

VIRTUTE·ET·INDUSTRIA

ABOUT 150 PIECES

ABOUT 150 PIECES

WINDSOR CASTLE

Manufactured by The Chad Valley Co., Ltd., Harborne, Birmingham.   Published by The Great Western Railway Company,

80. The lid of a box containing a jigsaw puzzle depicting Windsor Castle. It was produced by Chad Valley Co. Ltd for the GWR. Note the elaborate lettering. (Author's collection)

Below: 81. An enamel plate. (Author's collection)

Right: 82. A poster, published in the summer of 1904, advertising expresses. The train is hauled by a County Class 4-4-0. (Author's collection)

Great Western Railway.

CAUTION!

Unauthorised persons interfering with the Electric Gear will be

Instantly Dismissed

Engineer's Office
Loco Carriage & Wagon Dept
Swindon January 1910

BY ORDER.

GREAT WESTERN RAILWAY.
LONG DISTANCE TRAVEL
TO & FROM LONDON
WITHOUT A STOP

WEST of ENGLAND		THE MIDLANDS	
	MILES MINUTES		MILES MINUTES
BRISTOL	118 · 120	WORCESTER	120 · 135
EXETER	194 · 205	LEAMINGTON	106 · 110
PLYMOUTH	246 · 265	BIRMINGHAM	129 · 137

SOUTH WALES
MILES MINS
CORRIDOR TRAINS | NEWPORT 133 · 153 | DINING CARS
CARDIFF 145 · 172

JULY, AUGUST & SEPTEMBER, 1904.
SEE TIME-TABLES FOR DETAILS OF TRAIN ARRANGEMENTS
PADDINGTON STATION   JAMES C. INGLIS (General Manager)

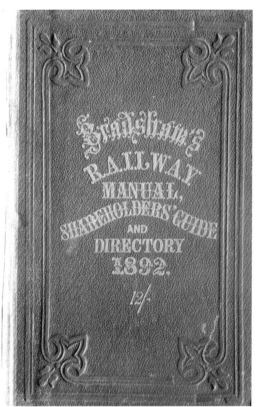

Left: 83. The cover of *Bradshaw's Railway Manual.*

Below: 84. A 1912 GWR poster comparing Cornwall with Italy. (Author's collection)

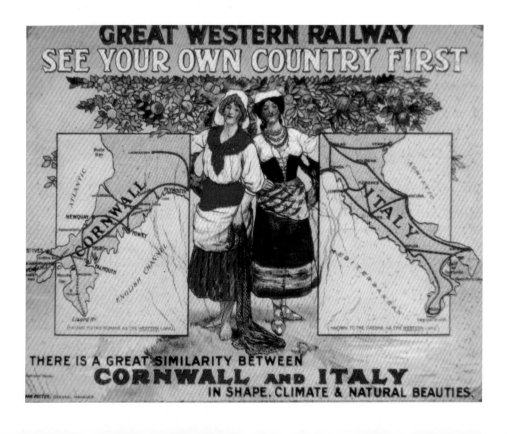

85. Enamel advertisement publicising the Fishguard–Rosslare steamer service. (Author's collection)

86. A King Class 4-6-0 heading the Cornish Riviera Express with 'Centenary' coaches. The poster was designed by Charles Mayo. (Author's collection)

87. Advertising poster shows a woman in a bathing suit drinking from a wine glass held by a seagull at Weston-super-Mare. (Amberley Archive)

The branch had largely supplanted the Somerset Coal Canal which carried most of the coal to Wiltshire and further east. The Camerton branch line continued to supply these traditional markets, but from Camerton trains set off in a westerly direction.

In 1898 plans were made to sink a new pit at Dunkerton, 2 miles to the east of Camerton, and this new colliery was to become the largest in Somerset. By now the Somerset Coal Canal was derelict. An Act of 15 August 1904 assented to the canal being abandoned and the site vested in the GWR, which was given powers to build a line to Limpley Stoke where it would join the Bathampton to Westbury main line.

Southampton was developing at this date and it was expected that much of Dunkerton Colliery's output would be sent eastwards along the valley floor to Limpley Stoke and on to Bathampton. Gradients would allow trains to be up to fifty wagons in length. Some parts of the line actually used the formation of the canal, one instance being the 66-yard-long canal tunnel at Combe Hay which was converted to railway use, while at Monkton Combe a footbridge cast in 1811 formerly spanning the canal then spanned the new railway.

The length from Camerton to Dunkerton was opened on 4 April 1907, coal being taken away via Hallatrow, but on 9 May 1910 the line was opened through to Limpley Stoke. A coal-cutting machine was installed at Dunkerton and by 1912 around 3,000 tons of coal were being raised weekly. Unfortunately due to the owners' policy of getting coal as cheaply as possible, coal supplies were exhausted in 1925. Coal continued to be wound at Camerton until 14 April 1950 when its coal was exhausted. As coal provided the main source of traffic on the branch, subsequent trains usually consisted of just a single van conveying raw material to a flock mill at Monkton Combe and coal and luggage for the school in the same village. The line closed completely on 15 February 1951.

Passenger traffic had not proved successful due to its geography. Most people in the Cam Valley, which the line traversed, wished to travel either northwards to Bath or southwards to Radstock. In order to do this they had to catch a branch train, which ran east or west along the valley, and then change either at Limpley Stoke or Hallatrow, whereas even before the line opened in 1910 motor buses were serving the area and giving a direct service to Radstock and Bath. The passenger service was withdrawn as a wartime economy measure on 22 March 1915. It was restored on 9 July 1923 but prospective users had learned to live without the railway and there was little incentive to walk to a railway station when the bus stopped outside their door. The passenger service ended on 21 September 1925. The section from Camerton to Hallatrow was not really required following the withdrawal of the passenger service, so freight services were withdrawn from this section on 8 February 1932 and the rails lifted.

Not having an intensive train service, the Camerton branch proved useful for film producers. In 1931 *The Ghost Train* was shot at Camerton and this led to GWR publicity folders being distributed to cinema audiences: 'See the Ghost Train Country'. In 1937 some of the night scenes for the Edgar Wallace thriller *Kate Plus Ten* were shot on the sidings at the disused colliery at Dunkerton, while in 1952 the branch formed the setting for *The Titfield Thunderbolt*.

By 1911 many railwaymen were aggrieved at their pay and conditions of work. The Government offered to set up a royal commission to examine the workings of the conciliation boards, which had been set up to enable employers and staff to discuss pay and conditions but made no promise that any recommendations would be implemented.

The four railwaymen's unions believed this offer unsatisfactory and on 16 August 1911 sent an ultimatum to all the railway companies stating that unless there was an immediate response within twenty-four hours all labour would be withdrawn from the railway industry. This was the first national railway strike.

The Prime Minister, H. H. Asquith replied:

> We cannot allow the commerce of the country to be interfered with in the way it would be by a national dispute, and we want you men to realise in the event of it reaching that stage, His Majesty's Government have decided that they will use all the civil and military forces at their disposal to see that the commerce of this country is not interfered with.

The Home Secretary, Winston Churchill, mobilised 58,000 troops who shot dead two strikers at Llanelli. This aggravated the situation by making the men more inclined to continue the fight and also caused many members of the public to sympathise with the men.

The strike began on 18 August when many lines, stations and goods yards became silent. Labour MPs persuaded the Cabinet that mediation and not bloodshed was the way forward and railway companies were told that they must agree to a meeting between their General Managers and the unions, which they had so far refused to recognise.

The companies agreed that if the strike was called off and all strikers reinstated that the railwaymen's grievances would be examined by a royal commission on which they would accept equal representation with the unions. The strike ended on 20 August.

With the increase in traffic, Paddington was becoming inadequate so in 1906 a programme of extensions and improvements was drawn and from 1909 until 1916 work was continuously in progress. The most important additions were three additional platforms, these requiring a new train shed on the arrival side, built to match the original structure and increasing the area of the glass roof to 3½ acres. Each of the three platforms was provided with an innovation as far as the GWR was concerned, in the shape of Ransomes & Rapier hydraulic buffer stops. These extra platforms were brought into use between November 1913 and December 1915.

The Development (Loans, Guarantees & Grants) Act of 1929 for the relief of unemployment provided £1 million for redevelopment work at Paddington and this started in May 1930 and finished in 1934. It consisted of extending Platforms 2 to 11 beyond Bishop's Road Bridge and the parcels depot being moved from the Lawn to Platform 1A, with a new parcels depot constructed above, thus releasing the Lawn to become a passenger concourse. Two new steel-framed office blocks were built either side of the Lawn.

Colour light signals and power-worked points replaced mechanical signalling. To cope with the increase in passenger traffic, especially to the fast developing outer suburbs, new platforms were made by rebuilding Bishop's Road station. The former Up and Down platforms were replaced by two islands and an engine siding was provided to facilitate changing steam to electric traction to work GWR trains over the Metropolitan lines. From 10 September 1933 the name Bishop's Road was dropped, the platforms becoming

Nos 13 to 16. On 22 May 1935 Paddington scored another first – the first Crown Post Office on a railway station was opened.

The GWR introduced piecework rates at Swindon in around 1910. This offered a financial encouragement to increase output, while in 1913 the GWR was the first British railway company to inaugurate a suggestion scheme for saving the company money.

Shipping

Following the GWR's takeover of the Channel Islands service on 1 July 1889 there was an enormous increase in traffic and by 1908 as many as 300 wagons were needed daily to convey flowers, new potatoes and tomatoes from the Channel Islands and broccoli and other vegetables from France. As these had a short shelf life, speedy transport was essential.

In 1897 the summer daylight service was augmented by a regular night service. In 1899 intense competition with the London & South Western Railway (LSWR) ended and the traffic was pooled. Both companies agreed to run three services weekly in winter while in summer the GWR only ran day services and the LSWR ran to the Channel Islands at night and returned during the day. Pooling continued after grouping.

In the autumn of 1897 the GWR directors turned their eyes to Fishguard. The controlling interest of the moribund North Pembrokeshire & Fishguard Railway (NPFR) had been acquired in 1892 by two men who also purchased the Rosslare Harbour works and who by the following year had obtained an Act for the Fishguard Bay Railway & Pier, which was to connect with it. They hoped to sell the Welsh side of the company to the GWR but it showed little interest until an Act was secured to link it with the London & North Western Railway near Carmarthen.

Although further extensions east to Swansea and the London & North Western Railway and the Midland Railway were defeated, the GWR realised the threat and so in February 1898 acquired control of the NPFR. In May 1899 an agreement was made between the GWR, the Great Southern & Western of Ireland and the Fishguard & Rosslare, the latter undertaking to construct harbours at both locations, construct a line from Waterford to Rosslare and provide ferry vessels. The GWR was to build a new, more direct line from Clarbeston Road to Fishguard and work the Welsh side including the shipping service, the Great Southern to work the railways and harbour on the Irish side.

The problem at Fishguard was to find a stretch of level land. After moving 2 million tons of rock, a level 27 acres was provided. A 1,120-foot-long quay enabled cattle to be landed at a lower level and passengers at the upper simultaneously. The cattle pens could accommodate over 1,000 animals and serve as a quarantine and inspection station as well as a rest camp for cattle. The 2,000-foot-long breakwater required 650 tons of stone for every foot extended. A power station was built for operating the electric cranes, haulage capstans and lighting.

On 23 August 1906, guests were taken from London to be entertained on board the GWR steamer, *St David*, overnight at Fishguard. The next day other guests arrived aboard the *St Patrick* on its maiden voyage from Glasgow and it was this vessel that conveyed the entire party to Rosslare and back later that day. The public service began on 30 August 1906 and services from New Milford to both Waterford and Cork were transferred to Fishguard on the same date.

The new service provided both a day and a night service in each direction, daily except Sundays. Boat trains left Paddington at 8.45 a.m. and 8.45 p.m. taking five and a half hours to Fishguard, where they arrived in time to work the return service. Efficiency was the watchword: no more than fifteen minutes was allowed between the train arrival and the ship's departure, and vice versa.

The GWR purchased three new turbine steamers capable of making the passage to Rosslare in three hours, while two new screw steamers replaced the old paddleboats working to Waterford.

New coaches were built for the trains which carried roof boards with gold lettering on a red ground: 'Irish Express via Fishguard' for the day service and 'Irish Mail via Fishguard' for the night service. Both trains had catering facilities and a sleeping car was included on the night train.

As four vessels were available, fuller use of them was made by running day excursions to southern Ireland, Douglas, or Dublin. These excursions for about a thousand passengers were generally fully booked. The excursions from Paddington to the lakes of southern Ireland involved travelling by special train leaving Friday evening and returning on Saturday night.

The first ocean liner to call at Fishguard was the SS *Lanfranc* on 2 April 1908. The water depth was insufficient for her to land passengers at the quay, but they transferred by tender. Nevertheless the boat train left Fishguard only fifty minutes after she dropped anchor. Cunard liners started to call in 1909, Fishguard being 40 miles nearer New York than any other port in Great Britain.

Liverpool had enjoyed a monopoly of transatlantic traffic until 1909 when German liners began calling at English Channel ports in order to reduce the journey time from New York to London. Competition between steamship companies led to the importance of saving a few hours. White Star lines began calling at Holyhead, saving 74 miles, while the Cunard Company decided to call at Fishguard, which was 115 miles nearer New York than Liverpool. Cunard continued to use Fishguard until the outbreak of the First World War, three to four special boat trains being run for each sailing. By the time transatlantic shipping services resumed after the First World War shipping companies had transferred to Southampton, and Fishguard was just left with Irish services.

On the outbreak of the First World War the newer steamers on the Channel Islands and Irish routes were commandeered, the GWR continuing services with older, or borrowed, vessels. SS *Ibex* on the Channel Islands service shot at and sank an enemy submarine, the captain and crew receiving £500 from the Admiralty for this act. Almost every night during the war a GWR steamer crossed St George's Channel with a load of cattle, taking its chance of encountering mines and submarines.

Following the Amalgamation Act of 1921, the GWR became the owner of the largest dock system in the world, covering 1,300 acres. Apart from Millbay, other main ones were sited at Cardiff, Swansea, Newport, Barry, Penarth and Port Talbot.

In the post-war period Millbay Docks at Plymouth were important and the number of liners using Plymouth more than doubled from 354 in 1921 to 788 in 1929. To cater for this traffic the GWR began running Pullman cars on the Ocean Liner expresses, but in 1931 substituted its own Super Saloons for the Pullmans. In 1927 an electrically driven belt was installed to carry post between the ships and stowage vans and required only a third of the manpower required by a human chain. By the mid-fifties, the number of liners using Plymouth fell to about 180 a year and the last Ocean Specials ran in 1962.

Signalling

On 27 July 1903 the signalling and telegraph departments were amalgamated and the signal works extended by the constructing of a new telegraph shop, stores and offices to house the 397 staff of the telegraph section transferred to Reading from Westbourne Park.

A very important advance in safety was made in January 1906 when ATC (Automatic Train Control) was introduced on the Henley branch. This consisted of a ramp formed by an insulated steel bar resting on a timber baulk laid centrally between the rails. A spring contact shoe was fixed on a locomotive so that when crossing the ramp it would be raised by 1½ inches. When the distant signal arm indicated 'all right' the ramp was electrified and the current passing through the shoe rang a bell in the locomotive's cab. If the signal stood at 'caution', or any failure occurred in the ATC apparatus, the ramp remained electrically dead and the raising of the shoe broke a local circuit on the engine and caused a steam whistle to sound in the cab until it was silenced by the driver.

As on single lines trains in both directions travelled over the same ramp, the only ATC signals picked up by the apparatus were those relating to the direction in which it was travelling. This was effected by interlocking between the single line train staff and switches controlling the current to the ramps.

These audible signals were found so reliable that when a more extended trial was carried out in December 1906, when ATC ramps were installed, distant signals were removed, though on main lines semaphore distant signals were retained with the ATC. Only engines fitted with ATC were allowed to work the branch.

An important feature of the system was that the failure of any part of the system invariably gave the danger signal and applied the brakes, so that no breakdown compromised safe working.

In November 1908, as some main line engines had been fitted with ATC apparatus, ramps were laid at all distant signals on the four roads extending between Reading and Slough, and in 1910 between Slough and Paddington. The distant signals remained as a visible reminder.

Later improvements to the ATC included an automatic device for lifting and clipping the ATC shoe at a safe height before entering sections of line electrified on the third rail principle, and for restoring it to the correct position on leaving.

The ATC was further improved by making the operation that caused the 'caution' signal to sound a whistle also open a valve admitting air to the vacuum pipe and thus apply the brakes on the engine and train. In 1929 a start was made on equipping all main and some secondary lines with this system. One great advantage was that trains could travel at much greater speed in dense fog as they could trust the audible signalling, rather than having to rely on visible signals. By 1931, 2,130 miles and 2,538 engines were equipped for ATC running.

Collett was a member of the second special committee set up in 1927 by the Ministry of Transport to consider a standard system of ATC for the whole country. The GWR system was unanimously considered the most satisfactory for adoption by all railways.

In 1938 ATC system was demonstrated to senior managers of the London & North Eastern Railway. A ten-coach express travelling at 69 mph approached a distant signal set at 'caution', the driver being instructed to ignore the warning siren which sounded. The ramp was 318 yards in front of the distant signal, which was 1,032 yards ahead of the home signal. The train stopped 450 yards before the home signal.

The reasons that other railway companies did not adopt this excellent safety feature were that it was a time of financial stringency and also that it had been invented by the GWR and not by them.

Another useful GWR invention was the detonator economiser. To provide against the failure of a detonator, two detonators were used in fog to repeat a home at 'danger'. The economiser was a cunning device consisting of a revolving iron bar alongside a rail, which used the explosion of the first detonator to pull the second off the rail before the engine reached it and thus prevented it from exploding unnecessarily.

In July 1905 Didcot North Junction signal box was opened, all its points and signals worked by electric power. It replaced two mechanical boxes. It was followed by similar boxes elsewhere, while electro-pneumatic power was adopted for the junction of the Windsor branch at Slough in 1913.

Another great improvement in safety was the introduction of track circuits on certain stretches of line. This is a device whereby an electric current passing through the rails allows the presence of at least one vehicle to be detected when the wheels and axles complete a circuit. In addition to indicating the presence of a vehicle, it can lock block instruments, signals and points to prevent any conflicting movement being made. They made their first appearance on the GWR in connection with the new semi-automatic signals at Basildon between Pangbourne and Goring. Semi-automatic, or intermediate block, signals are controlled from the signal box in the rear and provide an additional block section without the additional expense of an extra signal box.

The electric train staff, as opposed to the block telegraph or train staff and ticket, system was introduced in October 1891 between the Dawlish and Parson's Tunnel signal boxes. Then in January 1914 a modification was brought into use on the Great Marlow branch. Working on the same principle as the electric train staff, the bulky staffs were replaced by a small, key-shaped implement known as a token. Proving successful, this system was adopted by the GWR as standard.

Around the time of grouping, Reading signal works covered 8 acres and was served by extensive sidings. Power was supplied to the works by two steam engines, each supplied by one of two pairs of ex-locomotive boilers that received water from the locomotive depot's treatment plant.

Until 1921 the maintenance and repair of GWR clocks and watches was carried out by private contractors, the main one being Kay's of Worcester, but that year the work was transferred to a new clock shop established within the signal works. The staff of thirteen repaired 5,500 watches, 4,500 station and office clocks and 3,500 brass drum timepieces.

In October 1946 the GWR announced that the signal works was to be modernised at a cost of £300,000, but most of the work was delayed until after nationalisation. BR believed that semaphore signals should be standardised, meaning that the lower-quadrant Western Region signals would need to be converted to upper quadrant. The ex-GWR men were appalled! To appease BR, an experimental upper-quadrant signal was constructed and installed at Oxford North Junction in December 1950 where it remained until 1973, but eventually the idea of upper-quadrant signals on the Western Region was dropped.

By the early 1960s the BR modernisation plan was in full swing and mechanical signalling was being replaced by new electric panel boxes covering many miles of track. On 16 November 1970 the signal and telegraph headquarters were transferred from Caversham Road to Western Tower and then in 1983 it was decided to move the signal works to release the land, which had become a valuable asset. Caversham works closed on 29 June 1984.

Publicity

The GWR was the first British railway to publicise widely, and as far back as the early 1900s the GWR far outstripped its competitors with its excellent advertising. The company produced guidebooks in a good literary style, with clear, striking illustrations, all for three pence. Titles were produced such as *Smiling Somerset*, *The West Country* and *The Cotswold Country*, while later hardback books covered such features as castles, cathedrals and abbeys.

From its initial opening it advertised in local papers, first the regular timetable and then special excursions. In 1904 the GWR placed an illustrated advertisement in the *Daily Mail* whereas until then only single column advertisements with a small picture of a train at its head were allowed to be placed.

The *Great Western Railway Magazine* started in 1888. Published monthly, it gave details of staff movements and deaths, and details of the company's development. Originally managed by a part-time editor, Felix Pole took over in 1903 and under his management circulation grew from 2,000 copies monthly to over 20,000. From 1919 Pole handed the office to Edward Hadley, editor from 1919 to 1937, who increased its circulation to 46,000.

The first issue of *Holiday Haunts* appeared in 1906 giving details of holiday places on the GWR system and addresses for accommodation. The first edition contained 538 pages, but by the 1930s this had risen to a chunky one thousand or more pages.

In 1911 the GWR catered for locomotive spotters by producing the *GWR Engine Book* with details of all its locomotives. This was followed with a series of readable and popular books for 'boys of all ages' giving details about such things as how the railway was run, the docks, permanent way and signalling. Another way of appealing to boys was with a GWR board game, while the GWR also arranged for Chad Valley to produce railway jigsaw puzzles. The GWR was also the pioneer of organising trips to a locomotive works.

The GWR made capital of the fact that the outline of Cornwall's coast was like that of Italy and implied that perhaps, rather than travel all that distance on the Continent, one should use the Cornish Riviera Express instead.

During the winter months when demand for the GWR buses was less, some were covered with posters advertising the delights of holidays taken in the GWR country. These buses travelled all over Britain; Inverness was reached in 1907 and the bus was the first large motor vehicle seen in some of the remoter areas of Scotland.

In 1914 the company proclaimed 'GWR The Nation's Holiday Line' while 'Go Great Western' became a catchphrase in the 1920s and appeared on such things as inkwells.

The Big Four co-operated with each other for international marketing and shared premises in Paris and New York. The GWR also promoted the Continental services offered by the Southern Railway.

Pole retired in 1929 and was replaced as general manager by Sir James Milne who continued to develop the company's advertising. He introduced the Gill Sans typeface, while in 1934 the GWR monogram in a circle replaced 'Great Western Railway' on advertisements and locomotives.

First World War

War was declared at 11.45 p.m. on 4 August 1914 and fifteen minutes later the Government took over all British railways, ready for army mobilisation. Control was placed in the hands of the Railway Executive Committee, consisting of the presidents of the Board of Trade and general managers of the principal railway companies. Each line was worked as usual and the public was hardly affected. In the five days from 15 to 19 August, 900 special trains were run, entering southern ports at twelve-minute intervals. In the first fortnight of war, the GWR ran 632 special troop trains in addition to 41 Admiralty coal trains. Nevertheless, ordinary services were maintained, only excursions suffering suspension. Three of the Fishguard to Rosslare ferry vessels were commandeered for use as hospital ships, as were two from the Channel Islands service. Both services continued to be operated using other vessels.

The GWR was important for supplying steam coal for the fleet. Special coal trains were run from Pontypool Road to Warrington and on to Grangemouth on the Forth, where it was either stacked or sent by ship to the naval base at Scapa Flow. By 1918, seventy-nine of these specials ran weekly. Enormous quantities of iron ore were landed at Newport, while Avonmouth was very busy with troops, ammunition, guns, horses and mules. A shell-filling factory at Hayes had thousands of employees and was served by up to 100 trains daily.

Swindon works, in addition to maintaining GWR locomotives and rolling stock, provided sixteen fifteen-coach ambulance trains and constructed road vehicles, heavy howitzers and 60-pounder Hotchkiss and anti-aircraft guns, gun carriages, ammunition wagons, large quantities of medium- and heavy-calibre shells, fuses, bombs and parts for submarines and paravanes. A large quantity of Toluol was produced for use in the manufacture of TNT.

By the end of the first six months, 10,000 GWR employees had enlisted in the services and by 1918, 25,479, almost a third of the staff employed, had joined up; 2,524 were killed. The posts of those in the services were filled by women and older men, as passenger and goods traffic had increased. In 1914 the GWR had between 1,300 and 1,400 female employees, but by 1918 it had over 6,000 and over half the clerical work was done by women along with the majority of ticket collecting and carriage cleaning.

During the First World War the GWR ran over 37,000 special naval and military trains, including 6,000 ambulance trains. Large army camps were established in the Warminster and Salisbury area, causing congestion on the branch. A large ordnance depot and an aircraft depot were established in the Didcot area. All these and other military establishments involved laying many new sidings and consequently brought increased traffic to the GWR.

The result of all this activity was that from 1 January 1917 some expresses were cancelled, while others called at more stations; restaurant, sleeping cars and slip coaches were discontinued; seventy-seven stations and halts were closed and fares rose by 50 per cent. GWR goods and mineral traffic increased to a far greater extent than on other railways: similarly, passenger fares in 1917 compared with 1913 showed the GWR had an increase in traffic of 23 per cent, while the London & North Western

Railway and the Midland Railway showed an increase of only 3 and 2 per cent respectively. The Severn Tunnel proved invaluable, the number of trains passing through increasing from 18,099 in 1913, to 24,027 in 1917. In the First World War the GWR supplied to the War Department 95 locomotives, 105 tenders, 6,086 wagons, 49 miles of complete track, 15,000 tons of rail and 50,000 sleepers for overseas use.

To save labour, by 1915 locomotives were no longer lined out and difficulties in obtaining paint led to a sandy shade of khaki appearing. By 1917 matters had somewhat improved and green was obtainable, but there was no lining out and all bright and polished work was painted over. Coaches appeared in both black and khaki all over and, as the war progressed, became more and more shabby.

The end of the war was a joyful event and was celebrated by the GWR in different ways. The driver of the daily goods train along the Cam Valley south of Bath brought news of the armistice on 11 November 1918 by continuously sounding his locomotive whistle as he drove along the line.

Government control affected the GWR finances. On 1 February 1919 trade union demands for an eight-hour day were met and, coupled with the higher cost of coal, rates and taxes, made 1919 expenses double that of 1913, yet the GWR had to meet this cost from just the 50 per cent increase in fares, while the goods and mineral rates had been fixed by the Government as those charged in 1913. Rumours spread that the Government planned a £2 0s 0d a week minimum wage compared with the current £2 11s 0d and a pre-war minimum of 18 shillings.

The Government, which was still running the railways, in August 1919 craftily offered a rise to footplatemen believing that if a dispute arose over pay of other departments, as the wages of several grades were planned to be cut, the footplatemen would not support a strike. On 26 September 1919 the strike began, drivers and firemen joining in. Railwaymen pressed for overtime and night duty to be paid at a time and a quarter; for time and a half for Sunday duty; three weeks' holiday with pay and a minimum of twelve hours' rest between booked turns. On the GWR 65 per cent of the men went on strike. Stablemen continued to come and feed their horses and the union told the men employed on the Severn Tunnel pumps to continue working. There were some violent scenes, for example near Wootton Bassett an attempt was made to wreck a train by placing an obstruction on the rails. The public did not support the strike and of the 8,600 volunteers who offered their services at Paddington, 4,113 were taken on. Sir Edward Nicholl, MP for East Cornwall, who had served an apprenticeship on the GWR and had been a marine engineer before becoming a shipowner, fired an engine from Reading to Paddington and back. On 5 October 1919 the Government abandoned its plans to reduce wages and the strike ended.

Matters were settled by a further wage increase, the wage bill becoming over three times that of 1913. By 1 January 1920 charges were approximately doubled, but with the availability of inexpensive ex-army lorries and ex-servicemen who had been taught driving during the war, road transport raised its competitive head as the 1919 strike was a warning that rail transport could not be relied on.

On 6 August 1920 passenger fares were raised 75 per cent above those charged before 1917. This encouraged passengers to patronise new bus services operated by ex-servicemen, often using bus bodies on ex-service vehicles.

The Railway Executive Committee did not return control of the GWR and other railways to their owners until 15 August 1921. The railways were bankrupt as fares and goods cartage rates had not risen sufficiently and there had been no increase in passenger fares apart from the 50 per cent rise in 1917 and 25 per cent in August 1920, while until August 1920 goods and mineral traffic charges had been held at 1914 rates! In August 1920 they had risen 115 per cent, yet the GWR salary and wage bill in 1914 of approximately £6 million had risen in the post-war years to over £20 million.

Railway Amalgamation

These railway problems resulted in parliamentary discussion, some favouring nationalisation of the railway companies and others believing it was best to leave them in private hands.

The result was the Railways Act of 19 August 1921, which was a compromise, amalgamating 120 railway companies into four: the Great Western Railway, the London, Midland & Scottish Railway, the London & North Eastern Railway and the Southern Railway, the Act coming into force on 1 January 1923.

The GWR was the only company to retain its previous name. Most of the companies added to the GWR were in South Wales. Although the coal trade had hitherto been profitable, the industry reached its peak in 1923 and then suffered a decline.

The constituent companies of the new GWR were:

1. Alexandra (Newport and South Wales)
   Docks and Railway   10¼ miles
2. Barry Railway   68 miles
3. Cambrian Railways   295¼ miles
4. Cardiff Railway   11¾ miles

5. Great Western Railway	3005 miles
6. Rhymney Railway	51 miles
7. Taff Vale Railway	124½ miles

The Alexandra (Newport) Dock was incorporated on 6 July 1865 to construct docks and a connecting railway. From 31 December 1897 it absorbed the Pontypridd, Caerphilly & Newport Railway thus adding a 9¼-mile-long main line to its 100 miles of dock line. Apart from two railmotors, all its locomotives were tank engines.

The Barry Dock & Railways was incorporated in 1884 and the first dock opened on 18 July 1889. It gained running powers over other lines to make a system of about 70 miles including residential services in and out of Cardiff and excursions to Barry Island. In the record year of 1913 over 11 million tons of coal were shipped from Barry Docks.

The Cambrian Railways was incorporated by an Act of 25 July 1864, 'railways' being in the plural as it was formed from the Llanidloes & Newtown, the Oswestry & Newtown, the Newtown & Machynlleth, and the Oswestry, Ellesmere & Whitchurch, while the Aberystwyth & Welsh Coast Railway was added on 5 August 1865. On 1 July 1904 it took over the Mid-Wales Railway, which ran from Llanidloes to Talyllyn Junction. The narrow gauge Vale of Rheidol amalgamated on 1 July 1913 and the Tanat Valley Light Railway on 12 March 1921.

The Cardiff Railway was incorporated on 6 August 1897 and grew from the Bute Docks. Its route mileage was about 11½ miles compared with 120 miles of dock sidings. Like many Welsh companies, apart from two railmotors it only used tank engines. It was the only coal-carrying railway in South Wales that proved a financial failure, paying a dividend of only 1 per cent in 1921 when the Rhymney Railway paid 9 per cent.

The Rhymney Railway opened for goods on 25 February 1858 and for passengers on 31 March. Although the company paid no dividend in 1871, over the next twenty-two years it rose to 10½ per cent.

The Taff Vale Railway was the largest and oldest of the Welsh constituent companies, its Act being granted in 1836, so it was only a year younger than the GWR. Like the GWR, its engineer was Brunel, though due to the line's curvature he favoured the standard, rather than broad, gauge. The original main line ran from Cardiff to Merthyr Tydfil. It moved almost 20 million tons of coal annually and paid a dividend of a remarkable 17½ per cent.

Taking over the Taff Vale Railway brought the Pwllyrhebog Incline to the GWR. On a branch serving Clydach Vale Colliery, the 1¾-mile-long line was steeply graded, starting with half a mile at 1 in 13 before easing to 1 in 29/30 for the remainder. Empty wagons were hauled up by a cable connected to a descending loaded train. To guard against breakaways, a locomotive propelled the wagons up the incline, the cable passing below the train to be hooked to this engine.

In 1884 the Taff Vale locomotive superintendent Tom Hurry Riches designed special engines. Their wheels were 5 feet 3 inches, the railway's standard passenger engine size, to offer safe clearance to the winding cable sheaves. A slipper brake was fitted between the last two sets of wheels. The locomotives normally worked up the incline bunker-first, a steeply sloping firebox crown ensuring a depth of water above, while the tapered boiler offered ample steam space. The design also permitted the firebox crown to be fully covered and still have adequate steam space if the engine worked chimney-first.

Built by Messrs Kitson, the three engines became TVR Nos 141–3, the GWR renumbering them 792–4 and then 193–5 in 1946. Based at Treherbert, two engines worked the incline with the third kept as spare. Normally each worked for a month followed by a fortnight's rest.

When the incline closed on 1 July 1951 the engines were almost sixty-seven years old and their boilers thirty-five to thirty-six years of age. When the engines were withdrawn by BR, of 1951–3 No. 194 had covered the fewest miles (865,504) and No. 193 the most (943,197). Considering their duties, these figures were surprisingly high. Two were sold by BR to the National Coal Board, but were scrapped by 1960.

Three old tenders were kept at the head of the incline to act as a counterbalance and enable a train at the bottom to ascend without having to wait until a loaded train was ready at the summit. It is believed that the tenders ceased working in 1932.

In addition to the above constituent companies, the GWR took over the following subsidiary companies:

1. Brecon & Merthyr Railway	59¾ miles
2. Burry Port & Gwendraeth Valley Railway	21 miles
3. Cleobury Mortimer & Dittons Prior Light Railway	12 miles
4. Gwendraeth Valleys Railway	3 miles
5. Llanelli & Mynydd Mawr Railway	13 miles
6. Midland & South Western Junction Railway	63¼ miles
7. Neath and Brecon Railway	40 miles
8. Port Talbot Railway & Docks	35 miles
9. Rhondda & Swansea Bay Railway	29 miles

10. South Wales Mineral Railway   13 miles
11. Swansea Harbour Trust
12. Powlesland & Mason

The Brecon & Merthyr was a curious line as it consisted of two sections: Brecon to Merthyr Tydfil and then from Deri Junction to Bargoed South Junction and on to Bassaleg and Newport, running over the Rhymney Railway. The route included the Seven Mile Bank which proved expensive to work. The company never made a true profit. It was absorbed by the GWR on 1 July 1922.

The Burry Port & Gwendraeth Valley Railway was one of South Wales's westerly mineral lines. Opened to goods in July 1869, on 30 June 1909 it carried colliers unofficially. To comply with the Board of Trade, it was granted a Light Railway Order and official passenger services began on 2 August 1909. Until then, miners' wives and others going shopping at Llanelli travelled in brake vans and goods vehicles, as the railway was unauthorised to carry people but quite legally able to charge sixpence per package for the carriage of shopping baskets and other receptacles. The company was absorbed by the GWR on 1 July 1922.

The Cleobury Mortimer & Ditton Priors Light Railway conforms to the tradition of the longer the name, the shorter the railway. Although incorporated in 1901 it did not open until July 1908 for goods and November 1909 for passengers. Its principal use was to carry granite from Abdon Clee. The company was absorbed by the GWR on 1 January 1922.

The Gwendraeth Valley Railway was owned by the Kidwelly Tinplate Works, though the two companies were run separately. The Act was obtained by the Carmarthen & Cardigan Railway, but then powers were transferred in 1866. In its early years the line had been worked by the Burry Port & Gwendraeth Valley Railway, but in 1909 it purchased GWR No. 1378 *Margaret*. When the Gwendraeth Valley was taken over by the GWR in January 1923, its sale to the tinplate company had already been negotiated so it was never allocated a new GWR number in 1923. The company was absorbed by the GWR on 1 January 1923.

The Llanelli & Mynydd Mawr Railway (L&MMR) was incorporated in 1875 to purchase the Carmarthenshire Railway, which had opened between Llanelli and Gorlas in 1806. It had gone into liquidation in 1844 and been abandoned. A contractor, Messrs John Waddell & Sons of Edinburgh, agreed to construct the L&MMR, provide rolling stock and work the line in return for a percentage of the receipts. It opened on 1 January 1883, and Waddell continued to work the line until it was taken over by the GWR when it absorbed the company on 1 January 1923.

The Midland & South Western Junction Railway linked the Midland Railway at Cheltenham with the London & South Western Railway at Andover, though actually its line ended at Andoversford and used its running powers over the GWR to reach Cheltenham. Many trains ran from Cheltenham through to Southampton.

It began as the Swindon, Marlborough & Andover Railway, which opened on 27 July 1881 and which reached Andover on 5 February 1883. The associated Swindon & Cheltenham Extension Railway opened to Cirencester on 18 December 1883 and through to Cheltenham on 1 August 1891. It was absorbed by the GWR on 1 July 1923. It proved a vital line during the First World War, taking men and ammunition southwards and ambulance trains northwards. It ran two express trains called simply the North Express and the South Express.

The Neath & Brecon Railway was incorporated in 1862 as the Dulais Valley Mineral Railway and opened on 2 September 1864. It was extended through to Brecon on 3 June 1867. Although it was 72 miles in length, traffic was sparse because there were no towns between its termini. Coal was carried over the line from Neath and the Dulais Valley, but this was insufficient to provide a good revenue. Not surprisingly, the company passed into receivership in 1873 and four years later expenditure exceeded receipts by 238 per cent. The Midland Railway, anxious to secure a route from Birmingham to Swansea, obtained running powers over the Neath & Brecon and began running through-trains from 1877. Adeslina Patti, the famous Italian soprano, purchased Craig-y-Nos Castle in 1878 and built a private waiting room for herself and her many guests at Penwyllt station, which was renamed Craig-y-Nos.

Although the Neath & Brecon was vested in the GWR under the Railways Act of 1921, and absorbed by the GWR on 1 July 1922, the LMS operated the passenger and through goods services until the end of 1930.

The Port Talbot Railway & Docks was incorporated on 31 July 1894 to acquire and enlarge Port Talbot Docks. The main line from Port Talbot to Blaengarw involved a steep climb, partly at 1 in 40. The line prospered and the GWR took over working in 1908. The company was absorbed by the GWR on 1 January 1922.

The Rhondda & Swansea Bay Railway was constituted in 1882 to offer a shipping outlet for Rhondda coal to Port Talbot and Briton Ferry as Cardiff was choked with traffic. A terminus at Swansea Riverside opened on 7 May 1899. The company came under the control of the GWR in 1906, but was not actually absorbed by the GWR until 1 January 1922.

The South Wales Mineral Railway was incorporated on 15 August 1853 and included a cable-worked incline over which the locomotives travelled with the wagons. Leased and worked by the Glyncorrwg Coal Company until 1870, the incline fell out of use and was closed by the end of 1910. Although not actually absorbed by the GWR until 1 January 1923, it was taken over by the GWR with effect from 1 January 1908 and, with the Port Talbot Railway, worked as part of the PTR's system.

The first Swansea Harbour Act was passed in 1791 and there were connections with various horse-worked tramways, including the Mumbles Railway. The Swansea Harbour Trust was incorporated by an Act of 3 July 1854. Its railways were worked by contractors until locomotives were purchased in 1905. The trust was vested in the GWR on 1 July 1923.

From 1865 Powlesland & Mason hauled GWR traffic over the Swansea Harbour Trust's lines and also acted as GWR carting agents in the area. Although the Swansea Harbour Trust had been vested in the GWR on 1 July 1923, Messrs Powlesland & Mason were not taken over until 1 January 1924.

The 2-foot-3-inch-gauge Corris Railway was initially opened using horsepower, but steam traction was introduced in February 1879. A passenger service began on 4 July 1883. The line was purchased by Imperial Tramways of Bristol who in 1924 introduced bus services in the area. In 1929 the GWR acquired a substantial interest in the Crosville Motor Service Ltd which took over the Corris Railway's buses, while from 4 August 1930 the GWR took over the railway. Passenger services were withdrawn from 1 January 1931.

From having a staff of 1,101 in 1851, by 1925 the number of GWR employees had grown to an army of over 117,000, including 3,500 women. The staff consisted of:

76 capstanmen

3,281 carters and vanguards

1,242 carriage cleaners

839 carriage and wagon examiners

384 carriage and wagon oilers and greasers

1,638 checkers

18 crane men

314 crossing keepers

1,928 engine cleaners

6,120 engine drivers and motormen

6,114 firemen

1,114 foremen and chargemen (non-supervisory)

3,274 goods guards

1,111 passenger guards

5,864 labourers

340 lampmen

844 loaders, callers-off, ropers and sheeters

367 messengers

282 number-takers

12,350 officers and clerks

10,888 permanent way men

26 pointsmen

378 policemen

37 police inspectors

3,234 goods porters

4,607 passenger porters

630 shop and artisan staff (supervisory grades)

21,820 shop and artisan staff (excluding labourers and watchmen)

3,770 shunters

1,580 signal and telegraph men

4,954 signalmen

1,294 stationmasters and yardmasters

1,948 supervisory staff (other than shop and artisan and police staff)

721 ticket collectors

100 watchmen

13,626 miscellaneous

Narrow Gauge

The GWR possessed several narrow gauge lines. The Westleigh Quarries, near Burlescombe, Devon, were leased by a group led by J. C. Wall, General Manager of the Bristol & Exeter Railway. An agreement was made with the B&E to work the 3-foot-gauge line for twenty-five years from March 1873. The tramway, just over ¾ mile in length, opened on 12 January 1875. The B&E, having no engines of this gauge, built two 0-4-0WTs to work the line. When these engines were taken over by the GWR, the brass number plate had to be fixed to the rear of the cab, there being no suitable surface to display it on the side. When the B&E's lease expired, the quarry company converted the line to standard gauge and worked the line itself. Rail traffic ceased in around 1950.

The 1921 Amalgamation Act brought more narrow gauge lines to the GWR. The 2-foot-6-inch-gauge Welshpool & Llanfair Railway opened on 4 April 1903 and was initially worked by the Cambrian Railways and absorbed by the GWR on 1 January 1922. Although the passenger service was suspended on 9 February 1931, goods continued until 3 November 1956. It owned two Beyer Peacock 0-6-0Ts, *The Earl* and *The Countess*. The first portion of a mile running through the town was last used on 17 August 1963, but the rest has been preserved.

The 1-foot-11½-inch-gauge Vale of Rheidol Railway opened on 22 December 1902, was amalgamated with the Cambrian Railways on 1 July 1913 and was taken over on 1 January 1922 by the GWR. Closed in 1940, it reopened in 1945. The branch to Aberystwyth closed in 1924 and in 1968 the line from Llanbadarn to Aberystwyth was realigned so that it entered the main station. This highly scenic line has been preserved.

The 2-foot-3-inch-gauge Corris Railway opened on 30 April 1850 as the Corris, Machynlleth & River Dovey Tramroad using horse traction. In 1853 it was renamed the Corris Railway and steam traction was introduced in 1879. From 1879 until powers to carry passengers by rail were granted, the railway operated a service of road coaches. Passenger service started on 25 August 1887. The line was bought by Imperial Tramway Co., Bristol in 1878 and became GWR property in 1930. The passenger service was withdrawn on 1 January 1931 and the line closed on 20 August 1948. It is gradually being reopened.

Commercial Traffic

Today it is not always appreciated just how much of the nation's goods was handled by the railways in the 1930s. Apart from vast quantities of coal required for the railway's own use and for domestic and industrial needs, there was oil, milk, post and newspapers. The GWR carried more milk to London than any other line, bringing about 250,000 gallons daily.

Until about 1930 milk was carried in 17-gallon churns weighing 2¼ cwt when full. United Dairies at Wootton Bassett used the first rail bulk milk tanks to run in England and proved much more economical than churns. One man could rinse a tank with cold water and scrub it, then rinse it out with hot water and finally sterilise with steam, a much easier operation than carrying out these procedures with 176 17-gallon churns which held the equivalent of one tank. The 176 churns required three vans to transport them and weighed a total of 80 tons, whereas one tank was only 22 tons. Each tank was insulated with a 2-inch layer of cork which meant that the milk left the factory at 38 degrees Fahrenheit and the temperature rose by no more than one degree on its journey to Mitre Bridge Siding, Willesden.

Bananas required heated vans, meat and fish required refrigerated vans and flowers needed swift transport from Cornwall to various markets as did potatoes and tomatoes from the Channel Islands. Strawberries from the Cheddar Valley and fruit from Evesham were perishable traffic needing speedy handling, as were rabbits from North Devon. Raw materials were carried to factories and the finished products transported away. Most goods sold in shops travelled by rail. The introduction of containers eased transhipment from road to rail vehicle and vice versa.

Locomotives

Churchward retired as Chief Mechanical Engineer in December 1921, his deputy, Charles Benjamin Collett, taking his office. Collett built on Churchward's foundations, his Castle Class 4-6-0 which appeared in 1923 being a direct development of a Star; in fact, some Stars were converted into Castles. The Castles were followed four years later with Kings, these being the most powerful 4-6-0s in Britain.

Although the Castles were very satisfactory when burning Welsh coal, during the 1926 coal strike, when they had to burn imported coal, they were less satisfactory. The Southern Railway had produced the Lord Nelson Class in 1926 with a tractive effort superior to a Castle, so it was felt that something should be done to enable the GWR to regain its claim to have the most powerful passenger locomotive in Britain.

Collett explained that a GWR engine was limited to a maximum axle weight exceeding 20 tons, whereas a Lord Nelson had a limit of 20¾ tons. The GWR's General Manager, Sir Felix Pole, on investigation discovered that the GWR's chief engineer had provided for a maximum axle load of 22 tons in all new bridge work on the main lines, while on the West of England main line, only four bridges were subject to a 20-ton restriction.

Pole immediately ordered two directives: to J. C. Lloyd, the chief engineer, to bring those four bridges up to the new standards, and to Collett to design a new class of express passenger locomotive of maximum power having an axle load within the 22-ton limit.

It was initially planned to call these Super-Castles 'Cathedrals', but then in 1927 the Baltimore & Ohio Railroad was celebrating its centenary and Pole suggested the latest GWR express locomotive should be sent over and displayed. With his majesty's consent, the engine was named *King George V*.

On 10 August 1927, while *King George V* was still crossing the Atlantic, another King hauling the Down Cornish Riviera Express had its bogie derailed at 60 mph. Fortunately the driving wheels kept to the road, but this was a warning. Collett cabled to William Stanier who was accompanying *King George V* to tell him to prevent it doing any main line running until further notice.

It was found that the bogie's springing required modification and then all would be safe; indeed it reached a speed of 75 mph – far faster than contemporary American locomotives.

In 1924 Collett rebuilt a 4-6-0 Saint with 6-foot instead of 6-foot 8½-inch driving wheels. This produced a highly useful mixed-traffic engine capable of hauling goods trains during the week and holiday expresses on summer Saturdays. In 1946 the 4-6-0 Grange Class appeared, similar to the Halls but with 5-foot 8-inch wheels and incorporating the wheels and motion of withdrawn 43XX Class 2-6-0s. The Manor Class engines introduced in 1938 were similar to the Granges but of a lighter design thus giving them wider availability.

Collett did not forget motive power for branch or subsidiary lines. Churchward had built no six-wheel tender engines and following the 1923 grouping, there was a need for replacement 0-6-0s. In 1930 the first of the 2251 Class appeared with this wheel arrangement. Similarly the 517 Class 0-4-2Ts used on mainly branch lines were being withdrawn and a small modern replacement was required, capable of running over all GWR lines.

The Collett replacements were of two classes: the 48XX fitted with apparatus for working auto trains and equipped for ATC, and the 58XX Class built without either feature. The cabs fitted to both classes offered much greater protection to crews than on the 517 Class and the windows were unusually large. Despite their small size, they could be speedy.

Another light-weight class was the 4-4-0 Earl. By the 1930s Duke Class 4-4-0s were being withdrawn as their frames had failed and the trains hauled by them needed a light-weight replacement. Collett did this most economically by placing Duke cabs and various types of boiler on 4-4-0 Bulldog frames – a Bulldog, being a heavier engine, could not itself be a replacement. Names of Earls were allotted to this class, but then it was considered inappropriate to have such appellations on small engines and the grand names were transferred to new Castle Class locomotives.

Churchward's 2-8-0Ts were designed to haul coal in South Wales between pit and port or factory. Following the General Strike of 1926, this traffic declined and some of the 2-8-0Ts became superfluous. Collett realised that if the frames were extended by 4 feet 1 inch, the enlarged bunker could hold almost as much coal as a tender engine and thus allow the range of the class to be extended. The enlarged bunker was supported by a trailing radial axle, making the locomotive a 2-8-2T of most impressive appearance. These 72XX Class engines replaced the Aberdare 2-6-0s on medium- and long-distance mineral trains.

521 2-8-0s based on J. G. Robinson's Great Central Railway design and built for the Railway Operating Division of the Royal Engineers were built in the First World War. After the war, no single railway wished to purchase them all. In 1919 the GWR bought twenty that were virtually new and hired a further eighty-four. Most of the loaned engines had been used in France and were in various conditions. All the loaned engines were returned to the Government in 1921 and 1922, which dumped them in different locations until 1924 when they were offered for sale at a much reduced price.

In 1925 the GWR purchased eighty at £1,500 each. After only four months' use, they were withdrawn and sent to the dump at Swindon. It was decided that the best thirty would be 'thoroughly overhauled, fitted with copper fireboxes and painted G.W. standard green', while the other fifty were to be 'touched up and returned to traffic, with steel fireboxes and painted in the original ROD black' and scrapped when no longer fit for traffic. The Westinghouse brake gear was removed, but many engines retained the flat steel hangers welded to the smoke box to which it had been attached, some lasting into the BR era. All the ROD black batch of engines was withdrawn between October 1927 and December 1931. The highest mileage recorded was 70,937 and the lowest 22,693. Following the locomotives' withdrawal, the tenders were repainted green, and allocated to Aberdare Class 2-6-0s. When these were withdrawn from 1934 onwards, some of the tenders were transferred to 2251 Class 0-6-0s. All but five of the 'thoroughly overhauled' engines passed into BR stock, one achieving a mileage of 761,945. Having only steam brakes, they were confined to unfitted freight trains.

Diesel Railcars

As early as 1911 the GWR obtained a four-wheel railcar, powered by a 40 hp Maudslay petrol engine driving a dynamo supplying power to two electric motors. The four-wheel car, designed by British Thomson-Houston Company, seated forty-four passengers and had a maximum speed of about 32 mph. It worked on the Windsor branch, but was withdrawn in October 1919. It is believed that overheating of the valve seatings may have been why the idea did not generally find favour.

The GWR purchased Drewry petrol-engined inspection trolleys before 1910 and in 1923 a four-wheel Simplex petrol-engined shunting locomotive was purchased from the Motor Railway & Tram Co. Ltd. Proving successful for light work, particularly where shunting was intermittent rather than continuous, by 1927 the GWR owned a fleet of five of these machines.

In 1933 a four-wheel diesel-mechanical shunter was purchased from John Fowler & Co. Ltd, while in 1936 the GWR bought a 350 hp diesel-electric shunting engine from Hawthorn, Leslie & Co. Ltd. This was the forerunner of the later British Railways shunters. The GWR ordered six similar machines with English Electric power units and one with a Brush-built unit, the rest of the locomotives being manufactured at Swindon, though it was the British Railways era by the time they appeared from the workshops.

In 1933 a streamlined diesel-mechanical railcar, built by Associated Equipment Co. Ltd using a standard 130 hp road-vehicle engine with a Park Royal Coachworks body, was placed in service. It seated sixty-nine passengers in a three-plus-two format. Its maximum speed was 60 mph. The body was the result of wind-tunnel tests on models at the London Passenger Transport Board's laboratory at Chiswick. The car was exhibited at the 1933 commercial vehicle show at Olympia.

This first car proving successful, in its first year carrying 136,000 passengers and running more than 60,000 miles; the next three cars built were equipped with two 121 bhp engines which could achieve a speed of 75–80 mph. Seating forty-four passengers two-by-two-style at tables, it had two lavatories and a buffet. July 1934 saw them introduced on the first long-distance express diesel railcar service in Great Britain; this ran from Birmingham to Cardiff. A supplementary fare of 2*s* 6*d* was added to the normal third-class fare. As well as running regular services, railcars were used for outings of groups and societies and also mystery trips.

Car No. 17 was designed with hinged stowage racks fitted to its walls for parcels traffic. From 4 May 1935 it ran on weekdays between Reading and Oxford plus an early morning working from Kensington with Lyons's cakes. It bore the legend 'Express Parcels' on its side in large letters.

During the locomotive exchanges of 1948, the 8.30 a.m. Plymouth–Paddington slipped a coach at Reading. One day the slip occurred as normal and on arrival at Paddington the Southern enginemen and inspectors from the engine that had drawn the train from Plymouth were talking on the platform when a Southern inspector noticed No. 17 running into the parcels platform, causing him to remark, 'We must have been going some at Reading as our slip coach has just followed us in!'

The first seventeen diesel railcars were not fitted with standard drawgear, but were just equipped with a simple device for attaching a towing hook, while the buffers were just small, spring-loaded plungers.

Several problems had arisen with the early railcars. Following prolonged use, the internal expanding brake drums overheated and impaired their use. Another problem was that the wheels sometimes failed to provide electrical paths for track circuiting due to the wheels not being kept clean by the brake shoes rubbing on the tyres as was normal railway practice. A further disadvantage was that the vacuum only allowed the ATC to sound a short note when indicating 'caution'.

Initially a klaxon warning horn was fitted, but the sound was not sufficiently penetrating and could be confused with a road vehicle. The problem was solved by using a strident two-tone horn. The warning of a railcar's approach was particularly important because when running it made little track noise and, as it emitted no steam, was less visible. In tunnels the streamlining produced little forward draught and so tunnel workers were less likely to feel it.

In 1936 sixteen railcars worked 132 services covering over 3,000 miles daily. A Bristol-based railcar ran 402 miles daily. Their average fuel consumption was 8 miles per gallon on express services and 6–7 miles per gallon on stopping trains.

Railcar No. 18 had an AEC chassis and a Gloucester Railway & Carriage & Wagon Company body. It was fitted with standard GWR buffers and drawgear so could haul one or two coaches or vans as trailers up to a total weight of 60 tons. The exhaust-heated boiler, installed in the luggage compartment, heated the trailer. The car was used principally on the Lambourn branch where it frequently needed to haul horseboxes carrying animals to or from the racing stables. Its maximum load was six horseboxes. On market days it hauled a trailer coach. To cope with haulage work adequately, a dual-ratio gearbox was installed.

At the GWR's annual meeting in February 1938, the company's chairman said that the original intention was to use railcars to provide additional services where traffic was insufficient to justify the working of a train, but experience had shown that owing to the increasing cost of operating steam locomotives, considerable economies could be effected by replacing them with diesel railcars on certain sections – thus the GWR predated British Railways' plans by about twenty years.

He said that the twenty new cars would be fitted with standard buffers and drawgear and have electro-pneumatic controls so that two or more power cars could be run as a train. Fifteen of the new cars were intended for local or branch services and thus were geared to a maximum speed of 40 mph and capable of hauling 60 tons, or two standard coaches. Another parcels car was to be built and the other four cars were to consist of two twin units with vestibule connections

These twin sets had a top speed of 75 mph and seated 104 passengers. One car contained a buffet, while the other had a small luggage compartment and toilet. The twin sets could cope with an intermediate trailer.

Coaching Stock Improvements

The passenger coach livery of cream and brown from about 1880 displayed the garter crest in the lower panel if first class, while second and third class carried the entwined letter monogram. In 1904 this was changed to a garter crest with the crests of London and Bristol to either side for first-class compartments, while second and third continued to use the monogram until 1906.

In 1903 a rake of coaches was painted brown all over. The experiment proved successful – it was easier to keep clean than the cream – and from 1908 all stock was to be repainted thus. Roofs were still white and underframes black. Coaches were still lined but window mouldings were no longer painted black; then in 1913 coach livery was changed to lake. In 1923 the chocolate and cream livery returned.

In 1900 the Cork Boat Express had the first set of GWR coaches to be equipped with electric lighting and this form became more general in 1905, though gas-lit coaches still continued to be built until 1913, and this form of lighting showed a great improvement when incandescent mantles were adopted in 1905. Gas lighting had the severe disadvantage that in the event of a derailment, the danger was always present that gas escaping from the storage cylinders would aggravate a fire. Nevertheless, the last gas-lit coach was not withdrawn from service until 1959.

First-class dining cars were introduced in 1896, while third-class dining cars appeared in 1903. The second class was abolished in 1910.

Clerestory roofs where the central section of the coach roof was raised to give additional light and ventilation were popular around the end of the nineteenth century, but when Churchward succeeded Dean he favoured the elliptical style, which was much stronger and less expensive to build. In around 1907 a few six-wheel bogies were produced for sleeping and restaurant cars.

Until 1904, coaches had always been shorter than 60 feet but in the interests of efficiency and economy, Swindon designed stock which conveyed the maximum number of passengers in comfort for the minimum tare weight. This resulted in 70-foot-long stock with ten compartments seating a total of eighty third-class passengers. An unusual feature of these Dreadnought coaches was that their corridors changed from one side to the other at the centre of each coach and another was that their extreme width of 9 feet 6 inches made it necessary to recess the outside doors. Churchward's coaches had wooden bodies on steel underframes, but Collett's had steel panels. As these lengthy coaches were restricted to certain lines, 57-foot coaches had to be built for some routes. These coaches had elliptical, instead of clerestory, roofs and were 9 feet 6 inches wide at the waist. The fact that they only had three doors on each side instead of one per compartment made them disliked by the public. The fact that the locking bars of points had to be modified to cope with their length outweighed any operation economy gained by their greater carrying capacity. The GWR ceased building 70-foot coaches in 1925 because flange wear was found to be excessive; 57–60 feet length became the general standard in Britain for eight-wheel coaches.

In 1925 articulated coaches with two bodies sharing a bogie appeared, but were not found successful and in 1936–7 they were placed on separate bogies and the length of the bodies increased from 49 feet 7 inches to 57 feet. The two-coach 'B-sets' of the 1920s, which appeared on many branch lines, consisted of two close-coupled brake composites permanently coupled together. By 1930 galvanised steel panels were being fitted to coaches and also used for repair and found most durable.

In 1931 'Super Saloons' appeared on Plymouth boat trains and when the boat trains ceased in 1962, these coaches were used for up-market specials such as those to Newbury races. The interiors of the Super Saloons were quite up to Pullman standard and all were named after members of the royal family.

For the GWR centenary in 1935, new stock was built for the Cornish Riviera Express. Built exclusively for the service, the design took advantage of the wider GWR loading gauge on ex-broad gauge lines and they were built to a width of 9 feet 7 inches, these dimensions restricting them to only a few GWR lines and certainly not those of any other railway company.

The year 1935 also saw the introduction of Quick-Lunch-Bar cars and specially built excursion stock with centre aisles capable of a meal service being delivered to any seat; hitherto excursion trains had used old vehicles. A restaurant car pair built in 1935 could boast of being the first fully air-conditioned stock in Britain.

Post-Second World War, F. W. Hawksworth produced coaches of modern design with large windows, though one lady shareholder was adamant that seeing so much countryside rushing past, and the sun entering the compartments, would cause travel sickness.

The GWR operated slip coaches long after other companies abolished them. Until 1909, although a slip-coach guard could apply the vacuum brake, he had no means of releasing it, but that year the brakes were designed so that the vacuum could be restored to the brake cylinders. This had the advantage that slips could be made further in advance of stations. The last BR slip coach ran into Bicester in 1960.

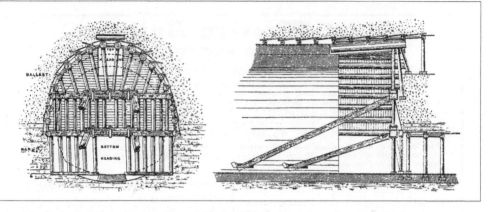

88. Completed timbering for a full-sized tunnel cut in soft ground.

GREAT WESTERN RAILWAY.—The public

are informed that this RAILWAY will be OPENED for the CONVEYANCE of PASSENGERS only between London, West Drayton, Slough, and Maidenhead station, on Monday, the 4th June. The following will be the times for the departure of trains each way, from London and from Maidenhead, (excepting on Sundays,) until further notice :—

Trains each way.

8 o'clock morning ; 4 o'clock afternoon.
9 o'clock   ditto   5 o'clock   ditto
10 o'clock   ditto   6 o'clock   ditto
12 o'clock   noon   7 o'clock   ditto

Trains on Sundays each way.

7 o'clock morning ; 5 o'clock afternoon.
8 o'clock   ditto   6 o'clock   ditto
9 o'clock   ditto   7 o clock   ditto

Each train will take up or set down passengers at West Drayton and Slough.

Fares of Passengers.

	First Class.		Second Class.	
	Posting Carriage.	Passenger Coach.	Coach.	Open Carriage
	s. d.	s. d.	s. d.	s. d.
Paddington Station ⎰ to West Drayton	4 0	3 6	2 0	1 6
Paddington Station ⎨ to Slough........	5 6	4 6	3 0	2 6
Paddington Station ⎱ to Maidenhead ..	6 6	5 6	4 0	3 6

Notice is also given that on and after Monday, the 11th June, carriages and horses will be conveyed on the railway, and passengers and parcels booked for conveyance by coaches in connexion with the Railway Company to the west of England, including Stroud, Cheltenham, and Glocester, as well as to Oxford, Newbury, Reading, Henley, Marlow, Windsor, Uxbridge, and other contiguous places. By order of the Directors,

CHARLES A. SAUNDERS, ⎰
THOMAS OSLER. ⎱ Secs.

89. Opening announcement of the GWR from *The Times*, 2 June 1838. In the event, road carriages were not conveyed by rail until 4 August and horses not until the following month.

Great Western Railway.
LONDON TO MAIDENHEAD.

On and after the 1st of May, the SOUTHALL STATION will be opened
For Passengers and Parcels.

An **Extra Train** to **Slough** will leave Paddington on **Sunday Mornings**, at **half-past 9 o'clock**, calling at **Ealing, Hanwell, Southall and West Drayton.**

Horses and Carriages, being at the Paddington or Maidenhead Station ten minutes before the departure of a Train, will be conveyed upon this Railway.

Charge for 4-wheel Carriage, 12s.   Two-wheel ditto, 8s.   For 1 Horse, 10s.   Pair of Horses, 16s.

Post Horses are kept in readiness both at Paddington and Maidenhead, and upon sufficient notice being given at Paddington, or at the Bull and Mouth Office, St. Martin's-le-Grand, would be sent to bring Carriages from any part of London to the station, at a moderate charge.

TRAINS.

From Paddington To Maidenhead.	From Maidenhead To Paddington.
8 o'clock morn. calling at - Southall and Slough	6 o'clock morning, calling at - Slough
9 do. - Slough	*(and on Wednesday Morning at Southall.*
10 do. - West Drayton and Slough	8 do - Slough and West Drayton
12 do. - West Drayton and Slough	9 do. - Slough and West Drayton
2 o'clock afternoon - West Drayton and Slough	10 do. - Slough and Southall
4 do. - Slough	12 do. - Slough and West Drayton
5 do. - Hanwell and Slough	2 o'clock afternoon - Slough and Southall
6 o'clock evening Ealing, West Drayton and Slough	4 do. - Slough
7 do. - Southall and Slough	5 do. - Slough and Hanwell
8 do. - Slough	6 o'clock evening - Slough and West Drayton
	7 do. - Slough and Ealing

The six o'clock up Train will call at Southall on Wednesday mornings, for the convenience of persons attending the market on that day.

SHORT TRAINS

From Paddington To West Drayton.	From West Drayton To Paddington.
½ past 9 o'Clock Morning,	before 9 o'Clock Morning,
½ past 1 do. Afternoon, calling at { Ealing, Hanwell, AND Southall,	before 11 do. calling at { Southall, Hanwell, AND Ealing.
½ past 4 do. do.,	before 3 Afternoon
½ past 8 do. Evening	before 7 o'Clock Evening

☞ *There are no second class close carriages in the short Trains*

Passengers and Parcels for Slough and Maidenhead will be conveyed from all the stations by means of the short Trains, waiting to be taken on by the succeeding long Train, as above ; and in like manner they will be conveyed from Maidenhead and Slough, to every station on the Line

On SUNDAYS.

From Paddington To Maidenhead.	From Maidenhead To Paddington.
8 o'clock Morn, calling at - Ealing and Slough	8 o'clock morn calling at - Slough
½ past 8 do. do. - West Drayton and Slough	8 do. do. - Slough Southall and Ealing
9 do. do. - Southall and Slough	9 do. do. Slough West Drayton and Hanwell
5 afternoon do. Hanwell West Drayton and Slough	5 afternoon do. - Slough and Hanwell
6 evening do. Ealing West Drayton and Slough	5 evening do. - Slough and West Drayton
7 do. do. - Southall and Slough	7 do. do. - Slough and Ealing

SHORT TRAINS,
PADDINGTON TO SLOUGH.
Half-past Nine o'Clock Morning, - - - calling at Ealing, Hanwell, Southall, and Drayton.

To West Drayton.	From West Drayton.
½ past 9 o'Clock Morning, } calling at { Ealing, Hanwell, & Southall and proceeding to Slough	before 8 o'Clock Morning, } calling at { Southall, Hanwell & Ealing.
½ past 8 do. Evening, Ealing, Hanwell & Southall	before 7 do. Evening,

FARES.

Paddington.	1st. Class.	Second Class.		Maidenhead.	1st. Class.	Second Class.	
	Coach.	Close.	Open.		Coach.	Close.	Open.
To Ealing	1 6	1 0	0 9	To Slough	2 0	1 6	1 0
Hanwell ...	2 0	1 6	1 0	West Drayton	3 0	2 6	2 0
Southall	2 6	1 9	1 3	Southall	4 0	3 0	2 6
West Drayton	3 6	2 0	1 6	Hanwell ...	4 6	3 6	3 0
Slough	4 6	3 0	2 6	Ealing	5 0	4 0	3 6
Maidenhead .	5 6	4 0	3 6	Paddington .	5 6	4 0	3 6

The same Fares will be charged from Slough to West Drayton as from Maidenhead to Slough.

OMNIBUSES and Coaches start from Princes Street, Bank, one hour before the departure of each Train, calling at the Angel Inn, Islington ; Bull Inn, Holborn ; Moore's Green Man and Still, Oxford Street ; Golden Cross, Charing Cross ; Chaplin's Universal Office, Regent Circus ; and Gloucester Warehouse, Oxford Street ; to the Paddington station.—**Fare 6d.** without Luggage.

90. The GWR train bill for 1 May 1839.

91. A lithograph by George Measom of the interior of the first engine shed at Paddington *c*. 1852. Leo Class 2-2-2 *Elephant* is on the left and Iron Duke Class 4-2-2 *Rover* on the right. The short turntable requires engine and tender to be turned separately.

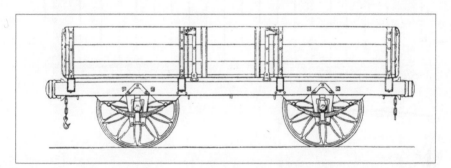

92. A third-class coach of 1840. The low sides proved dangerous as a sudden jerk when starting or stopping could throw a passenger overboard.

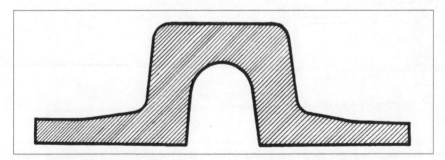

93. A section of Brunel's bridge rail.

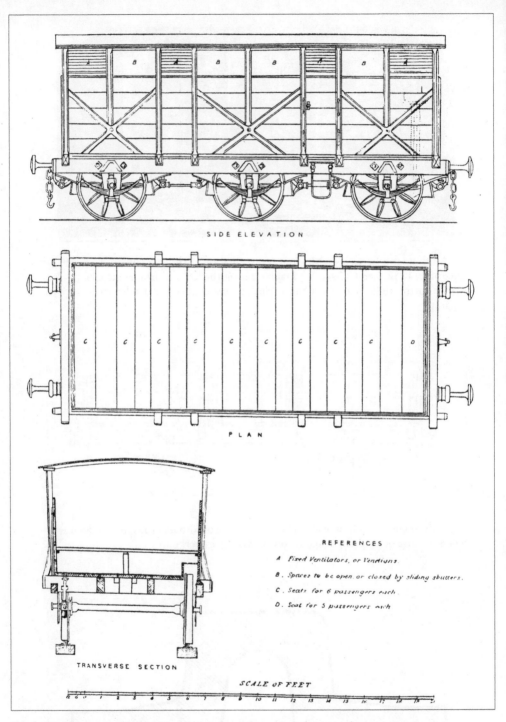

SIDE ELEVATION

PLAN

TRANSVERSE SECTION

REFERENCES

A Fixed Ventilators, or Venetians.

B. Spaces to be open or closed by sliding shutters.

C. Seats for 6 passengers each.

D. Seat for 5 passengers each.

SCALE OF FEET

94. A third-class coach of 1844. Unlike the earlier third-class coaches, passengers were so enclosed that there was no danger of being thrown out; the problem was gaining access through the 2-foot-wide doorway.

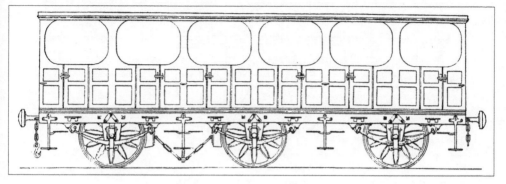

95. A second-class coach of 1844.

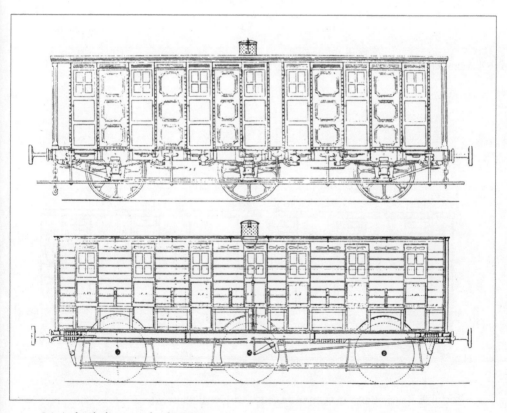

96. A third-class coach of 1848.

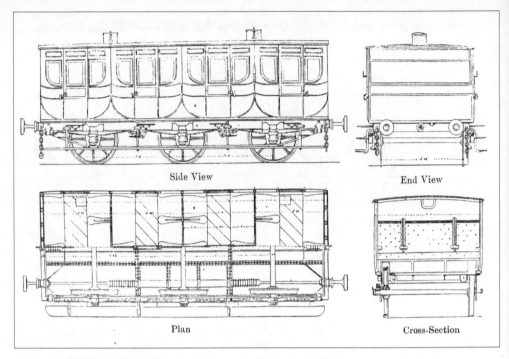

Side View

End View

Plan

Cross-Section

97. A first-class coach *c.* 1851.

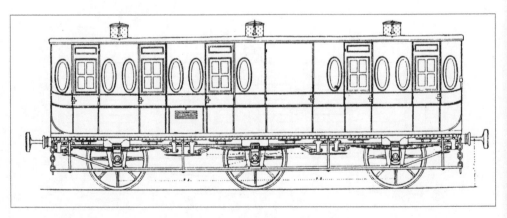

98. A Bristol & Exeter Railway composite coach with oval windows.

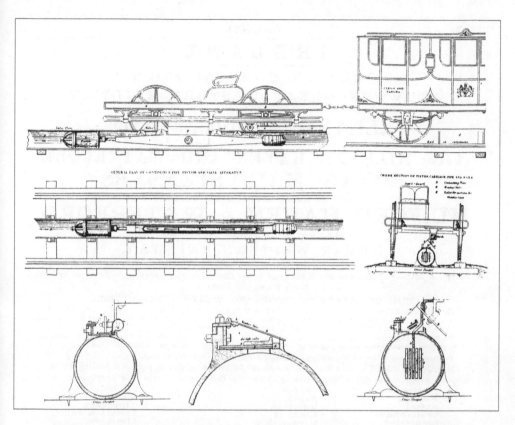

GENERAL PLAN OF CONTINUOUS PIPE PISTON AND VALVE APPARATUS

CROSS SECTION OF PISTON, CARRIAGE, PIPE AND RAILS

Above: 99. Diagram showing the elevation of a section of the atmospheric railway and a piston carriage cross section showing details of the valve sealing mechanism; a closed valve and an open valve.

Right: 100. The original form of a disc and crossbar signal.

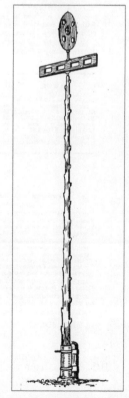

IRELAND.

THROUGH COMMUNICATION

BETWEEN GREAT WESTERN RAILWAY

AND

IRELAND, *via* Milford Haven.

THE MILFORD HAVEN AND WATERFORD
ROYAL MAIL STEAMERS

Sail as under between the Ports of

MILFORD HAVEN & WATERFORD,

In connection with the EXPRESS TRAINS of the

GREAT WESTERN RAILWAY,

And the Trains on the Waterford and Limerick, Waterford and Kilkenny, and other Railways in the South of Ireland, Carry Her Majesty's Mails, and afford the most Direct Communication between the South of Ireland, South Wales, and England.

TIME OF DEPARTURE (WIND AND WEATHER PERMITTING).

The Waterford Steamers will start from the Pier at the New Milford Terminus Daily (Sundays excepted), on the arrival of the 9.15 a.m. Express and 6.0 a.m. Third Class Trains, at 6.50 p.m., reaching Waterford so as to secure the departure of the 6 0 a.m. Train from Waterford for Limerick and Cork, and the 12 noon Train for Kilkenny and Dublin.

The Waterford Steamers will leave the Adelphi Wharf at 3.15 p.m. on the arrival of the Train from Cork and Limerick, an arrive at New Milford (circumstances permitting) in time for passengers to proceed by the 8.55 a.m. Train.

Passengers arriving at New Milford on Sunday Mornings, will proceed by the 10.40 a.m. Train.

THROUGH TICKETS, for a Single Journey, available for Three Days, with the privilege of breaking the journey at either Gloucester or New Milford (Milford Haven), and Waterford or Clonmel, are issued to and from the following stations:—

Paddington	**Cardiff**		**Cahir**
Reading	**Neath**		**Clonmel**
Oxford	**Swansea**		**Tipperary**
Cheltenham	**Llanelly**	**and**	**Limerick June,**
Gloucester	**Carmarthen**		**Limerick**
Newport	**Waterford**		**Kilkenny**

Tickets will also be granted from the Stations on the Great Western Railway, as also from Bristol, via the Midland Railway, to Waterford, with the privilege of breaking the journey at either Gloucester, or New Milford; also at the Steam Ship Offices of Messrs. Jackson, and Co., 36, Cannon-street, London; or Mr. Downey, Adelphi Wharf, Waterford.

1st and 2nd Class **RETURN TICKETS** will be issued at a Fare-and-a-Half for the Double Journey, available for the Return Journey within One Month of the date of issue.

Through Fares by Steamer and Railways.

FARES.	SINGLE TICKETS. 1st Class & Saloon		2d Class & Cabin.		3d Class & Deck.		RETURN TICKETS. 1st Class & Saloon		3d Class & Cabin.		FARES.	SINGLE TICKETS. 1st Class & Saloon		2d Class & Cabin.		3d Class & Deck.		RETURN TICKETS. 1st Class & Saloon		2d Class & Cabin.	
	s.	d.	s.	d.	s.	d.	s.	d.	s.	d.		s.	d.	s.	d.	s.	d.	s.	d.	s.	d.
LONDON and LIMERICK or Limerick Junction	60	0	47	0	30	1	90	0	70	6	SWANSEA and KILKENNY	31	0	23	13	16	1	46	0	35	0
Gloucester and ditto	45	6	35	4	23	1	67	9	52	6	Merthyr and ditto	36	6	27	4	17	1	62	9	40	8
Newport, Cardiff and ditto	34	6	28	4	30	1	57	3	42	0	LONDON and WATERFORD	50	0	40	0	24	6	75	0	60	0
Swansea and ditto	38	6	28	4	20	1	67	3	42	0	Gloucester and do ...do	36	0	28	0	17	6	53	6	42	0
LONDON & KILKENNY	55	6	44	4	27	1	82	0	66	0	Newport, Cardiff and do...do	28	0	21	0	14	6	42	0	31	6
Gloucester and ditto	40	6	32	4	20	1	60	3	49	0	Swansea and do...do	25	6	19	6	13	6	38	6	29	6
Newport, Cardiff and ditto	33	6	26	4	17	1	49	9	37	6	Bristol & Waterford via Milford	40	0	31	6	....		60	0	47	3
											" New Passage	33	0	24	6	....		49	6	36	6

Fares by Steamer.	SINGLE TICKETS. Saloon.		Deck.		RETURN TICKETS. Saloon.		Fore Cabin.	
	s.	d.	s.	d.	s.	d.		
New Milford and Waterford	12	6	7	0	18	9	..	

Passengers on the Steamers with 2nd Class Tickets can exchange from the Cabin to the Saloon on payment of 1s. 6d. each.

Passengers for Cork via Waterford, should book to Limerick Junction, from whence they may obtain Tickets to Cork.

GOODS, CATTLE, PARCELS, FISH, &c., will be forwarded by these Steamers to all Stations on the South Wales and Great Western Railways, the Vale of Neath, Waterford and Limerick, and Waterford and Kilkenny Railways; Birmingham, and the principal towns in the Midland Counties. Rates and Fares can be learnt on application at Paddington, or any of the Stations on the respective Railways; of Messrs. Ford and Jackson, 36, Cannon-street, London; of Mr. Downey, Adelphi Quay, Waterford; of Mr. Jacob, Waterford and Limerick Railway, Limerick; or of Mr. Chadwick, Kilkenny.

NOTICE.—The Companies receive Goods for shipment on the following terms ONLY.—They reserve the right to carry BY ANY, not by particular vessels, with liberty to tow Ships, and call at other ports, and will not be accountable for injuries or losses arising from delay, accidents of the Seas, Rivers, Fire, the Queen's enemies, defective Navigation, or Accidents from any other cause, nor for any loss which might have been covered by Insurance, nor for Leakage, Breakage, Condition, Quality, or Contents of any Parcels or Packages, unless specially entered and *ad-valorem* freight paid. Goods not removed, to be stored at the Risk and Expense of the Consignees. All Goods will be considered as subject to a general lien, and held not only for all arrears of Freight, but for Storage, or other Charges due by the Importer, Owner, or Consignees to the Company.

SPACIOUS LOCK-UP WAREHOUSES are now opened at the Adelphi Wharf, Waterford, where Goods and Cattle will be received on the days of the Sailing of the Packets, and Warehoused without charge, when duly consigned by the STEAMERS.

SHED ACCOMMODATION and Water for the Live Stock, is provided at New Milford. Pasturage, Hay, and Corr, can be procured by the Drovers at the New Milford Terminus, on reasonable terms.

HORSES and CARRIAGES can now be booked through between LONDON and WATERFORD.

THE SOUTH WALES HOTEL AT NEW MILFORD IS OPEN ON THE ARRIVAL AND DEPARTURE OF THE BOATS AND TRAINS.

101. A page from the June 1865 GWR timetable giving details of services to Ireland.

CHANNEL ISLANDS.

THROUGH COMMUNICATION

BETWEEN GREAT WESTERN RAILWAY

AND THE

CHANNEL ISLANDS,

Via WEYMOUTH.

SUMMER SERVICE, 1865—(May to October inclusive.)

DAY PASSAGES.—SHORTEST SEA ROUTE BY SEVERAL HOURS.

The unpleasantness and dangers of Night Travelling avoided.

ONE OF THE WELL-KNOWN, FAST, IRON PADDLE STEAM SHIPS,

"Aquila," "Brighton," or "Cygnus,"

Carrying H.M. MAILS,

Will leave WEYMOUTH HARBOUR (Weather and circumstances permitting) with PASSENGERS and GOODS every Monday, Wednesday, and Friday, at 6.0 a.m., for Guernsey and Jersey.

RETURNING every Tuesday, Thursday, and Saturday from Jersey, at a quarter before 7.0 a.m., and Guernsey at about 9.0 a.m.

Through Fares to Guernsey or Jersey.

From the following Stations.	Single Journey.		Return. Within One Month.		From the following Stations.	Single Journey.		Return. Within One Month.	
	1st Class	2nd Class	1st Class	2nd Class		1st Class	2nd Class	1st Class	2nd Class
	s. d.	s. d.	s. d.	s. d.		s. d.	s. d.	s. d.	s. d.
PADDINGTON	31 0	21 0	45 0	35 0	WELLINGTON	62 0	37 0	68 0	58 0
READING	31 0	21 0	45 0	35 0	SHREWSBURY	52 0	37 0	68 0	58 0
BRISTOL	31 0	21 0	45 0	35 0	CHESTER	58 0	41 0	74 0	64 0
BATH	31 0	21 0	45 0	35 0	BIRKENHEAD for LIVERPOOL	61 0	43 0	80 0	70 0
EXETER	31 0	21 0	45 0	35 0	MANCHESTER	61 0	43 0	80 0	70 0
OXFORD	33 0	23 0	47 0	37 0	SWINDON	31 0	21 0	45 0	35 0
LEAMINGTON	40 0	28 0	58 0	48 0	STROUD	35 0	25 0	50 0	40 0
WARWICK	40 0	28 0	58 0	48 0	GLOUCESTER	38 0	28 0	53 0	43 0
STRATFORD-ON-AVON	44 0	31 0	60 0	50 0	CHELTENHAM	38 0	28 0	53 0	43 0
BIRMINGHAM	44 0	31 0	66 0	50 0	HEREFORD	43 0	33 0	60 0	50 0
WOLVERHAMPTON	46 0	32 0	62 0	52 0	CHIPPENHAM	31 0	21 0	45 0	35 0
					SALISBURY	31 0	21 0	45 0	35 0

The holders of Family and Excursion Tickets to Weymouth will have the privilege of proceeding to Guernsey or Jersey and back at Single Fares for the Double Journey upon production of their Railway Tickets.

Local Fares.

	Single Journey.		Return. Within One Month.	
	1st Class.	2nd Class.	1st Class.	2nd Class.
	s. d.	s. d.	s. d.	s. d.
WEYMOUTH to JERSEY or GUERNSEY	18 0	12 0	30 0	20 0
STEWARD'S FEE (each way)	2 0	1 0	2 0	1 0
JERSEY to GUERNSEY, or vice versa	4 0	2 6	6 0	4 0

Children under 2 years of age, free—above 2 and under 12, half price.

Tickets for any of the above Stations may be obtained at the Offices of the Company in Jersey or Guernsey, or on board the Ships.

Return Tickets can be extended beyond the Month, upon payment of (prior to commencing the Return Journey, and before the expiration of the Ticket) Ten per cent. for the first fifteen days after the expiration of the Ticket, and Five per cent. additional for every Week or portion of a Week beyond the first fortnight.

Single Tickets from London to Guernsey and Jersey, or vice versa, are available for Three Days by any Train over the Great Western Railway; they include Railway and Steam Packet Fares only; and are not transferable.

Passengers may break the Journey at Chippenham, Dorchester, Weymouth, or Guernsey, either going to or returning from Jersey.

Passengers are requested to be on board ten minutes before the hours mentioned for departure.

Passengers walk on board at the Custom House Quay, Weymouth, at any time of tide.

BAGGAGE.

All Goods other than Personal Baggage belonging to Passengers, although not entered on the manifest as Merchandise, to pay accustomed freight. Passengers are requested to have all Packages comprising their Luggage distinctly marked with their names and addresses, and to take the whole on board with them. The Company is not liable for any loss or damage to Baggage.

PROVISIONS MAY BE OBTAINED ON BOARD AT MODERATE RATES.

☞ To prevent delay in the Shipment of Goods, particulars of the contents and value of each Package should be forwarded by Post to the Company's Agents, as under. In the case of BONDED or EXCISEABLE GOODS, the Goods WITHOUT SUCH ADVICE CANNOT BE SHIPPED.

The Company is not liable for unavoidable delays, accidents, or sea-risks of any kind. The Company do not undertake to carry Passengers or Goods by any particular Vessel, or to meet any particular Train.

Further particulars may be known on application to the following Agents, viz.:—Mr. HENRY BUDD, Weymouth; Mr. JOHN JONES, Quay, Guernsey; Mr. JOHN WIMBLE, 9, Bond-street, Jersey; and at the Paddington and all other Stations of the Great Western Railway Company.

WEYMOUTH,
June 1st, 1865.

JOSEPH MAUNDERS,
Manager and Secretary.

102. A page from the June 1865 GWR timetable giving details of services to the Channel Islands.

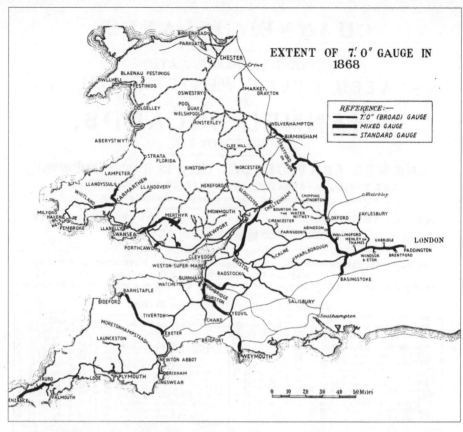

103. Map showing the extent of the GWR broad gauge in 1868.

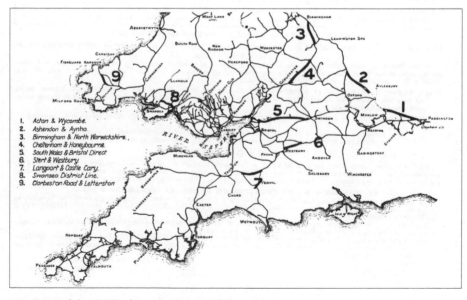

104. Map of the GWR showing the cut-off lines.

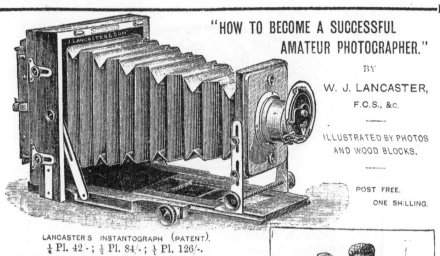

105. The last Down broad gauge Flying Dutchman in Sonning Cutting – an advertisement
from *The Official Guide to the Midland Railway*, 1893.

1. **Excellent Sites for Works and Factories.**
2. **Cheap Land and Rates.**
3. **Economic Handling.**
4. **Efficient Transit.**
5. **Private Sidings.**
6. **Sea and Canal Access.**
7. **Plentiful Labour Supply.**

————

The Business Man who contemplates erecting a Factory, or extending his existing works, cannot do better than consult the CHIEF GOODS MANAGER, DEVELOPMENT DEPARTMENT, GREAT WESTERN RAILWAY, PADDINGTON STATION, W.2. who will furnish full particulars, and also give useful information respecting freight charges, etc., on application.

Above: 106. A page from the booklet *Commerce & the Great Western*, published in August 1924.

Below: 107. A bookmark placed in GWR publications.

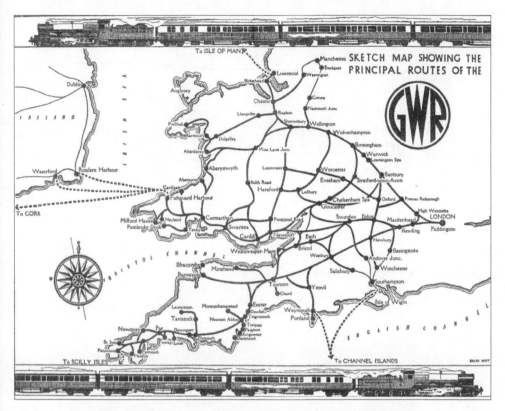

Above: 108. End paper to *Locos of the Royal Road*, published in 1936.

Below: 109. Cartoon from the *South Wales News*, 27 November 1922, showing that the GWR was little affected by the Railways Act of 1921.

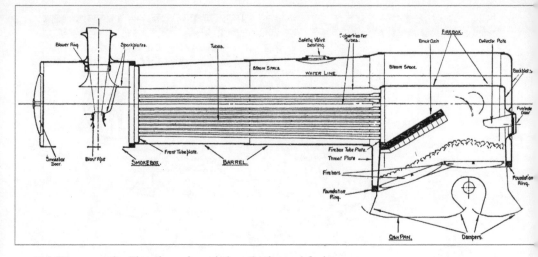

110. Diagram of a Churchward smokebox, boiler and firebox.

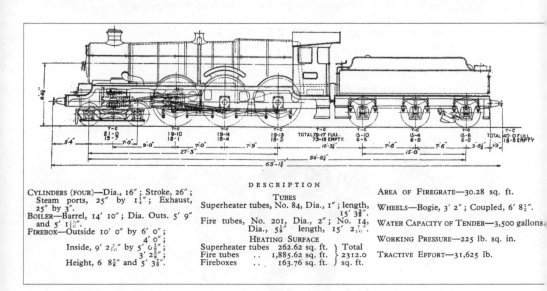

DESCRIPTION

CYLINDERS (FOUR)—Dia., 16″; Stroke, 26″;
Steam ports, 25″ by 1¼″; Exhaust,
25″ by 3″.
BOILER—Barrel, 14′ 10″; Dia. Outs. 5′ 9″
and 5′ 1¹³⁄₁₆″.
FIREBOX—Outside 10′ 0″ by 6′ 0″;
4′ 0″;
Inside, 9′ 2⁷⁄₁₆″ by 5′ 0¹⁄₈″;
3′ 2⅜″;
Height, 6 8⅞″ and 5′ 3⅜″.

TUBES
Superheater tubes, No. 84, Dia., 1″; length,
15′ 3⅜″.
Fire tubes, No. 201, Dia., 2″; No. 14,
Dia., 5⅛″ length, 15′ 2⁷⁄₁₆″.
HEATING SURFACE
Superheater tubes   262.62 sq. ft. ⎫ Total
Fire tubes   ..   1,885.62 sq. ft. ⎬ 2312.0
Fireboxes   ..   163.76 sq. ft. ⎭ sq. ft.

AREA OF FIREGRATE—30.28 sq. ft.
WHEELS—Bogie, 3′ 2″; Coupled, 6′ 8½″.
WATER CAPACITY OF TENDER—3,500 gallons.
WORKING PRESSURE—225 lb. sq. in.
TRACTIVE EFFORT—31,625 lb.

111. Diagram of a Castle Class locomotive.

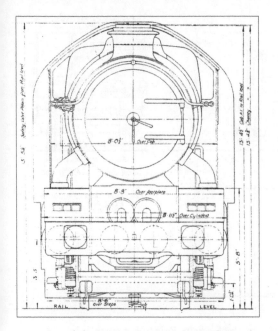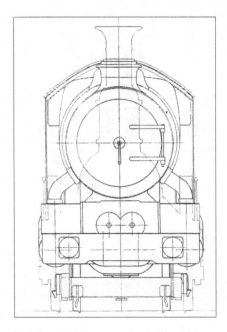

Above left: 112. Dimensions of a King Class locomotive.

Above right: 113. Contrast in outline between the broad gauge *North Star* and a King Class locomotive; the width is similar, but *North Star*'s boiler is set considerably lower and thus has a lower centre of gravity.

Below: 114. Diagram of a slip coach apparatus: train on the left, the slip coach on the right.

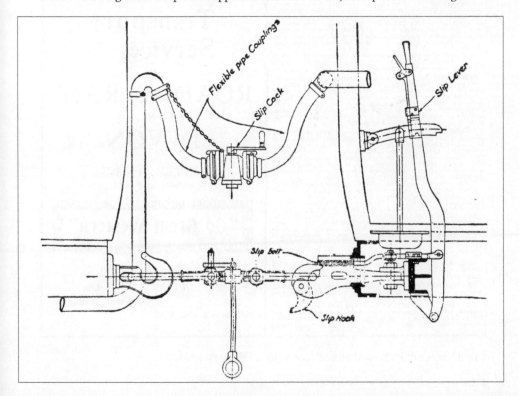

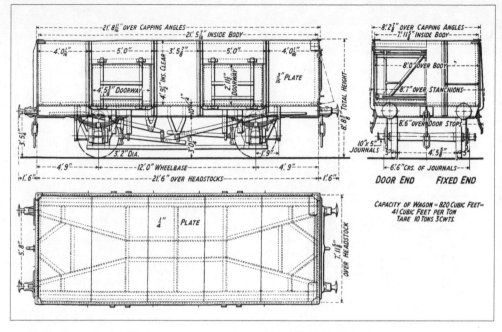

115. Diagram of a 20-ton coal wagon advocated by Sir Felix Pole to cut costs.

G.W.R. Road Motor Car Services.

GENERAL NOTICES AND REGULATIONS.

TIME TABLES.—The Company gives notice that the Road Motor Car Services are run subject to the condition of roads and circumstances permitting, and that the times are approximate, and liable to alteration. The Company does not undertake that the cars shall either start or arrive at the time specified in the Time Tables, or that there shall be sufficient room in the cars to accommodate intending passengers or their luggage ; and the Company will not be accountable for any loss, inconvenience, or injury, which may arise from delay or detention from any cause whatsoever.

On occasions when snow or fog prevails, or the state of the roads is unusually difficult, it may be necessary to vary the times of the Road Motor Cars, or to suspend the running of certain services without notice.

PASSENGERS.—Train passengers and passengers for the more distant points on the car route, will, as far as is REASONABLY PRACTICABLE, be given preference over persons desiring to travel short distances only.

The cars will call to pick up or set down passengers at the fare stages shown in the Time Tables. Passengers may also join the cars at other points en route on payment of the fare from the previous stage. Intending passengers are requested to give a clear and distinct signal to the driver of their desire for the car to stop.

PASSENGERS' TICKETS.—Passengers are requested to obtain tickets (punched in their presence) in exchange for fares paid ; also to see that they are given a receipt for luggage charges, &c. Conductors will punch tickets in the stage number to which the passenger is entitled to travel. Passengers are asked to verify the stage number so indicated by means of the fare lists exhibited in all cars. Tickets must be retained until completion of the journey and produced for inspection on the request of an official of the Company. Tickets are not transferable.

Books of 24 tickets, which are transferable and available on any G.W. Road Motor Car service, can be obtained at Stations from which Road Motor Car Services operate, or from the Car Conductors, at the following reduced rates :—1d. tickets, 1/9 ; 2d. tickets, 3/6 ; 3d. tickets, 5/3 ; 4d. tickets, 7/- ; 5d. tickets, 8/9 ; 6d. tickets, 10/6 ; 7d. tickets, 12/3 ; 8d. tickets, 1 1/- ; 9d. tickets, 15/9 ; 10d. tickets, 17/6 ; 11d. tickets, 19/3 ; 1/- tickets, £1 1s. 0d. ; and at proportionate rates for tickets over 1/- in value.

Books of 24 scholars' and apprentices' tickets, available for properly accredited scholars and apprentices up to 18 years of age, are issued at half rates, viz., when the ordinary single Adult fare is 2d., 2/- ; 3d., 3/- ; 4d., 4/- ; 5d., 5/- ; 6d., 6/- ; 7d., 7/- ; 8d., 8/- ; 9d., 9/- ; 10d., 10/- ; 11d., 11/- ; 1/-, 12/- ; and at proportionate rates over 1/ .

CHILDREN.—Children over 3 years of age and under 12 years are carried at approximately half fares. Children under 3 years of age are carried free of charge.

THE EXTERIOR FRONT SEATS OF CLOSED CARS are intended for gentlemen only. Ladies occupying them are charged threepence extra.

The Company desires to run the car services as efficiently and punctually as possible. Passengers can materially assist by entering and leaving the cars quickly. Passengers are warned not to enter or leave cars in motion.

(G.D.)

G. W. R.

Transport Services :

BY

ROAD & RAIL

IN

DEVON

WINTER, 1923-24

FEBRUARY (1924) ISSUE

"Go Great Western"

For Index see next page

FELIX J. C. POLE,
General Manager.

PADDINGTON STATION, W.2.
(R. T. 272)

116. Details of GWR road motor car services, February 1924.

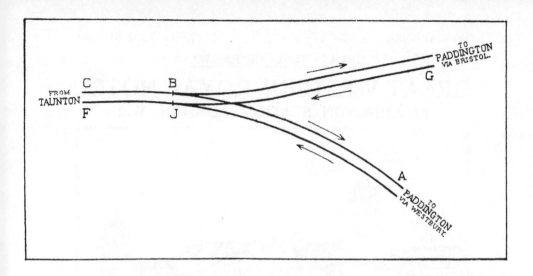

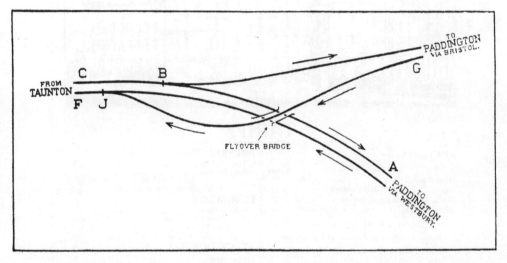

117. Sketches to explain how the flying junction at Cogload, near Taunton, avoids having conflicting routes.

GREAT WESTERN RAILWAY

GREAT WESTERN ROYAL HOTEL
PADDINGTON STATION, LONDON, W.2

TARIFF

APARTMENTS—

BEDROOMS

	PER DAY
Single rooms	from 10/-
„ „ with private bathroom .. „	13/6
Double rooms with private bathroom .. „	21/-

All Bedrooms have hot and cold running water.

Sitting-rooms 15/- per day.

Reception or Meeting Rooms from 15/- per day.

Telephone in every bedroom.

EARLY MORNING TEA—

Tea, Biscuits, or Bread and Butter, per person   1/-
Pot of Tea only .. .. 6d.

BREAKFASTS—

Table d'Hote	.. 4/-
Plain Breakfast	.. 2/-
„ „ with 2 boiled eggs ..	.. 3/-

Served in Bedroom, 6d. extra.

LUNCHEONS—

Table d'Hote	.. 4/-
Three Course Luncheon	.. 3/6

Also a la carte.
Served 12.30 p.m. to 2.45 p.m.

AFTERNOON TEA 1/6

DINNERS—

Table d'Hote	.. 6/6
Three Course Dinner	.. 5/-

Also a la carte.
Served 6 p.m. to 8.30 p.m.

VISITORS' SERVANTS—Board 10/- per day;   Bedroom 7/6.

Additional Charge for Luncheons and Dinners Served in Private Rooms, each, per meal, 1/-

SPECIAL LUNCHEONS AND DINNERS ARE SERVED TO PARTIES IN PRIVATE
SITTING ROOMS.

EXCELLENT ACCOMMODATION FOR WEDDING RECEPTIONS AND MEETINGS.

The hotel has been internally remodelled and vies favourably with London's finest hotels. The Public Rooms are spacious, air-conditioned, and provide the acme of comfort and quietude, whilst the Bedrooms —almost all of which have private bathrooms, etc., adjoining—have to be occupied to be appreciated.

GRILL ROOM AND RESTAURANT OPEN TO NON-RESIDENTS.

Separate entrance from Station to Hotel, and from Praed Street.

LUGGAGE

Hotel Porters meet all the principal trains and visitors' luggage is conveyed to and from the Hotel free of charge.

**FOR PARTICULARS OF OTHER HOTELS UNDER THE MANAGEMENT OF THE
GREAT WESTERN RAILWAY COMPANY, SEE PAGE 276.**

118. Tariff for the GWR Royal Hotel, Paddington, 1939.

By the late 1930s the use of four-wheel passenger coaches was restricted to remote branch lines and South Wales workmen's trains. The last ones ran on the Burry Port & Gwendraeth Valley branch until their withdrawal in 1953. In around 1935 sixteen four-wheelers were converted to camping coaches.

Following nationalisation, Swindon was responsible for producing a new standard BR bogie.

In BR times, although from 1949 lined crimson was used for non-corridor stock, until 1951 the majority of auto-trailers for push-and-pull trains were in the crimson and cream livery normally used just for corridor stock. The special duty saloons retained their GWR livery. In 1956 the Western Region painted some BR standard coaches used on named expresses in chocolate and cream, though this was discontinued in 1962.

Goods Stock

Ahrons, in *Locomotives & Train Working in the Latter Part of the Nineteenth Century*, describes a contemporary GWR milk train:

> This train [the Up Milford boat express], which left Swindon at 9.5 a.m., was also combined with a Bristol express and the load was about 160 and frequently up to 180 tons. But the Great Western Railway in those days was nothing if not economical in train mileage, so they also utilised this heavy important express as a West of England milk train, and at Swindon a tail was added to it consisting of six large milk vans.
>
> Now the Great Western Railway milk van was not the milk van of other companies, *ie* a moderate-sized four-wheeled vehicle. The Great Western Railway variety was a long six-

219

wheeled arrangement like a prison on wheels; it was intended to hold milk churns and plenty of them and succeeded admirably. I should think that the weight of one of those vans loaded with churns was at least 16 tons. Nearly every cow in the West of England contributed its quota to the load of the 9.5 a.m. up, and 250 to 260 tons was the weight with which the train had to try to keep time. The allowance for the 41¼ miles from Swindon to Reading was 50 minutes, and this had to include time lost for a slack through Didcot to about 25 miles per hour. It was really hard work, and though time could be kept in fine weather, there were many occasions when a minute or sometime even two minutes were dropped to Reading.

Although double-bogie goods wagons were built in 1888, the GWR found it difficult to get full loads for them and as an average load was just over 7 tons, the use of the four-wheel 10-ton wagon continued. The GWR encouraged pit owners to use larger wagons, but due to tight curves on many colliery lines, these larger wagons were generally impracticable. In 1897 the GWR introduced 20-ton steel wagons for its locomotive coal and then 40-tonners in 1905. In the 1920s the GWR had adapted the South Wales coal hoists to take 20-ton-capacity wagons. In 1931 the problem of tight curves was solved by building new 20-ton wagons, which did not exceed the length of a standard 12-ton wagon.

In 1930 the GWR introduced a 20-ton van with an exceptional length for a four-wheeler of 33 feet. It was equipped with Instanter couplings instead of screw couplings. With an Instanter, the central link of the otherwise standard three-link coupling was triangular in shape and could be turned to a vertical position to reduce the slack. This was a faster operation than laboriously tightening a screw coupling, yet avoided buffering up when a train braked, or a coupling snatching when accelerating.

From 1897 oil axle boxes were fitted to ordinary goods stock, replacing the former grease axle boxes and in 1903 some goods stock was fitted with the vacuum brake for working in express goods trains, or as tail traffic on passenger trains.

Permanent Way

The GWR track was individualistic, its chairs being secured by bolts when other railways used screwed spikes; its rail section was 97½ lb/yard when other lines used 95 lb/yard and its rail length was 44 feet 6 inches when others used 45 feet. The GWR gradually adopted the standard weight and length, but retained the bolting of chairs. In 1947 experiments were made using flat-bottomed rail – an innovation which became standard under British Railways.

In 1917–8 to obviate the timber shortage concrete transverse and pot sleepers were tried, but the transverse sleepers proved a failure. In the Second World War pot sleepers with a steel connecting bar at every third pot were used in sidings and goods loops and over half a million pot sleepers were cast.

Road Services

In 1902, F. C. A. Coventry, assistant carriage works manager at Swindon, prepared a report on the use of steam wagons for railway cartage services. That year a Thornycroft steam wagon was placed in service from the GWR's Hockley depot in Birmingham. Its performance failed to fulfil expectations and it was returned to the makers within a year. In 1908 the GWR built an electric vehicle powered by a battery, but the distance it could travel was severely limited.

By 1910 the GWR had acquired a fleet of twenty-five petrol-driven lorries and after the First World War numbers of ex-Army AEC lorries were purchased. An increased demand for cartage services brought a need for larger-capacity vehicles, among which were Thornycroft 10-ton tipping wagons and 12-ton Foden steam wagons. The introduction of the mechanical horse and trailer was the final stage in road transport before nationalisation.

The Big Four railway companies jointly purchased Pickfords and Carter Paterson road freight services in 1933.

On 17 August 1903 the GWR inaugurated the first motor bus service in England to work to a regular timetable. The Helston to Lizard route was operated by two second-hand Milnes Daimler buses previously owned by Sir George Newnes, the newspaper proprietor associated with the Lynton & Barnstaple Railway. He had decided to sell them after opposition from horse bus proprietors who had found out that he had exceeded the speed limit of 12 mph. The GWR had contemplated building a light railway between Helston and the Lizard, so the bus service was to test the potential.

The GWR service actually operated contrary to the legal requirements, which demanded that a man carrying a red flag should walk ahead of vehicles weighing 3 tons and over. As a bus travelling at walking pace would not have attracted much custom and manufacturers were unable to build a public-service vehicle below that weight limit, the difficulty was overcome by removing some equipment, painting '2 tons 19 cwts, 2 qrs' on the chassis and then replacing the equipment.

From this humble beginning the GWR increased its bus fleet to thirty-four by the end of 1904 and progressively to 300 in 1927, whereas at this date the other three main line railway companies had only about fifty vehicles in service between them.

On 11 July 1904 the first motor bus service to run parallel with an existing GWR line ran between Torquay and Paignton and by the end of the first week carried 600 passengers daily.

Although petrol was only four pence a gallon, the solid rubber tyres were very expensive – about £200 for a set – and only lasted for about 10,000 miles. Some buses carried double-decker bodies and some single-deck. Two passengers were allowed to sit in the open beside the driver, but ladies were discouraged from occupying this position in case they distracted the driver's attention. The discouragement was by making them 'smokers only' seats. Some ladies took up smoking, so a 'gentlemen only' notice was displayed.

Drivers were supplied with a cap, jerkin, waistcoat, breeches, gaiters and greatcoat, all made of leather. If a bus broke down and the driver was unable to repair it, he had to call on a local farmer to provide a team of horses to draw the disabled vehicle back to the depot. In around 1908 a telegram was sent to the leading driver at Slough by a member of his staff experiencing problems: 'Mr West, do your best, am in a sewer, down at Clewer'.

One short-legged driver had to have wooden blocks fitted to the pedals and could only just peep above his steering wheel, so policemen on point duty believed a driverless vehicle was approaching! Some GWR lorries had their bodies removed in summer and replaced with charabanc bodies for tour use.

In the early days of GWR buses, country roads were untarred and therefore became dusty in dry weather. The conductor of one small GWR bus had to stand on the rear step if his bus was full. In this position he became dusty and thirsty.

The route required the bus to climb a hill where the road curved round two sides of a brewery. As it approached, the conductor stepped off, entered the brewery, seized a foaming pint poured when the bus was heard approaching, and the conductor then left the premises on the other side and stepped neatly back on his bus as it slowly climbed the rise.

During the First World War some GWR buses and parcels vans were converted to run on coal gas stored in a rubber bag on the roof. Sometimes the gas bag became detached and the conductor or conductress had to chase across fields to retrieve it.

The railway grouping in 1923 had little effect on the GWR's Road Motor Department as none of the railways joining the GWR owned any buses. In the 1920s the GWR inaugurated several land cruises lasting several days, while in 1928 a service operated by a three-axle Morris Commercial ran from Devil's Bridge to the top of Plynlimmon, 2,008 feet above sea level.

The Railways Act of 1927 allowed the railway companies to purchase existing bus companies in order to eliminate competition and operate bus services instead of running unremunerative branch lines. In 1928 legislation allowed the speed of buses on pneumatic tyres to rise from 12 to 20 mph and then in 1931 to 30 mph.

In 1929 the GWR linked its road interests with the National Omnibus & Transport Co. Ltd and later with the British Electric Traction Co. Ltd. On the final day of 1933, the last bus in chocolate and cream livery was handed over to the Southern National Omnibus Co. at Weymouth. Although the GWR owned no buses, it held shares in all the major bus companies in its area, often held jointly with one or more of the other main line railways.

In addition to local bus services the GWR had a share in London Coastal Coaches, which owned, among other things, Victoria coach station. The GWR also had a share in Black & White, Greyhound and Royal Blue coaches.

Air Services

On 21 May 1929 the Big Four railway companies obtained parliamentary powers enabling them to operate air services. The GWR was the first company to take the initiative and on 12 April 1933 opened a service between Cardiff, Haldon (sited just inland from Dawlish and serving Teignmouth and Torquay) and Plymouth. The plane, a three-engined, six-seater Westland Wessex, built appropriately in GWR territory at Yeovil, was painted in chocolate and cream livery. Its interior decor was similar to a standard first-class railway compartment. Imperial Airways supplied the plane, pilot and ground staff for the twice-daily flights. It took about fifty minutes to cover the 80 miles, compared with almost four hours and 140 miles by rail. Initially the single fare from Cardiff to Plymouth was a very expensive £3 10s 0d or a return £6 0s 0d. The GWR provided buses to connect with Cardiff General, Torquay and Plymouth North Road stations and the enquiry bureau at Teignmouth Town Hall. On 22 May 1933 the service each way was extended to Birmingham.

Birmingham to	Time by rail between stations	Time between airports	Single fare Rail	Air
			£ s d	£ s d
Cardiff	170 minutes	70 minutes	1 2 6	2 0 0
Torquay	298 minutes	140 minutes	1 19 10	2 0 0
Plymouth	320 minutes	170 minutes	2 5 3	3 0 0

From 15 May 1933 the GWR received permission from the Postmaster General to carry mail on the service. Letters were required to be handed in at a GWR air booking office and on arrival at the airport at the end of the flight were posted for delivery in the ordinary way. A special GWR airmail stamp costing 3*d* had to be fixed in addition to the ordinary 1½*d* GPO stamp. When the seasonal service ended on 30 September 1933, only 714 passengers had been carried by air and the operation lost the company £6,526.

In 1934 the four main line railway companies, in association with Imperial Airways, formed the Railway Air Services Limited (RAS) and this restarted the former GWR service on 7 May 1934 using a two-engined, eight-seater De Havilland Dragon, the service being extended to Speke, Liverpool. As in the previous year, it only operated from May until September. From 1936 the RAS ran a Bristol–Weston-super-Mare–Cardiff–Haldon–Plymouth service, Haldon being a request stop. The service was permanently withdrawn on 3 September 1939.

In 1938 the Great Western Air Service and the Southern Air Service united to form the Great Western & Southern Air Service and thus eliminate competition on the Channel Islands routes.

In 1944 the Big Four published a plan for the development of air transport to Europe. However, a change of government in 1945 altered the ownership plan and brought to an end the railway involvement in air transport. British European Airways took over the railway airlines on 1 April 1947. The Railways Act of 1993 extinguished the 1929 air powers which BR had inherited in 1948.

The 1926 Strike

A serious fall in the quantity of coal traffic caused the GWR to have financial problems and Sir Felix Pole told its employees' representatives that there were three proposals:

1 The suspension of the guaranteed day and week.
2 Redundancies.
3 Reduction in pay for all grades on a percentage basis.

The unions refused to countenance proposals one and three, thus leaving dismissal as the only option.

  It was agreed that redundancies should be that casual, temporary and supernumerary workers to go first; should further reductions be necessary then juniors should follow.

  There was trouble too in the mining industry: costs were rising and output falling, so the mine owners offered the some proposals as the GWR. The miners' union said, 'Not a minute on the day; not a penny off the pay.' Due to economics, this simply could not be, so the miners called a strike on 3 May 1926 and were joined by many railwaymen.

  Despite the unions undertaking to run food trains, fish was delayed at Milford Haven resulting in 2,000 women being threatened with unemployment unless it was removed. The GWR arranged for it to be carried.

  Some trains still ran, worked by non-strikers and volunteers. On 4 May 194 trains ran and by 14 May no less than 1,517.

The GWR continued to deal with ocean passengers and mails at Plymouth. As well as the more glamorous jobs of engine driving, firing and signalling, volunteers took on such tasks as portering, ticket collecting and van driving.

The railway strike was declared illegal and ended on 14 May, the GWR taking strikers back as soon as work could be found for them. The miners' strike, however, continued throughout the summer and into the early winter; this inconvenienced the GWR as it had to run on imported coal for which its fireboxes were not designed.

The GWR's plans to modernise and develop coal-handling facilities at the South Wales ports that it inherited from the new companies acquired in the grouping were thrown awry. The export markets were lost forever, while the railway strike had caused many firms to seek road transport, and once they changed some never returned to rail. The strike cost the GWR over £4,000,000.

When the Labour Government came into power following the General Election of 1929 over a million men were out of work. To alleviate this situation, the Loans & Guarantees Act was passed, the Government undertaking to guarantee and pay the interest on large public schemes. The GWR was one of the first to put forward such projects:

1 Paddington station – lengthen the platforms to accommodate longer trains; provision of a large parcels depot away from the passenger platforms; enlargement of Bishop's Road station to facilitate suburban traffic.
2 Bristol – enlargement of Temple Meads station; quadrupling of track on either side; reconstruction of Bath Road locomotive depot.

3 Cardiff – enlargement of General station; widening lines Newtown to Cardiff and on to Ely Paper Mills.

4 Olton to Rowington Junction – extension of quadrupling.

5 Taunton – quadrupling line either side of station to include Norton Fitzwarren Junction; enlargement of Taunton goods depot and locomotive depot.

6 Westbury and Frome deviations to avoid speed restrictions.

7 Wolverhampton – reconstruction and modernisation of locomotive repair shops; reconstruction of Herbert Street goods depot and provision of a warehouse.

8 Banbury – construction of a hump yard for shunting.

9 Severn Tunnel Junction – enlargement of marshalling yard.

10 Rogerstone – enlargement of marshalling yard.

11 Swindon – modernisation of engine repair and spring shops.

12 Bugle to Goonbarrow Junction – doubling of the line.

13 Paignton – new goods depot and improvement of passenger station.

14 Scorrier to Redruth – doubling of the line.

15 Cardiff (Cathays) provision of new carriage and wagon repair shop, new locomotive depots at various sheds in South Wales

Notice that almost all the largest works undertaken were improving facilities for handling passenger traffic. This was because long-distance road coaches were starting to make inroads into railway passenger traffic.

The economic slump of 1931 affected the GWR, the reduction in receipts compared with 1930 showing diminution of almost 10 per cent while a coal strike that January exacerbated the situation.

The quantity of coal shipped from GWR docks in South Wales fell from 30 million tons in 1929 to 22 million tons in 1931. The local iron and steel industry in South Wales was in decline: imports increased from 721,000 tons in 1929 to 887,000 tons in 1931, while exports of iron and steel declined by 52 per cent. However the GWR was the only one of the Big Four whose financial stock retained full trustee status in both England and Scotland.

In the 1930s the railways were pressing for a square deal as regards road haulage competition. Railways were required to pay local rates in every district through which the line ran, whereas road hauliers did not have a comparable charge. Road hauliers were able to select traffic and take the most profitable, whereas the railways had to carry anything that was offered. The railways were compelled to publish their cartage rates, which road hauliers could then undercut. Unfortunately the 'Square Deal' campaign left the average rail passenger cold as they were only interested in getting from A to B and unconcerned about freight. The first year that the GWR ever had to declare a dividend of less than 3 per cent was 1938.

Another example of the GWR being in the forefront of developments was when, in February 1938, the electrical consultants Messrs Metz & McLellan were commissioned to prepare a scheme for electrifying all lines west of Taunton. The price of locomotive coal was escalating; Taunton and the West was some distance from South Wales, so there was the cost of haulage; the routes west of Taunton had considerable gradients, which could be more easily climbed by electric locomotives than by steam. It was envisaged that any branches west of Taunton not electrified would be diesel-worked, thus avoiding any steam depots west of Taunton.

The consultants preferred the overhead system at 3,000 volts, but observed that, owing to the unusually high proportion of curved track, shorter distances than normal would be required between the supporting posts in order to maintain the wire over the centre of the track. The net capital cost was estimated to be over £4,000,000, while saving in annual working costs under electrification would have been £100,500 and from this sum payment of interest on the capital expenditure would have to be paid.

The conclusion was that the line was not particularly suited to electrification due to the nature of the traffic and the wide variation between winter and summer traffic, when on summer Saturdays passenger traffic was particularly dense. The high cost of electric locomotives was another factor against the scheme.

Second World War

As early as 1938 the GWR started making preparations in the event of war. Some staff were sent to the Home Office Air Raid Precautions School and in turn trained their colleagues. Important signal boxes had the equipment on the ground floor temporarily protected with sandbags, while later lower windows were bricked up.

In late September 1938 the Railway Executive Committee was formed, the GWR represented by the General Manager James Milne. The REC offered the GWR a grant of £472,000 to cover wartime measures needed, one of which was dispersing the headquarters from Paddington to Beenham Grange close to Aldermaston station, Berkshire.

On Sunday 29 January 1939 a test exercise was carried out between 1.00 a.m. and 4.00 a.m. in the Paddington–Old Oak

Common district. It was imagined an air raid was going to take place. Lighting was reduced, colour light signals fitted with extra long shields to prevent them from being spotted from the air; all trains passing through had their blinds drawn and locomotives had sheets over the cabs to conceal any light issuing from fireboxes. At Paddington staff acted as casualties for first-aid staff to treat and the Paddington Auxiliary Fire Brigade was called out.

It was envisaged that in the event of war, London would receive air attacks, so plans for the evacuation of children were drawn up catering for 100,000 from London alone. It was thought that this task could well have to be carried out while an air attack was taking place.

Almost on the eve of the Second World War, 4-6-0 No. 4086 *Builth Castle* made an exploit which has been little recorded. On 31 July 1939 with a load of seven coaches it ran on a Paddington–Worcester express, and held a speed of 100 mph for no less than 4½ miles near Honeybourne.

The order for evacuation was given on Thursday 31 August 1939 and so efficient were the GWR's plans that the first special train left Ealing Broadway at 8.30 a.m. the next morning. Every train consisted of twelve coaches and accommodated 800 passengers. Fifty train sets were required and these were assembled from all over the GWR system. An emergency timetable specified the times the empty trains should leave the depots for the entraining point. Between 8.30 a.m. and 5.30 p.m. on each of the four days, sixty-four trains, sixty of them from Ealing Broadway, could leave at nine-minute intervals. They travelled non-stop at express speeds.

When a train departed, a telegram was sent to the reception station advising the approximate number of evacuees it carried, the stationmaster in turn informing the local reception officer. During the four days, 163 specials were run from London carrying 112,994 evacuees, all this in addition to catering for holidaymakers returning home and others making their own arrangements for evacuation.

In the early stages of the Second World War, all West of England expresses, with reduced scheduled speeds, were diverted via Bristol and restaurant and sleeping cars withdrawn. At night, as the blinds did not cut out all light, reduced lighting was necessary. Locomotives with side window cabs had them replaced with steel plates and a tarpaulin stretched from roof to tender to obscure the fire – though this made conditions in the cab uncomfortable. Footplate crews and signalmen were given steel helmets as protection against flying debris. Glass was removed from station roofs and canopies as flying glass splinters could inflict dreadful wounds.

The Government requisitioned 100 Dean Goods 0-6-0s, which were then fitted with the Westinghouse brake and some additionally fitted with pannier tanks and condensing gear. They were chosen for their light axle loading and thus could be used on most overseas lines. When France yielded to the Germans seventy-nine were lost.

It was not disputed that it was right for the Government to take control of the railways in wartime, but the question of payment was important. The GWR was private property: although some proprietors were rich men, many were small investors who needed the dividend as a pension. Shareholders had accepted low dividends in the past so that the GWR infrastructure could be made efficient, and were certainly entitled to a return on its use by the Government, yet the

Government made no announcement and the Government took all the revenue. Merchandise and mineral traffic increased by 47 per cent between August and December 1939, but no weekly traffic returns had been made. The *Financial Times* urged that the matter be brought to arbitration.

On 7 February 1940 the Minister of Transport announced in the Commons that each of the railway companies would be paid an average of its net revenue for the years of 1935, 1936 and 1937. After payment of these net revenues any balance in the pool up to an amount of £3½ million would be paid to the railways in proportion to their net revenues. Provision was made for maintenance and restoring any war damage, but just over a year later the Government said that war damage would have to be paid from revenue. The GWR shareholders received a dividend of 3½ per cent and 4 per cent in 1940 and 1941.

When the British Expeditionary Force was stranded on the beaches of Dunkirk in 1940, GWR ships assisted in the evacuation. Even the Kingswear to Dartmouth ferry, the SS *Mew*, went to Dover, but was not used as her draught was too great to get close to the beach and she was too small to carry large numbers from offshore.

On 26 May 1940 the code-word 'Dynamo' was sent to the GWR and other main line companies warning them that the evacuation was commencing, the GWR providing 40 of the 186 trains required. The GWR was restricted in the type of locomotive it could employ over the SR as clearance and weight restriction had to be taken into consideration. Most engines used were the relatively light 2-6-0s and the Manor Class 4-6-0s.

Following the evacuation from Dunkirk, the GWR and SR evacuated the civilians wishing to leave the Channel Islands, the last sailing being on 28 June 1940. The Germans occupied the islands from 1 July.

In GWR goods yards, men and women worked heroically through bombing raids, not infrequently saving ammunition trains from exploding. Shunter Tunna at Birkenhead spotted incendiary bombs falling on a train of high explosive bombs. Although covered with sheets, some incendiaries had penetrated this covering. He sped to the engine, collected a bucket of water and threw it on the bomb. This failed to extinguish the incendiary so he tore the sheet off and used a stirrup pump and bucket of water brought by a driver and fireman. Still unsuccessful, the only answer was to get the bomb out. With his shunter's pole he forced the two 250-lb bombs apart and with his bare hands lifted the incendiary bomb out and threw it on the ground out of harm's way. For this gallantry he received the George Cross.

At another station an incendiary bomb fell into a truckload of pigs. Had Porter Harris released them they would have run away in panic and been lost and he wished to look after animals in his company's care. He entered the wagon with the screaming pigs and put the incendiaries out.

By February 1941, 8,401 GWR employees had enrolled in the forces, about 7.5 per cent of the company's workers.

Initially a speed limit of 60 mph was imposed on expresses, but in April 1941 this was raised to 75 mph in order to encourage the recovery of lost time. Train loads were very heavy – the author remembers that many of the Paddington–Bristol trains consisted of sixteen coaches, their length requiring trains to pull up twice at such stations as Chippenham and Bath.

When one lengthy train drew up at Bath in the blackout, a sailor from one of the rear coaches stepped out on to what he imagined was the platform. Unfortunately it was the girder of a river bridge and when he took another pace, he fell into the river. He survived but, as it could have had a fatal ending, a fence was erected on the girder to prevent a repetition.

Trains were very crowded, for instance when the author travelled from Bath to Torquay on Saturday 29 July 1944, sixteen passengers and a baby were in a packed compartment for which there were only eight seats. Some got out at Weston-super-Mare which made a little more room. Returning on 8 August, as the train was full when it arrived at Torquay, my parents and I had to stand in the corridor as far as Newton Abbot where we changed into another train to reach Bristol. Having to travel in such conditions made some passengers vow that after the war when petrol and cars were available they would never again travel by train.

Unknown to the author when he was in that crowded compartment on 29 July 1944, a great drama was being played out at Paddington. That June and July the German V1 rockets had started to rain on the capital and Londoners took the opportunity to escape. Paddington became choked with thousands of potential passengers. It was not just a matter of running extra trains, because sanction for these had to be sought.

Had a V1 fallen in the vicinity of Paddington that day, the number of casualties would have been colossal. GWR made urgent requests to the Prime Minister's Office and sixty-three extra trains were permitted to be run to alleviate the situation.

The increased traffic in the Second World War demanded longer running loops on some stretches of line; the lengthening of crossing loops on the Didcot, Newbury & Southampton line and new connections to create alternative routes in case of blockage by enemy action, or to expedite taking materials and troops to the south coast for D-Day.

One interesting gesture was that following the Battle of Britain, some Castle type engines were renamed after British aircraft used in the fighting. The displaced names were used when further engines were built in the post-war period.

On 11 December 1942 the first of the American-built 2-8-0s was handed over to the Minister of War Transport at Paddington. Following the invasion of France in 1944, these engines were sent over to the Continent.

With the Japanese attack on Pearl Harbour and the consequent entry of the USA into the war, preparations were made for events leading up to D-Day.

One method of shortening the time a train needed to stay at a platform was the use of women travelling porters. They were responsible for seeing that each parcel loaded on the train went into the correct van and that the pile of parcels for each station lay by the most convenient door ready to be unloaded. While the train was in transit between stations the porter passed from van to van through the connecting gangways adjusting the stowage.

Sometimes volunteers were used at weekends to unload wagons and at one weekend in October 1943, 27,000 wagons were dealt with by shopkeepers, dustmen, clerks, students and housewives.

Only two GWR engines were destroyed by enemy action: 4-6-0 No. 4911 *Bowden Hall* at Keyham on 29 April 1941 and 0-6-0PT No. 1729 at Castle Cary on 3 September 1942.

Locomotives

F. W. Hawksworth was appointed Chief Mechanical Engineer in July 1941, rather unfortunate timing as wartime expediency prevented him from creating an express engine larger and more powerful than a King. Even authority to build a prototype was prohibited and instead the Government ordered Hawksworth to build LMS Class 8 2-8-os for use on the GWR and elsewhere.

Halls, being mixed traffic engines, were permitted to be built and Hawksworth set about improving their design. A visual difference was that with his Halls the main frames were carried through to the buffer beams, while an internal improvement was a larger superheater. The modified Halls were called the 6959 Class after the running number of the first one to appear. To save brass, they initially appeared unnamed. Footplate crews acknowledged that they were better than the original Halls and could reach 75 or 80 mph. They were placed on passenger duty and worked turn and turn about with Castles.

Hawksworth's first completely new design of locomotive was the County Class mixed traffic 4-6-0 which appeared in the summer of 1945. In some ways it was a development of an Improved Hall, but it had several different features. The boiler pressure was 280 lb compared with the 250 lb of a King, or the 225 lb of a Castle, and the driving-wheel diameter was a non-standard 6 feet 3 inches. The boiler, too, was non-standard, while the tender was of a new design, produced by welding instead of riveting, and had flat sides. Above the driving wheels was a continuous splasher, rather than a separate one over each wheel.

The boiler pressure and the driving wheels were actually a try-out for the 4-6-2 that Hawksworth hoped to build, but never did. Like all GWR 4-6-0s the Counties could display rapid acceleration and perhaps showed their best work over hilly roads such as the Cornish main line and between Wolverhampton and Chester.

Although the Castle design was twenty-three years old, more were built in 1946 as the GWR post-war policy was to run relatively light trains frequently, rather than long ones at longer intervals; hence there was no requirement for a Pacific such as were being built by the LMS, LNER and the SR. Castles were popular with their crews and economical in running costs.

In 1947 Hawksworth produced the 94XX 0-6-0PT, designed for heavy shunting duty, while in the BR era of 1949 the 15XX Class 0-6-0PT appeared, both classes having a tapered boiler, which initially looked odd on a pannier tank. The 15XX Class differed from GWR practice in several respects: there was an absence of platforms above the wheels and the widespread use of welding, while externally Walschaert's valve gear gave easy access for oiling. The wheelbase allowed the engine to traverse curves of 3½ chains at normal speed and 3 chains at slow speed. The short wheelbase made them unsteady at speed.

The 16XX Class was just a new edition of the 2021 Class of 1897, the dimensions being similar, but the 16XX had a boiler pressure of 165 lb instead of 150 lb. They were built to a restricted loading gauge enabling them to operate over routes with low overbridges such as the Burry Port & Gwendraeth Valley line. Ten of the class were kept for working over the Severn Bridge between Berkeley Road and Lydney. One was allocated well away from ex-GWR territory: in February 1957 No. 1646 worked the Highland Railway's Dornoch branch.

After the Second World War, to obtain foreign currency, the best coal was exported leaving poor quality for home use. To alleviate the shortage of good steam coal, in 1945 the GWR decided to equip some locomotives for oil firing. Engines chosen were from the 28XX 2-8-0 Class and 4-6-0 Hall Class. It involved fitting an oil tank in the tender, and a burner in the firebox where the oil was atomised in a steam jet prior to combustion. The GWR anticipated converting all engines used in Cornwall to oil firing, this area being the furthest from coal mines. When converted for oil firing, the GWR renumbered its 2-8-0s into a 48XX series and Halls into 39XX. On changing back to coal burning, they received their original numbers.

When drawing a heavy load, an oil-fired 2-8-0 burned 6.5 gallons per mile, compared with 72 lb of coal, which meant that the range of an oil-fired engine was approximately half as much again as one using coal. There were the additional advantages that there was no ash disposal or fire cleaning required at the end of a trip and that there were no lineside fires as no cinders were being ejected.

The Ministry of Transport believed it an excellent scheme and authorised other main line companies to convert 1,217 engines from coal to oil firing. Then, after many locomotives had been converted and money invested on oil fuelling plants, the Treasury announced that there was not enough foreign exchange available to purchase the oil! The left hand was ignorant of what the right hand was doing!

Keen on innovation, in 1946 the GWR ordered a gas-turbine locomotive from the Swiss firm of Brown-Boveri, only the third such machine in the world. It did not arrive in England until 1950 when it ran chiefly on Paddington–Bristol expresses. It was nicknamed 'Kerosene Castle'.

A second gas-turbine was ordered, this time from Metropolitan-Vickers, and delivered in December 1951. Both engines suffered from the defect that they consumed almost as much fuel when idling as when hauling a train, so diesel-electric propulsion proved more efficient. With a light load, the Metropolitan-Vickers locomotive consumed 2.97 gallons a mile, approximately three times the consumption of a diesel-electric.

The Western Region of BR continued the GWR tradition of being individualistic. Its engineers saw Germany using hydraulic rather than electric transmission for diesels and were impressed by the fact that it was lighter and thus gave an excellent power/weight ratio. The result was the Warship Class. For the first three years they performed well, but then expensive troubles started. In 1961 the larger and more colourful Western Class diesel-hydraulics appeared, but by now diesel-electric designs had improved, were cheaper to build and weighed only very little more.

Swindon Works

In 1919 Erecting Shop 'A' was almost doubled in size to cover 11½ acres, which at the time of building made it the largest permanent workshop in Europe. An interesting feature was that the offices and toilets were situated on the roof to allow maximum use of the ground floor space. A further feature of the works was that locomotive boilers were sent beneath Rodbourne Road from the boiler shop to the boiler testing shop.

In 1935, the GWR's centenary year, over 1,000 locomotives were repaired and the works had a capacity for building two new engines each week, while the annual capacity of the carriage works was the construction of 250 passenger vehicles of various types and the repair of no less than 5,000, 3,000 of these being in the nature of heavy repairs. The 1,800-foot-long carriage stock shed, paid for by a government loan, was completed in 1938. It was built on the south side of the Paddington–Bristol line on the site of Newburn, home of the GWR chief mechanical engineers. It was capable of storing 265 coaches awaiting use on the summer services on its ten roads. The wagon works could turn out 4,500 new wagons annually and repair approximately 8,000.

In the 1939 trip week 27,000 workers and their families left Swindon in thirty special trains. Although normally shops in Swindon closed at lunchtime on Wednesdays, during trip week they closed for the whole day, practically everyone going off and leaving it like a ghost town.

Children with prams and four-wheel 'bogies' transported, for a couple of pence, the luggage of those going on the trip. The favourite accommodation while away was 'room and attendance', with the trippers supplying food for the landlady to prepare and some families even taking their own vegetables.

Trip week was really a lock-out for the workmen until 1938 when they were granted a week's paid holiday, extended to a fortnight ten years later. With the increase in car ownership, numbers using the trip trains dwindled until they stopped in 1960, scheduled services being able to cope with those who still wished to travel by rail.

In the Second World War the works assisted in building gun mountings; turret rings for armoured cars; pom-pom guns; the first 2,000- and 4,000-lb bombs, more than 2,000 of the latter being produced; armour plating for armoured fighting vehicles;

timber components for Bailey portable bridges; Short Stirling bombers; fifty midget submarine superstructures and artificial limbs. The wagon shop built a large number of motor landing craft. Anti-aircraft posts armed with machine guns were set up on the roofs of some of the shops.

The USA servicemen who lived in coaches outside of No. 19 Carriage Lifting Shop were employed in various shops in converting stock into ambulance trains. American locomotives were received in the AE Shop and prepared for working on the GWR. Dean Goods 0-6-0 locomotives were again converted for war service and LMS Stanier Class 8F 2-8-0 freight locomotives Nos 8400–79 were produced for use in the United Kingdom. In BR use they actually outlived GWR locomotives built at Swindon, No. 48476 being one of the engines used on the Railway Correspondence & Travel Society's last steam-hauled special on 4 August 1968.

At nationalisation in 1948 the works covered 326 acres, 77½ of which were roofed. By this time most of the machinery was electrically driven, absorbing approximately a quarter of the output from Moredon power station.

Class D800 Warship Class diesel-hydraulic locomotives were built at Swindon in 1957 and in 1959 a new points and crossings shop was opened, bringing the roofed area up to approximately 85 acres. The last steam engine built for BR, No. 92220 *Evening Star*, was turned out from Swindon on 18 March 1960, though the last GWR-type steam engine built there was 0-6-0PT No. 1669 in May 1955.

In the late 1950s and early 1960s Swindon was turning out diesel-mechanical shunters, diesel-hydraulic D8XX and D10XX Class locomotives and Inter-City and Cross-Country DMUs.

The 'Main Workshops Future Plan' of 1962 called for the closure of fifteen of the thirty-one BR works in the country. At Swindon the carriage and wagon works closed in 1967 and the locomotive works was modified to undertake repair of carriages and wagons in addition to locomotives. The staff was reduced during this period from 9,000 to 6,000.

Under the 1968 Transport Act, BR workshops were turned into a limited company, British Rail Engineering Limited (BREL), wholly owned by BR but self-accounting. This Act gave BREL the right, when it had spare capacity, to accept outside tenders. Many bus operators were pleased to make use of the facilities offered to keep their fleets in operation, not only for engine work but also for repairs and modifications to the bodies and upholstery. In 1979 Swindon built its first locomotive for fourteen years as well as its first ever locomotive for export, producing twenty of the thirty-six shunters ordered by Kenyan Railways from Hunslet. As they were metre gauge, a track of this width was laid and if an engine could negotiate a kink in the layout without being derailed, it was deemed satisfactory.

Unfortunately the works closed completely in 1986. All the shops had sparrows living in them and as they had dwelt there for about 130 years, they had become modified. In contrast with a standard sparrow, the Swindon-works sparrow had two flight feathers missing on each wing and had yellow feathers round its throat. They were fed by the men and never went out, workmen going in during the holidays to feed them and also the cats. Rabbits were also found within the works, some having rust in their intestines due to the rusty land on which they grazed. At one time Irishmen cleaning out boiler tubes and sleeping in old coaches caught rabbits for making stews.

In the works' heyday workers arrived on thousands of bicycles and some people whose gardens were near the works entrance stored machines for a certain sum per week, a worthwhile supplementary income considering that whole gardens were filled.

The works had more first-aid boxes than an average factory and an above-average number of workers trained as St John's Ambulance men with all apprentices taught first aid.

Until about 1968 Wiltshire used Swindon works' fire brigade for fighting fires in the town, the works supplying two crews. Part-time firemen, they normally worked in the factory. Firemen's houses in the railway village were connected to the fire station by an electric alarm.

One unusual feature of the works was underground fires. In many places the land on which the works was constructed had been built up with cinders, clay and coke and would continue to burn for years, following spontaneous combustion. Sometimes the ground reached a temperature of 500 degrees Celsius and the clay turned to brick. Water failed to stop the fire's progress and the only way to halt it was to remove it by bulldozing to the original ground level.

Shipping Services

The GWR's Channel Island service was withdrawn during the Second World War, but the service to the Republic of Ireland continued, the *St Patrick* steaming quickly to make herself a difficult target. It was more vulnerable to U-boat than air attack, because it was some distance from enemy airfields. The *St Patrick* had been bombed and machine-gunned twice early in the war but on 13 June 1941, when only 25 miles from Fishguard, it was attacked by a German bomber. She sank with her master, seventeen of the crew and twelve passengers.

Four GWR vessels were used in the evacuation from Dunkirk: *St Andrew, St David, St Helier* and *St Julien*. Three were hospital ships and the *St Helier* was a troop transport. Despite being bombed and machine-gunned, although hospital ships by convention should never have been attacked, there were no casualties aboard.

Although the Channel Islands were liberated on 9 May 1945, a shortage of vessels prevented immediate restoration of the passenger service until 16 June 1946.

The Norton Fitzwarren Accident of 4 November 1940

On 4 November 1940 No. 6028 *King George VI*, with thirteen vehicles behind the tender, drew into the Down relief platform at Taunton eight minutes late with the 9.50 p.m. Paddington–Penzance sleeping car express.

Shortly after its arrival, the Taunton Station West signalman was informed by his Athelney Junction colleague that the 12.50 a.m. ex-Paddington, a newspaper train of five bogie vans hauled by another King, was running ahead of schedule. As it was not booked to call at Taunton, the Taunton signalman correctly decided to let it run through on the main line and send the express as far as Norton Fitzwarren on the parallel relief line, instead of crossing the express to the Down main immediately west of the station as was normal practice.

At 3.44 a.m. the express drew out of Taunton and, shortly after, the newspaper train passed through at approximately 55 mph. Unfortunately driver Stacey on the express, not realising he was on the relief, mistook the main line signal, set at 'clear', for his own. Not until the other King drew alongside just before Norton Fitzwarren station did he realise his error.

He immediately closed the regulator and applied the brakes, but at 40 mph there was no time to stop before *King George VI* was derailed at the trap points protecting the main line at the spot where the relief line ended.

The first six coaches of the express spread across all four roads. Of the 900 passengers aboard 27 were killed, 13 of whom were naval ratings, and injuries numbered 75.

In blackout conditions, guard Baggett of the newspaper train did not notice the express, but when struck by an object flying through a window, applied his brake and brought the train to a stand about a mile beyond Norton Fitzwarren. After a word with his driver, they proceeded carefully to Wellington station for a more thorough examination, but found nothing wrong.

The object which struck guard Baggett was a rivet head from the bogie of *King George VI* and the lower panels of the last newspaper van were found to be marked by the ballast flung by the derailed express. The newspaper train had not quite cleared the scene before the derailed express crashed across her path, the second coach of the express actually taking off one of its rear buffers. Had the newspaper train been just a few seconds later, it would have crashed into the crowded coaches with an even more appalling result.

Driver Stacey on the express was uninjured and hurried back to protect the line, but his fireman was killed. Driver Stacey was treated sympathetically because, apart from having to cope with the difficulties of driving in the blackout, his home at Acton had been damaged by bombing. The Automatic Train Control siren would have warned him as he passed Norton

Fitzwarren's distant signal at 'danger', but he must have cancelled it subconsciously.

It was believed locally that the signalman at Taunton had already set the road for the express to cross from the Down relief to the Down main just west of the station before he received the advice from Athelney that the newspaper train was near. Unfortunately, so the story goes, he did not wait for the express driver to whistle, thus acknowledging that he had seen the altered route, before clearing the signals for the express train to travel along the relief line.

Personalities

Charles Benjamin Collett, born in 1871, was educated at Merchant Taylors and the City & Guilds College, South Kensington, and became a pupil of Maudslay Sons & Field Ltd, marine engineers. In 1897 he was employed as a draughtsman at Swindon. His great ability was recognised and in 1898 he was appointed assistant to the chief draughtsman, being elevated in 1900 to technical inspector at Swindon works before becoming assistant works manager later the same year. In 1912 he was given the post of works manager and on 1 January 1922 succeeded Churchward, continuing the policy of standardisation. He retired in 1941 and died in 1952, aged eighty-one.

Frederick William Hawksworth was born in Swindon in 1884 and in 1898 became a GWR apprentice. Appointed draughtsman in 1905 he made drawings for *The Great Bear*. In 1925 he was made chief draughtsman and in 1932 assistant chief mechanical engineer. He played a large part in modernising the stationary locomotive testing plant in the 1930s and his principles of locomotive testing were adopted as BR Standard. He became chief mechanical engineer in 1941. He retired in December 1949, and from then onwards unified control of Swindon works ended as the locomotive works, running department, and carriage and wagon department were each placed under separate authority. Hawksworth died on 13 July 1976, aged ninety-two.

James Charles Inglis, born in 1851, was educated in Aberdeen. He worked for the South Devon and Cornwall railways before joining the GWR in 1878. In 1892 he was appointed chief engineer, and in 1903 general manager. Being elected president of the Institution of Civil Engineers in 1909 and 1910, he was knighted the following year but enjoyed the honour for only a short while as he died on 19 December 1911.

It was under the aegis of Inglis that the Great Western's publicity machine really developed and the Cornish Riviera Express was so named.

In January 1912 he was succeeded by his chief assistant, Frank Potter, who had joined the GWR in 1869 as a lad clerk in the goods office at Paddington. Eventually promoted to the general manager's office, he was transferred to the traffic department in 1881. After several years of being stationmaster, in 1888 he was made chief clerk and assistant to the superintendent of the London Division and rejoined the general manager's office in 1894 before becoming chief assistant to Inglis in 1904.

Potter proved a very able and popular general manager. In office throughout the First World War, the strain of the war years affected his health. To recuperate, he travelled to St Ives in March 1919 but died there on 23 July 1919. He had twice been offered, but declined, a knighthood.

He was succeeded by Charles Aldington who had enjoyed the experience of being superintendent of the line for eight years before being appointed assistant general manager in March 1919, when Potter had gone to take a rest. The war years had also taken their toll on Aldington and he was forced to go away for a respite early in 1921 and then to resign in June.

Aldington was succeeded by Felix John Clewett Pole, born on 1 February 1877, who in 1891 entered the GWR's telegraph department at Swindon and in 1896 transferred to the chief engineer's office and then to that of the general manager in 1904, one of his tasks being to edit the *Great Western Railway Magazine*. On Aldington's promotion he became assistant general manager in 1919.

As general manager, Pole was responsible for preparing for the amalgamation of twenty-one Welsh companies including their docks. In 1924 a simple, but useful, change was that regular main line services from Paddington left at regular intervals, obviating the need for passengers to consult a timetable.

Trains left Paddington at the following minutes past the hour: 00.10 to Birmingham and the North; 00.15 to Bristol; 00.30 to the West of England and Weymouth; 00.45 for the West Midland line and 0.55 to South Wales. Similarly, Up services departed at standard times: Birmingham–Paddington on the hour; from Cardiff at fifteen minutes past and so on.

Pole arranged for inspectors to count the number of passengers on trains and where traffic was light trains were withdrawn. Pole thus saved nearly 4,000 train miles daily. Pole also arranged for coaches to be used more intensively, arranging matters so that as many train sets as possible could make two journeys daily. He was knighted in 1924 but in 1928 left the GWR when he became the chairman of Associated Electrical Industries. He died in 1956.

James Milne took over from Pole. Milne, born in 1883, had graduated in engineering at Manchester before joining the GWR locomotive department aged twenty-one. He moved to the head office at Paddington where he gained operational and traffic experience. He then moved to the Ministry of Transport when it was set up in 1919, but returned to the GWR as assistant general manager in 1922.

When Milne was appointed general manager he faced a difficult task. The 1926 strike had wrecked coal exports, the depression was taking its toll and road competition for goods and passengers was raising its ugly head. Milne, keeping abreast of the times, helped to set up the Railway Air Services and examined electrification for the GWR, but found it unsuited to the GWR's traffic needs. Knighted in 1932, he steered the GWR through the Second World War to nationalisation. He was strongly opposed to state ownership of the railways, and although offered chairmanship of the Railway Executive of the British Transport Commission, declined it. He died in 1958.

The Main GWR Locomotive Classes

Year first built	Wheel arrangement	Designer	Class
Broad Gauge			
1837	2-2-2	Stephenson	Star
1840	2-2-2	Gooch	Firefly
1840	2-2-2	Gooch	Sun
1841	2-4-0	Gooch	Leo
1842	0-6-0	Gooch	Hercules
1846	2-2-2	Gooch	Prince
1846	0-6-0	Gooch	Premier or Ajax
1847	0-6-0	Gooch	Pyracmon
1847	4-2-2	Gooch	Iron Duke
1849	4-4-0T	Gooch	Corsair
1851	0-6-0	Gooch	Caesar
1852	0-6-0	Gooch	Standard Goods
1852	0-6-0ST	Gooch	Banking
1854	4-4-0T	Gooch	Sappho
1855	4-4-0	Gooch	Waverley
1856	2-4-0	Gooch	Victoria
1862	2-4-0T	Gooch	Metropolitan
1865	0-6-0T	Gooch	Sir Watkin

1865	2-4-0	Armstrong	Hawthorn or Avonside
1865	0-6-0	Armstrong	Swindon

Standard Gauge

1855	0-6-0	Gooch	57
1855	2-2-2	Gooch	69-76
1857	0-6-0	Gooch	79
1857	0-6-0	Gooch/Beyer Peacock	77
1861	0-6-0	Gooch	167
1862	0-6-0	Gooch	131
1862	2-2-2	Gooch	157
1862	2-4-0	Gooch	Chancellor
1863	2-4-0	Armstrong	111
1864	0-6-0	Beyer Peacock	Bayer
1864	0-6-0ST	Armstrong	302
1866	2-2-2	Gooch	Sir Daniel
1866	0-6-0	Armstrong	360
1866	0-6-0	Armstrong	Standard Goods
1867	0-6-0ST	Armstrong	1016
1868	2-4-0	Armstrong	Bicycle
1868	0-4-2T	Armstrong	517
1869	2-4-0	Armstrong	481
1869	2-4-0T	Armstrong	Metropolitan
1870	0-6-0ST	Armstrong	1076
1871	2-4-0	Armstrong	56
1871	0-6-0T	Armstrong	633
1872	0-6-0ST	Armstrong	645
1873	2-2-2	Armstrong	Queen
1873	2-4-0	Armstrong	806
1874	0-6-0	Armstrong	Coal Engines
1874	0-6-0ST	Armstrong	850
1879	2-2-2	Armstrong	Sharpies
1881	2-4-0	Dean	2201

1882	0-6-0T	Dean	1813
1883	0-6-0	Dean	Dean Goods
1885	2-4-0	Dean	Stella
1885	0-6-0	Dean	2361
1885	2-4-0T	Dean	3511
1886	0-6-0ST	Dean	1661
1887	4-4-0	Dean	3521
1889	2-4-0	Dean	3226
1889	2-4-0	Dean	Barnum
1890	0-6-0ST	Dean	1854
1891	2-2-2	Dean	3001
1892	2-4-0	Dean	3232
1892	0-6-0ST	Dean	655
1895	2-4-0	Dean	River
1895	4-4-0	Dean	Duke
1897	0-6-0ST	Dean	2021
1897	0-6-0ST	Dean	2721
1899	2-6-0	Dean	Kruger
1899	4-4-0	Dean	Bulldog
1900	2-6-0	Dean	Aberdare
1900	2-4-2T	Dean	36XX
1900	0-6-0	Dean	Sir Daniel
1901	4-4-0	Dean	Cities
1902	4-6-0	Churchward	Saint
1903	2-8-0	Churchward	28XX
1906	2-6-2T	Churchward	3150
1906	2-6-2T	Churchward	45XX
1907	4-6-0	Churchward	Star
1910	2-8-0T	Churchward	42XX
1910	0-6-0ST	Churchward	1361
1911	2-6-0	Churchward	43XX
1911	2-8-0	Robinson	ROD
1919	2-8-0	Churchward	47XX
1923	4-6-0	Collett	Castle
1924	4-6-0	Collett	Hall

1924	0-6-2T	Collett	56XX
1926	0-4-0T	Avonside	1101
1927	4-6-0	Collett	King
1928	2-6-2T	Collett	51XX
1929	0-6-0PT	Collett	57XX
1930	0-6-0	Collett	2251
1931	0-6-0PT	Collett	54XX
1932	0-4-2T	Collett	48XX/58XX
1934	2-8-2T	Collett	72XX
1934	0-6-0PT	Collett	1366
1936	4-6-0	Collett	Grange
1936	4-4-0	Collett	Dukedog
1938	2-6-2T	Collett	31XX
1938	4-6-0	Collett	Manor
1945	4-6-0	Hawksworth	County
1947	0-6-0PT	Hawksworth	94XX
1949	0-6-0PT	Hawksworth	15XX
1949	0-6-0T	Hawksworth	16XX

Engine Classification: Power Groups and Route Colours

GWR locomotives bore a disc on the cabside, the colour indicating the maximum axle load and the approximate tractive effort on starting.

Group letter	Tractive effort in pounds, not exceeding
Ungrouped	16,500
A	18,500
B	20,500
C	25,000
D	33,000
E	38,000
Special	Above 38,000

Route colour	Axle load
Uncoloured	Up to 14 tons
Yellow	Up to 16 tons
Blue	Up to 17 tons 12 cwts
Red	All engines over 17 tons 12 cwts except King Class
Double Red	22 tons 10cwts (King Class)

Table of Opening Dates, Mileage and Gauge

B.G. = Broad Gauge. M.G. = Mixed Gauge. S.G. = Standard Gauge.
M = Miles C = Chains
Italics indicate changes of gauge or loss of mileage.

Date	Section of line	B.G.		M.G.		S.G.	
		M	C	M	C	M	C
GREAT WESTERN RAILWAY (INCLUDING LINES WORKED)							
1838							
4 June	Paddington (Old Station)–Maidenhead (Old Station)	22	43				
1839							
1 July	Maidenhead (Old Station)–Twyford	8	18				
	31 December 1839	30	61				
1840							
30 Mar.	Twyford–Reading	4	77				
1 June	Reading–Steventon	20	44				
20 July	Steventon–Faringdon Road (now Challow)	7	29				
31 Aug.	Bristol (Old Terminus)–Bath	11	43				
17 Dec.	Faringdon Road–Hay Lane (80¼ mp)	16	29				
	31 December 1840	91	43				
1841							
31 May	Hay Lane–Chippenham	13	57				

Date	Section of line	B.G.		M.G.		S.G.	
		M	C	M	C	M	C
31 May	Cheltenham & Great Western Union Railway, Swindon Junction–Kemble	13	58				
31 May	Kemble–Cirencester	4	17				
14 June	B&ER Bristol, Harbour Bridge Junction–Bridgwater	33	20				
14 June	Weston Junction–Weston-super-Mare	1	38				
30 June	Chippenham–Bath	12	73				
	31 December 1841	170	66				
1842							
1 July	B&ER Bridgwater–Taunton	11	45				
	31 December 1842	182	31				
1843							
1 May	B&ER Taunton–Beambridge (171 m. 52 c.)	8	40				
	31 December 1843	190	71				
1844							
1 May	B&ER Beambridge–Exeter	22	23				
12 June	Didcot Junction–Oxford (Old Station)	9	57				
	31 December 1844	222	71				
1845							
12 May	Kemble Junction–Gloucester (Standish Junction to Gloucester (7 m 30 ch) opened by Bristol & Gloucester Railway 8 July 1844)	23	9				
	31 December 1845	246	0				
1847							
28 July	B&ER Yatton–Clevedon	3	45				
23 Oct.	Gloucester, Tramway Junction–Cheltenham, Lansdown Junction, GWR portion			3	11		
23 Oct.	Cheltenham, Lansdown Junction–St James's station	1	6				

Date	Section of line	B.G.		M.G.		S.G.	
		M	C	M	C	M	C
23 Oct.	Gloucester Avoiding Line (Millstream Junction–Barnwood Junction)		56				
23 Oct.	Gloucester T Line (Tramway Junction–T station)		20				
21 Dec.	Reading–Hungerford	25	32				
	31 December 1847	276	79	3	11		
1848							
12 June	B&ER Tiverton Road–Tiverton	4	60				
5 Sept.	Wilts, Somerset & Weymouth Railway, Thingley Junction–Westbury	13	54				
1 Nov.	Southcot Junction–Basingstoke	13	49				
	31 December 1848	309	2	3	11		
1849							
1 May	B&ER Company took over its own line	85	31				
8 Oct.	Slough–Windsor, and West Curve at Slough	3	5				
	31 December 1849	226	56	3	11		
1850							
2 Sept.	Oxford, Millstream Junction (62 mp)–Banbury (Single Line)	24	15				
7 Oct.	Westbury–Frome (Single Line)	5	61				
	31 December 1850	256	52	3	11		
1851							
9 Sept.	Westbury–Warminster (Single Line)	4	73				
19 Sept.	Gloucester & Dean Forest Railway, Gloucester–Grange Court (Junction with South Wales Railway)	7	36				
	31 December 1851	269	1	3	11		
1852							

Date	Section of line	B.G.		M.G.		S.G.	
		M	C	M	C	M	C
1 Oct.	Oxford, Millstream Junction–Birmingham (Standard Gauge began at Isis River Bridge, 63 mp)	1	0	66	24		
1 Oct.	*Oxford, Millstream Junction–Banbury, mixed and doubled*	24	15				
	31 December 1852	245	66	69	35		
1853							
11 July	Grange Court–Hopesbrook	5	5				
	31 December 1853	250	71	69	35		
1854							
16 Jan.	Paddington New Station, departure side		20				
20 Mar.	Over Junction–Gloucester Docks	1	16				
29 May	Paddington New Station, arrival side	0	0				
29 May	*Bristol, Midland Junction–Terminus*		34		34		
1 Aug.	Wycombe Railway, Maidenhead, Wycombe Junction–High Wycombe	9	71				
1 Sept.	Shrewsbury & Birmingham Railway					22	59
1 Sept.	Shrewsbury & Chester Railway					54	58
14 Nov.	Birmingham–Priestfield Junction with OWWR			10	72		
14 Nov.	Wolverhampton, Cannock Road Junction–Stafford Road Junction				56		
14 Nov.	*Stafford Road Junction–Oxley Viaduct and Victoria Basin*			1	10	1	10
14 Nov.	Frome–Radstock (Mineral Line)	8	19				
	31 December 1854	270	3	82	47	76	27
1855							

Date	Section of line	B.G.		M.G.		S.G.	
		M	C	M	C	M	C
2 June	Hereford, Ross & Gloucester Railway, Hopesbrook–Hereford (Barr's Court)	17	46				
	31 December 1855	287	49	82	47	76	27
1856							
2 June	Abingdon Railway, Abingdon Junction–Abingdon	1	70				
30 June	Warminster–Salisbury	19	50				
1 Sept.	Frome–Yeovil	25	62				
8 Sept.	West Drayton–Uxbridge	2	51				
22 Dec.	*Oxford, Isis Bridge (63 mp)–Didcot, North Junction*	9	4	9	4		
22 Dec.	Didcot Loop, North Junction–East Junction			1	2		
22 Dec.	*Didcot, East Junction–Reading, West Junction*	15	66	15	66		
22 Dec.	Reading Loop, West Junction–Oxford Road Junction				45		
22 Dec.	*Reading, Oxford Road Junction–Basingstoke*	14	50	14	50		
	31 December 1856	298	2	123	54	76	27
1857							
20 Jan.	Yeovil–Dorchester Junction	20	66				
20 Jan.	Dorchester Junction–Weymouth			6	49		
2 Feb.	Bradford Junction–Bathampton	9	12				
1 June	Twyford–Henley	4	47				
1 July	Holt Junction–Devizes	8	17				
12 Nov.	Bridport Railway, Maiden Newton–Bridport	9	21				
	31 December 1857	350	5	130	23	76	27
1858							
9 Nov.	East Somerset Railway, Witham–Shepton Mallet	9	3				

Date	Section of line	B.G.		M.G.		S.G.	
		M	C	M	C	M	C
1 Dec.	Reading, West Junction–Junction with Staines & Wokingham Railway (SER)					1	45
	31 December 1858	359	8	130	23	77	72
1859							
1 June	Wednesbury, Branch to S. Staffordshire Railway				14		
18 July	Great Western & Brentford Railway, Southall–Brentford goods only, passengers 1 May 1860	3	77				
	31 December 1859	363	5	130	37	77	72
1860							
2 Aug.	Llantrissant–Tonyrefail (goods)	4	77				
10 Oct.	Stratford-on-Avon Railway, Hatton–Stratford (Old Station)			9	43		
	31 December 1860	368	2	140		77	72
1861							
1 July	Wellington & Severn Junction Railway, Ketley Junction–Lightmoor					4	41
24 July	Stratford-on-Avon Railway, connecting line to WMR at Stratford				32		
1 Oct.	*Reading, West Junction–Paddington*	36	78	36	78		
	Reading West Junction to east of Reading station					1	17
	Southall–Brentford (Up line only)	3	77	3	77		
1 Nov.	Bordesley Junction Branch to Midland Railway				21		
	31 December 1861	327	7	181	48	81	16
1862							
1 Jan.	South Wales Railway	174	65		40		
8 Jan.	Ely Valley Railway (goods) Mwyndy and Brofiskin Branch	2	63				

Date	Section of line	B.G.		M.G.		S.G.	
		M	C	M	C	M	C
8 Jan.	Branch to Gellyrhaidd	1	24				
1 Mar.	East Somerset Railway, Shepton Mallet–Wells	4	62				
Mar.	*Slough–Windsor, and West Curve at Slough*	3	5	3	5		
Mar.	*Reading, Station Junction–Oxford Road Junction*		59		59		
22 May	Wrexham & Minera Railway, Croes Newydd Junctions–Junction with old branch from Wheatsheaf at Brymbo					3	33
	Old line between Moss and Brymbo abandoned						60
2 June	Vale of Llangollen Railway, Ruabon, Llangollen Line Junction–Llangollen (goods June 1863)					5	40
1 Aug.	Wycombe Railway, High Wycombe–Thame	13	72				
11 Nov.	Berks & Hants Extension Railway, Hungerford–Devizes	24	32				
Dec.	Ely Valley Railway, Tonyrefail–Dinas (Penygraig)	2	10				
	31 December 1862	547	31	185	72	89	29
1863							
1 April	West London Junction–North Pole Junction				34		
1 June	*Didcot station, East Junction–North Junction*	1	12	1	12		
	1 August 1863	546	19	187	38	89	29
1 Aug.	West Midland Railway			2	9	280	67
7 Sept.	Milford Railway, Johnstone–Milford	4	0				
8 Sept.	Bristol & South Wales Union Railway, Bristol–New Passage Pier	11	37				
1 Oct.	Wycombe Railway, Princes Risborough–Aylesbury	7	27				

Date	Section of line	B.G.		M.G.		S.G.	
		M	C	M	C	M	C
20 Oct.	Nantwich & Market Drayton Railway, Market Drayton–Nantwick Junction					10	65
29 Oct.	Calne Railway, Chippenham–Calne	5	24				
28 Dec.	Maesycwmmer Branch						58
	31 December 1863	574	27	189	47	381	59
1864							
1 Jan.	Portskewett–Pier		74				
14 Apr.	Marlborough Railway, Savernake–Marlborough	5	49				
18 Apr.	Quaker's Yard Junction–Middle Duffryn Junction (passengers 5 October)					4	73
1 June	Faringdon Railway, Uffington–Faringdon	3	49				
13 June	Yeovil, Clifton Maybank Branch		36				
13 Aug.	Tenbury & Bewdley Railway, Bewdley–Tenbury Junction					15	17
14 Oct.	Wycombe Railway, Thame–Kennington Junction, Oxford	12	75				
1 Nov.	Lightmoor–Coalbrookdale					1	34
1 Nov.	Wenlock Railway, Buildwas Junction–Coalbrookdale						69
5 Dec.	Much Wenlock–Priesthope					2	75
	Ely Valley Railway, Llantrissant–Maesaraul Jc. and Brofiskin	3	28	3	28		
	31 December 1864	594	42	192	75	407	7
1865							
1 Feb.	Vale of Neath Railway		45	43	37		
8 May	Llangollen & Corwen Railway, Llangollen–Corwen					10	10
16 Oct.	Ogmore Valley Railway, Gellyrhaidd–Gilfach Goch	2	36				

Date	Section of line	B.G.		M.G.		S.G.	
		M	C	M	C	M	C
	31 December 1865	597	43	236	32	417	17
1866							
1 Jan.	Stourbridge Railway, Cradley–Old Hill					1	35
2 July	Wallingford & Watlington Railway, Wallingford Road–Wallingford					3	20
16 July	Corwen & Bala Railway, Corwen–Llandrillo					4	61
16 July	*Hereford, Barr's Court–Rotherwas Junction*	1	15	1	15		
1 Sept.	Swan Village–Horsley Fields Junction					1	45
1 Sept.	Swan Village Basin Branch						23
	31 December 1866	596	28	237	47	428	41
1867							
1 Apr.	Handsworth Junction–Smethwick						65
	Stourbridge Railway, Old Hill–Galton					4	23
16 Oct.	Wellington & Drayton Railway, Wellington–Market Drayton					16	12
16 Dec.	Wenlock Railway, Presthope–Marsh Farm Jc., Craven Arms					11	3
	31 December 1867	596	28	237	47	460	64
1868							
1 Apr.	Corwen & Bala Railway, Llandrillo–Bala					6	11
25 May	Forest of Dean Central Railway, Awre Jc.–New Fancy Colliery	4	57				
4 Aug.	Bala & Dolgelley Railway, Bala (Old Station)–Dolgelly Jc.					17	64
13 Oct.	*Princes Risborough–Aylesbury*	7	27			7	27
	31 December 1863	593	58	237	47	492	6
1869							

Date	Section of line	B.G.		M.G.		S.G.	
		M	C	M	C	M	C
1 Apr.	Oxford–Wolverhampton			80	11	80	11
	Bordesley Junction Branch				21		21
	Wednesbury Branch				14		14
	Hatton–Stratford-on-Avon			9	43	9	43
	Southcot Junction, Reading–Basingstoke			13	49	13	49
14 Aug.	Grange Court–Rotherwas Junction, Hereford	21	36			21	36
27 July	Rotherwas Jc.–Hereford, Barr's Court			1	15	1	15
20 Aug.	Tramway Junction, Gloucester–Grange Court	7	66	7	66		
	Gloucester Docks Branch	1	16	1	16		
	31 December 1869	563	20	141	56	618	35
1870							
23 Aug.	Wycombe Junction, Maidenhead–Kennington	36	58			36	58
	31 December 1870	526	42	141	56	655	13
1871							
6 Oct.	West Drayton–Uxbridge	2	51			2	51
	31 December 1871	523	71	141	56	657	74
1872							
Feb.	Didcot–Swindon	24	73	24	73		
11 May	Grange Court–Cardiff, Bute Street Junction	48	47			48	47
	Cardiff, Bute Street Junction–station				40		40
	Cardiff station–Carmarthen Bridge Junction	74	56			74	56
	Carmarthen Bridge Junction–Whitland	13	45			13	45
	Whitland–New Milford	26	34			26	34
	Forest of Dean Branch	7	20			7	20
	Bullo Pill Dock Branch		53				53
	Forest of Dean Central Railway	4	57			4	57

Date	Section of line	B.G.		M.G.		S.G.	
		M	C	M	C	M	C
	Portskewett–Pier		74				74
	Cardiff Docks Branch	1	19			1	19
	Ely Valley Railway	7	66	3	28	11	14
	Llynvi & Ogmore Railway, Ely Valley Extension	2	36			2	36
	Briton Ferry Dock Branch		45				45
	Swansea Vale Junction Branch		30				30
	Landore–Swansea, High Street	1	25			1	25
	Swansea North Dock Branch		56				56
	Johnston–Milford	4	0			4	0
	Swansea Wind Street–Middle Duffryn			28	54	28	54
	Swansea Harbour Line				60		60
	Swansea Vale Branch at East Dock				13		13
	Neath Junction–Neath station				50		50
	Gelli Tarw Junction–Merthyr			6	23	6	23
	Dare and Amman Branches			6	77	6	77
	Gloucester station–Grange Court			7	36	7	36
	Gloucester Docks Branch			1	16	1	16
25 May	*Swindon–Tramway Jc., Gloucester*	35	57			35	57
	Tramway Junction–Gloucester station				30		30
	Kemble–Cirencester	4	17			4	17
	Tramway Junction, Gloucester–Lansdown Junction, Cheltenham, GWR portion			3	11	3	11
	Cheltenham, Lansdown Junction–station	1	6			1	6
	Gloucester Avoiding Line and T Line, long derelict, written off		76				
25 Nov.	*Abingdon Junction–Abingdon*	1	70			1	70

Date	Section of line	B.G.		M.G.		S.G.	
		M	C	M	C	M	C
26 Nov.	*Didcot station–Oxford*			10	71	10	71
	Didcot Loop, East Junction–North Junction			1	2	1	2
	Oxford, Millstream Junction–Old Station closed		66				
	31 December 1872	259	3	95	18	967	38
1873							
1 Jan.	Llanelly Railway					35	79
15 Jan.	East Gloucestershire Railway, Witney Jc.–Fairford					14	10
28 June	Great Marlow Railway. Marlow Road–Bourne End					2	60
1 July	Llynvi & Ogmore Railway					27	0
1 Aug.	Ross & Monmouth Railway, Ross–Monmouth, May Hill					12	32
	Bristol, Midland Junction–North Somerset Jc.		36		36		
7 Aug.	*South Wales Junction, Bristol–New Passage Pier*	11	37			11	37
3 Sept.	Bristol & North Somerset Railway, North Somerset Jc.–Radstock					15	10
8 Sept.	Abingdon Branch extended to new station at Radley						61
	31 December 1873	247	10	95	54	1087	7
1874							
1 May	Monmouth, Troy–May Hill						59
2 May	Bromyard Jc.–Yearsett					7	5
June	*Swindon–Thingley Junction, Chippenham*	18	68	18	68		
	North Somerset Junction, Bristol–Bathampton	12	75	12	75		
	Thingley Junction–Frome	19	35			19	35
	Frome–Dorchester	46	19			46	19
	Dorchester–Dorchester Junction		29				29

Date	Section of line	B.G.		M.G.		S.G.	
		M	C	M	C	M	C
	Dorchester Junction–Weymouth			6	49	6	49
	Bradford Junction–Bathampton	9	12			9	12
	Westbury–Salisbury	24	43			24	43
18 June	*Frome–Radstock*	8	19			8	19
	Witham–Wells	13	65			13	65
	Yeovil, Clifton Maybank Branch		36				36
	Maiden Newton–Bridport	9	21			9	21
26 June	*Hungerford–Holt Junction*	32	49			32	49
1 July	*Savernake–Marlborough*	5	49			5	49
	Southcot Junction, Reading–Hungerford	23	52			23	52
	Reading–Southcot Junction			1	60	1	60
	Reading West Junction–Oxford Road Junction				45		45
3 Aug.	Kington & Eardisley Railway, Titley–Eardisley Jc.					6	74
14 Aug.	*Chippenham–Calne*	5	24			5	24
17 Sept.	Pontypool Road South Jc.–Maindee West Jc.					8	73
	Maindee North Junction–East Junction						17
1 Dec.	Bristol, Narroways Hill Junction–Ashley Hill Jc.						36
21 Dec.	Pontypool Road North Junction–Panteg Jc.					1	18
	Pontypool Road, West Junction–Middle Junction						15
	31 December 1874	16	54	118	43	1320	31
1875							
1 Feb.	Pontypool Road, East Junction–Coedygric Junction						43
1 Mar.	*Thingley Junction–Bathampton*	8	38	8	38		
4 June	*Southall–Brentford*			3	77	3	77

Date	Section of line	B.G.		M.G.		S.G.	
		M	C	M	C	M	C
1 Aug.	Monmouthshire Railway					51	19
1 Sept.	Llynvi & Ogmore Railway, Black Mill–Hendreforgan					3	30
9 Sept.	Leominster & Kington Railway, Titley–Presteign					5	53
25 Sept.	Kington & Eardisley Railway, Kington–New Radnor					6	43
Nov.	*West London Junction–North Pole Junction*				34		34
Dec.	Cardiff, Penarth Junction Lines to Taff Vale Railway						66
	31 December 1875	8	16	122	50	1392	76
1876							
1 Jan.	Bristol & Exeter Railway	125	41	69	47	18	36
	Bristol Harbour Railway				65		
1 Feb.	South Devon Railway	123	26		34		
	Cornwall Railway	70	7				
	West Cornwall Railway			25	69	10	22
1 Mar.	*Taunton–Exeter*	29	47	29	47		
24 Mar.	*Twyford–Henley*	4	47			4	47
	Lydford–Tavistock Junction	19	33	19	33		
	Tavistock Junction–North Road, Plymouth	3		3			
	North Road–Devonport Jc. (Loop)				24		
	Devonport Junction–Keyham Junction	2	17	2	17		
29 May	Culm Valley Light Railway, Tiverton–Hemyock					7	29
June	Bristol Harbour Extension to Wapping Wharf				39		
27 Aug.	Ponkey Branch, Aberderfyn–Legacy					3	6
4 Sept.	Alcester Railway, Bearley–Alcester					6	40

271

Date	Section of line	B.G.		M.G.		S.G.	
		M	C	M	C	M	C
2 Oct.	Llynvi & Ogmore Railway, Cardiff and Ogmore Line, Llanharen– C&O Junction, Black Mill					8	24
25 Oct.	Garw Branch, Brymnenyn Junction–Blaengarw					5	54
1 Nov.	Wye Valley Railway, Wye Valley Junction,Chepstow– Monmouth					13	8
13 Nov.	Llynvi & Ogmore Railway, Pyle Junction Branch						42
	31 December 1876	268	26	274	25	1470	64
1877							
25 Oct.	Acton–Acton Wells Junction						49
1 May	Llynvi & Ogmore Railway, Bryncethin Jc.–Tynycoed Jc., Tondu					1	77
1 June	St Ives Road (St Erth)–St Ives	4	22				
1 Oct.	Cornwall Minerals Railway	3	10			43	48
3 Oct.	*Hayle Wharves Branch*				55		55
22 Oct.	Yearsett–Bromyard					3	62
18 Dec.	Malmesbury Railway, Dauntsey–Malmesbury					6	43
	31 December 1877	275	58	275	0	1526	48
1878							
1 Feb.	*Plymouth, Laira Jc.–Friary Junction*		59		59		
1 Mar.	Netherton–Old Hill					2	65
	Old Hill–Halesowen					1	43
April	Llantarnam Jc.–Cwmbran Jc.						67
1 June	Kidderminster Junction– Bewdley					3	3
18 June	*Plymouth, North Road Junction–Millbay*		45		45		
	Cornwall Junction–Devonport Junction		24		24		

Date	Section of line	B.G.		M.G.		S.G.	
		M	C	M	C	M	C
1 July	Llynvi & Ogmore Railway, Tywith–Cymmer					2	22
	Junction Branch to South Wales Mineral Railway						19
10 Aug.	Ely & Clydach Valleys Railway, Dinas (Penygraig)–Blaen Glydach					1	68
	Uffington–Faringdon	3	49			3	49
	31 December 1878	270	41	276	48	1542	64
1879							
1 Jan.	Par–St Blazey						27
	Newport, Gaer Junction–Park Junction						63
10 Mar.	Withymoor (Netherton Goods) Branch						67
30 June	*Durston–Yeovil, Pen Mill*			20	35	20	35
	Yeovil Town–Hendford made into siding						74
	Weston Junction–Weston-super-Mare			1	38	1	38
1 Sept.	Llanelly Loop, Main Line to Llandilo Branch						13
18 Sept.	Monmouthshire Rly, Talywain Branch					4	5
27 Sept.	*Yatton–Clevedon*	3	45			3	45
1 Oct.	Stourbridge Junction–Stourbridge						73
6 Nov.	Plymouth, Sutton Harbour, North Quay Branch		32				
31 Dec.	*Lostwithiel & Fowey Railway closed*	4	60				
	31 December 1879	262	48	254	55	1574	36
1880							
24 Jan.	*Portishead Junction–Portishead*	9	49			9	49
	31 December 1880	252	79	254	55	1584	5
1881							

Date	Section of line	B.G.		M.G.		S.G.	
		M	C	M	C	M	C
9 May	Swansea, Hafod Junction–Morriston					2	3
14 May	*Norton Fitzwarren–Barnstaple*	42	50			42	50
1 June	Bourton-on-the-Water–Lansdown Junction, Cheltenham					16	50
22 Aug.	Carmarthen & Cardigan Rly					18	58
	31 December 1881	210	29	254	55	1664	6
1882							
1 Mar.	Bristol & North Somerset Railway, Hallatrow–Camerton					3	50
13 Apr.	Didcot, Newbury & Southampton Railway, Didcot East Junction–Newbury East Junction					17	27
11 May	Moss Valley Line, Junction near Wrexham–Jc. with old branch from Wheatsheaf					1	72
14 Sept.	Cardiff, Riverside Branch					1	18
9 Oct.	Teign Valley Railway, Chudleigh Road (Heathfield)–Ashton					6	16
28 Oct.	*Norton Fitzwarren–Minehead*	22	60			22	60
1 Nov.	Bala & Festiniog Railway, Bala Junction–Festiniog					22	9
	31 December 1882	187	49	254	55	1740	60
1883							
1 Jan.	Torbay & Brixham Railway	2	6				
9 May	Swindon & Highworth Railway, Highworth Railway					5	46
30 June	*Slough–Windsor, and Slough West Curve*			3	5	3	5
11 Aug.	Princetown Railway, Yelverton Junction–Princetown					10	43
1 Sept.	Coleford Railway, Wyesham Junction, Monmouth–Coleford					5	20

Date	Section of line	B.G.		M.G.		S.G.	
		M	C	M	C	M	C
10 Sept.	Festiniog & Blaenau Railway					3	36
	31 December 1883	189	55	251	50	1768	50
1884							
1 Jan.	Watlington & Princes Risborough Railway					8	66
1 Mar.	Weston-super-Mare Loop					3	74
	Weston Junction–Weston-super-Mare closed					1	38
	Leominster & Bromyard Railway, Leominster–Steens Bridge					3	69
31 Mar.	Bridport Railway, Bridport–West Bay					2	
28 June	*Tiverton Junction–Tiverton*	4	60			4	60
1 Aug.	2 m 17 ch north of Tiverton–Morebath Junction					6	37
9 Aug.	Staines & West Drayton Railway, West Drayton–Colnbrook					2	60
7 Nov.	Oldbury Railway, Langley Green–Oldbury					1	21
	31 December 1884	184	75	251	50	1800	79
1885							
1 May	Exe Valley Line, Stoke Canon Junction–2 m 17 ch north of Tiverton					12	71
4 May	Didcot, Newbury & Southampton Railway, Enborne Junction, Newbury–Winchester					25	74
July	Forest of Dean Branch, Bilson Junction–Speedwell Siding					1	69
27 July	Newent Rly, Over Junction–Dymock					12	58
	Ross & Ledbury Railway, Dymock–Ledbury					4	59

Date	Section of line	B.G.		M.G.		S.G.	
		M	C	M	C	M	C
2 Nov.	Staines & West Drayton Railway, Colnbrook–Staines					3	20
9 Nov.	Abbotsbury Railway, Upwey Junction–Abbotsbury					6	8
	31 December 1885	184	75	251	50	1868	38
1886							
15 Feb.	Didcot West Curve						35
10 Mar.	'Hall's Tramroad', Penar Junction–Manmoel Colliery					3	63
22 Mar.	Cymmer–Abergwynfi					2	77
6 Apr.	Newport, Western Loop, Ebbw Junction–Park Junction						56
29 May	Bristol Loop, North Somerset Junction						31
1 Sept.	Severn Tunnel Line, Pilning Junction–Severn Tunnel Junction (passengers 1 December)					7	34
	Whitland & Cardigan Rly					14	14
	Crymmych Arms–Cardigan					11	4
1 Dec.	*Pilning Jc.–New Passage Pier closed*					2	59
	Portskewett–Pier closed						74
	31 December 1886	184	75	251	50	1905	59
1887							
6 Apr.	Banbury & Cheltenham Direct Railway, King's Sutton–Chipping Norton					15	34
9 May	Helston Rly., Gwinear Road–Helston					8	67
27 May	Bodmin Road–Bodmin					3	43
1 June	Barnstaple, Loop to LSWR					1	27
	31 December 1887	184	75	251	50	1934	70
1888							
3 Sept.	Bodmin–Boscarne Junction with LSWR					2	56

Date	Section of line	B.G.		M.G.		S.G.	
		M	C	M	C	M	C
Oct.	*Cornwall Minerals Railway, Treamble– Gravel Hill closed*					1	9
	St Erth–Lelant Quay	1	8	1	8		
	31 December 1888	183	67	252	58	1936	37
1889							
1 July	Moreton-in-Marsh–Shipston-on-Stour					9	7
2 Dec.	Kemble–Tetbury					7	19
	31 December 1889	183	67	252	58	1952	63
1890							
19 May	Woodstock Road–Blenheim & Woodstock					3	56
	31 December 1890	183	67	252	58	1956	39
1891							
1 Apr.	Plymouth, Lipson Junction–Mount Gould Jc.						36
18 July	*Creech Junction–Chard*	12	61			12	61
1 Oct.	Winchester–Shawford Jc.					2	6
	31 December 1891	171	6	252	58	1971	62
1892							
10 Apr.	Bristol Relief Line, East Depot–Pylle					1	6
20 May	*Paddington–Exeter*			194	7		
	Exeter–City Basin Junction (Down Line mixed in 1871)	1	25				
	City Basin Junction–Tavistock Jc.	47	57				
	Tavistock Junction–Millbay Docks Junction, Plymouth			3	45		
	Plymouth, Millbay station		10				
	North Road–Devonport Junction				24		
	Cornwall Junction–Keyham Junction			2	41		

Date	Section of line	B.G.		M.G.		S.G.	
		M	C	M	C	M	C
	Keyham Junction–Truro	50	78				
	Truro–Penzance			25	69		
	Swindon, on Gloucester Line				60		
	Bristol, Harbour Bridge Junction–Old GWR terminus				15		
	Bristol Harbour Line			1	24		
	Dunball Wharf Branch				36		
	Bridgwater Docks Branch				76		
	Exeter City Basin Branch				34		
	Newton Abbot–Moretonhampstead	12	13				
	Newton Abbot–Kingswear	14	54				
	Churston–Brixham	2	6				
	Ashburton Junction, Totnes–Ashburton	9	20				
	Totnes Quay Branch		62				
	Tavistock Junction–Lydford			19	33		
	Lydford–Launceston	12	34				
	Laira Junction–Friary Junction				59		
	Friary Junction–Sutton Harbour and North Quay	1	35				
	Burngullow–Drinnick Mill	3	10				
	Truro–Falmouth	11	68				
	Hayle Wharves Branch				55		
	St Erth–Lelant			1	8		
	Lelant–St Ives	3	14				
	23 May 1892	171	6	252	58	423	64
21 Nov.	Llynvi & Ogmore Line, Brymnenyn Loop						20
	Tondu North Loop						16
	31 December 1892					2397	8
1893							
13 Nov.	Hengoed–Ystrad Mynach Junction with Rhymney Railway						47

Date	Section of line	B.G.		M.G.		S.G.	
		M	C	M	C	M	C
30 Nov.	Bird-in-Hand Junction, Pontllanfraith–Tredegar Junction						22
19 Dec.	Brent–Kingsbridge					12	35
	31 December 1893					2410	32
1894							
6 June	Birmingham & Henley-in-Arden Railway, Rowington Junction–Henley-in-Arden (goods 2 July)					3	7
	31 December 1894					2413	39
1895							
10 Mar.	Bradford Loop						25
1 July	Llandyssil–Newcastle Emlyn					6	78
16 Sept.	Lostwithiel–Fowey					5	32
	31 December 1895					2426	14
1896							
12 Feb.	Pontycysyllte Branch, Trevor–LIwynenion					3	44
1 July	Goonbarrow Branch					3	8
	Pembroke & Tenby Railway					28	13
	31 December 1896					2460	79
1897							
1 July	Hatton North Loop						31
1 Sept.	Bromyard–Steens Bridge					9	9
	31 December 1897					2470	39
1898							
17 Jan.	Plymouth, Mount Gould Junction–Cattewater Junction						27
	Plymstock Junction–Yealmpton					6	44
4 Apr.	Newport, East Usk Branch					1	52
1 July	North Pembrokeshire & Fishguard Railway					17	12
	31 December 1898					2496	14
1899							

Date	Section of line	B.G.		M.G.		S.G.	
		M	C	M	C	M	C
1 July	Letterston–Goodwick					6	14
1 Aug.	*High Wycombe–Princes Risborough transferred to Great Western & Great Central Joint Committee*					8	38
17 Dec.	Reading, New Junction Line to the South Eastern Railway						27
	31 December 1899					2494	17
1900							
5 Feb.	Avonmouth & Severn Tunnel Line, Pilning Junction–Avonmouth					7	53
29 July	Patney & Chirton–Westbury (passengers 1 Oct.)					14	35
	31 December 1900					2516	25
1901							
1 May	Golden Valley Line, Pontrilas–Hay Junction					18	52
Aug.	East Usk Branch extended						40
1 Oct	Stourbridge Town Branch altered and extended						22
	Wrexham, Rhos Junction–Rhos					3	19
25 Nov.	Gloucester, Cheltenham Loop						66
4 Dec.	Wrington Vale Light Railway, Congresbury–Blagdon					6	41
	31 December 1901					2546	25
1902							
2 Apr.	Halesowen Canal Branch						54
	31 December 1902					2546	79
1903							
1 Jan.	Wootton-Bassett–Badminton (passengers 1 July)					17	9
20 Apr.	Llanelly, Dafen Branch Extension						63
1 May	Badminton–Patchway					12	51
	Stoke Gifford–Filton						75

Date	Section of line	B.G.		M.G.		S.G.	
		M	C	M	C	M	C
3 June	West London Junction (Old Oak Common)–Park Royal					1	17
1 July	Exeter Railway, City Basin Junction–Christow Junction					8	7
	Alphington Road goods line						26
6 July	Chacewater, Blackwater East Jc.–Perranporth					7	45
	Blackwater West Loop						18
2 Nov.	Cardiff, Roath Dock Branch					1	22
	31 December 1903					2597	12
1904							
1 May	Park Royal–Hanwell					4	79
	Exeter Railway, Jc. Line to City Basin Branch						20
1 July	Drayton Green–West Ealing						20
1 Aug.	Honeybourne, East and North Junctions–Broadway					5	22
	Broadway–Toddington					4	43
1 Oct.	Greenford, East Loop Junction–station						53
	Greenford, West Loop						33
	31 December 1904					2613	42
1905							
2 Jan.	Perranporth–Shepherds Junction with Treamble Branch					4	31
1 Feb.	Toddington–Winchcombe					2	44
1 July	Castle Cary–Charlton Mackrell					6	73
	Barnstaple, East Loop						24
	Lambourn Valley Railway					12	33
16 July	'Hall's Tramroad', Manmoel–Markham Colliery					1	52
6 Sept.	Grafton Curve, Savernake (to MSWJR)						44
20 Nov.	Greenford–Northolt Junction					2	26
	31 December 1905					2644	49

Date	Section of line	B.G.		M.G.		S.G.	
		M	C	M	C	M	C
1906							
8 Jan.	Chipping Norton Junction (Kingham) Direct Loop						54
	Cheltenham, Hatherley Loop						39
	Rhondda & Swansea Bay Railway					28	63
12 Feb.	Somerton–Curry Rivel Junction (passengers 2 July)					5	21
5 Mar.	Swansea, Landore West Loop						52
2 Apr.	Athelney–Cogload Junction					2	67
20 May	Charlton Mackrell–Somerton (passengers 2 July)					3	26
1 June	Winchcombe–Bishop's Cleeve					4	76
1 July	Manchester & Milford Railway					41	25
1 Aug.	Bishop's Cleeve–Malvern Road Junction, Cheltenham					3	67
30 Aug.	Clarbeston Junction–Letterston Junction					10	47
	Fishguard & Goodwick–Fishguard Harbour						47
4 Oct.	Bristol Harbour Lines:						
	Ashton Junction–Wapping Wharf Jc.					1	26
	Ashton Swing Bridge Junction–Canon's Marsh					1	7
	Canon's Marsh–Corporation Railway						15
	Portishead Junction West Loop						30
	31 December 1906					2750	71
1907							
1 May	Denham East Junction–Uxbridge, High Street					1	77
	Denham West Loop						28
28 June	Honeybourne South Loop						41
1 July	*Aylesbury Branch transferred to GW and GC Joint Committee*					7	27

Date	Section of line	B.G.		M.G.		S.G.	
		M	C	M	C	M	C
1 Aug.	Cradley, Spinners End Branch (goods)						55
26 Aug.	Camerton–Dunkerton Colliery (goods)					1	10
4 Nov.	Gwaun-cae-Gurwen Branch					2	8
	Part of old Gwaun-cae-Gurwen Branch renamed Cawdor Branch, remainder closed						59
	Forest of Dean Branch, Speedwell–Drybrook						41
9 Dec.	Birmingham & North Warwickshire Line, Tyseley Junction–Bearley West Junction					17	67
	Henley-in-Arden Branch extended to new line						32
	Bearley East Loop (part of old Alcester Branch)						33
	Alcester Branch shortened						40
	Courtybella Jc.–Dock Street & Llanarth Street Jc. closed					1	15
	31 December 1907					2767	2
1908							
1 Jan.	Port Talbot Railway					33	47
	South Wales Mineral Railway					12	59
24 Feb.	Stirchley Branch, Hollinswood (goods only)					1	16
9 Mar.	Westerleigh West Junction–Yate Junction					1	25
	Westerleigh East Loop						41
	Berkeley Loop, Midland Railway–Severn & Wye Railway					1	22
April	Cinderford, Bilson Loop						33
4 May	Reading, Coley Branch from Southcot Junction					1	61

Date	Section of line	B.G.		M.G.		S.G.	
		M	C	M	C	M	C
Oct.	*Wrexham, Old Line Gwersyllt–Moss closed*						40
	31 December 1908					2819	26
1909							
1 Jan.	Liskeard & Looe Railway					9	12
	Liskeard & Caradon Railway					12	60
	31 December 1909					2841	18
1910							
4 Apr.	Ashendon Junction–Aynho Junction					18	29
9 May	Stoke Gifford–Holesmouth Junction, Avonmouth					6	58
	Filton West Loop						54
	Dunkerton Colliery–Limpley Stoke					6	52
31 May	*South Wales Mineral Line, Briton Ferry–Tonmawr Junction*					4	45
	31 December 1910					2869	6
1911							
10 Apr.	Lampeter, Aberayron & New Quay Light Railway					12	14
	Monmouthshire Line, Cwrncarn Branch						72
	31 December 1911					2882	12
1912							
	Swansea District Lines:						
18 Feb.	Skewen East Junction–Felin Fran					2	70
	Jersey Marine South–Lonlas Junction					2	24
1 July	Retew Branch Extension, Melangoose Mill–Meledor					1	39
Sept.	Hall's Tramroad, Hall's Road Junction–Penar Junction					4	67
	31 December 1912					2893	52

Date	Section of line	B.G.		M.G.		S.G.	
		M	C	M	C	M	C
1913							
	Swansea District Lines:						
14 July	Felin Fran–Morlais Junction South					7	76
	Morlais Junction East–Hendy Junction						48
	31 December 1913					2902	16
1914							
8 May	Swansea District Lines, Morriston–Felin Fran					1	18
	31 December 1914					2903	34
1915							
9 May	Neath Loop, Dynevor Junction North–Jersey Marine Jc. North						48
	31 December 1915					2904	2
1917							
1 Jan.	*Rowington Junction–Henley-in-Arden*					2	59
	Moorswater–Caradon, etc.					12	45
	Wyesham Junction–Coleford					4	17
	Wrexham, Aberderfyn–Legacy					1	25
16 Apr.	Ealing–Wood Lane Junction					4	15
	Branch to West London Joint Railway						68
	31 December 1917					2888	19
1920							
1 May	Trenance Valley Branch, (Lansalson) St Austell					1	53
	31 December 1921					2889	72

SHREWSBURY & BIRMINGHAM RAILWAY

1849							
1 June	Wellington–Oakengates					2	42

Date	Section of line	B.G.		M.G.		S.G.	
		M	C	M	C	M	C
12 Nov.	Oakengates–Wolverhampton, High Level, and Victoria Basin					16	21
1854							
1 June	Madeley Junction–Lightmoor					3	76
	Mileage, 1 September 1854					22	59

SHREWSBURY & CHESTER RAILWAY

Date	Section of line	B.G.		M.G.		S.G.	
1846							
4 Nov.	Chester, Saltney Junction–Ruabon (with powers over Chester & Holyhead Railway, Chester station to Saltney Junction 1 m 67 c)					15	8
	Branch to Saltney Quay						56
1847							
July	Wheatsheaf Junction–Minera					6	20
Nov.	Short branches to collieries and works at Ffrwd, Brymnally, Westminster, South Sea, Brymbo, and Vron					5	0
1848							
14 Oct.	Ruabon–Shrewsbury					25	23
23 Dec.	Gobowen–Oswestry					2	31
	Mileage, 1 September 1854					54	58

SOUTH WALES RAILWAY

Date	Section of line	B.G.		M.G.		S.G.	
1850							
18 June	Chepstow–Landore	73	28				
	Landore–Swansea, High Street	1	25				
1851							
19 Sept.	Grange Court (Junction with GWR)–Chepstow East	18	70				
1852							

Date	Section of line	B.G.		M.G.		S.G.	
		M	C	M	C	M	C
June	Swansea, Branch to North Dock		34				
19 July	Chepstow East–Chepstow (single line; doubled 18 April 1853)	1	0				
11 Oct.	Landore–Carmarthen (single from Pembrey; doubled 8 February 1853)	30	14				
1854							
2 Jan.	Carmarthen–Haverfordwest (single; doubled 1 July 1857)	31	14				
17 Jan.	*Cardiff, Bute Street Junction (with TVR) station*		40				40
24 July	Forest of Dean, Bullo Pill–Churchway, etc. (tramway converted)	7	20				
	Bullo Pill Dock Branch		53				
1856							
April	Haverfordwest–'New Milford' (Neyland) (single; doubled 1 July 1857)	9	16				
1857							
Feb.	Branch to Swansea Vale Railway		30				
1858							
19 Apr.	Cardiff, Bute Docks Branch	1	19				
1859							
Sept.	Swansea, North Dock Branch extended		22				
	Mileage, 1 January 1862	174	65		40		

WEST MIDLAND RAILWAY (INCLUDING LINES WORKED)

1860							
1 July	Oxford, Worcester & Wolverhampton Railway			2	9	109	17

Date	Section of line	B.G.		M.G.		S.G.	
		M	C	M	C	M	C
	Newport, Abergavenny & Hereford Railway					52	6
	Worcester & Hereford Railway					9	51
July	Worcester, Rainbow Hill Junction–Shrub Hill						17
	31 December 1860			2	9	171	11
1861							
1 July	Coleford, Monmouth, Usk & Pontypool Railway (Little Mill Junction–Usk opened 2 June 1856, Usk–Monmouth (Troy) opened 12 October 1857, Monmouth (Troy)–Wyesham opened 1 July 1861)					17	2
13 Sept.	Malvern Wells–Shelwick Junction					18	5
14 Nov.	Witney Railway, Yarnton–Witney					8	13
	31 December 1861			2	9	214	31
1862							
1 Feb.	Severn Valley Railway, Hartlebury–Sutton Bridge Junction (with Shrewsbury & Hereford Railway)					39	44
	Much Wenlock & Severn Junction Railway, Buildwas–Much Wenlock					3	40
1 Mar.	Bourton-on-the-Water Railway, Chipping Norton Junction–Bourton-on-the-Water					6	47
1 July	Leominster Junction–Kington (opened 20 August 1857, and worked by Brassey till June 1862, then leased by WMR)					13	28
	31 December 1862			2	9	277	30

Date	Section of line	B.G.		M.G.		S.G.	
		M	C	M	C	M	C
1863							
1 Apr.	Stourbridge Railway, Stourbridge Junction–Cradley					2	21
	Cradley–Corngreaves Yard (goods)						34
June	Lye–Hayes Lane (goods)						62
	Mileage, 1 August 1863			2	9	280	67

OXFORD, WORCESTER & WOLVERHAMPTON RAILWAY

Date	Section of line	B.G.		M.G.		S.G.	
1850							
5 Oct.	Worcester–Norton					3	8
	Norton–Abbot's Wood Junction (with Midland)						66
1852							
18 Feb.	Worcester–Droitwich					5	49
	Droitwich–Stoke Works Junction (with Midland)					4	3
1 May	Droitwich–Stourbridge					16	37
	Norton Junction–Evesham					10	48
16 Nov.	Stourbridge–Dudley (for passengers Dec. 20)					5	46
1853							
4 June	Evesham–Wolvercot Junction					40	48
	Doubled:						
	Wolvercot–Handborough 18 Nov. 1853						
	Handborough–Charlbury 1 Aug. 1854						
	Campden–Evesham 20 March 1855						
	Charlbury–Campden 2 August 1858						
1 Dec.	Dudley–Tipton					1	4
	Tipton–Junction with Stour Valley Railway (L&NW)						52

Date	Section of line	B.G.		M.G.		S.G.	
		M	C	M	C	M	C
1854							
April	Tipton–Priestfield (passengers 1 July)					3	17
	Priestfield–Wolverhampton, Cannock Road (passengers 1 July)			2	9		
July	Cannock Road–Bushbury Junction (with L&NWR) for goods; passengers 1 January 1864						75
1855							
10 Aug.	Chipping Norton Junction–Chipping Norton					4	42
Oct.	Priestfield–Walsall Street (goods)					1	0
1858							
14 Nov.	Kingswinford Junction–Bromley Basin					1	45
1859							
12 July	Honeybourne–Stratford-on-Avon					9	37
	Mileage, 1 July 1860			2	9	109	17

NEWPORT, ABERGAVENNY & HEREFORD RAILWAY

Date	Section of line	B.G.		M.G.		S.G.	
1854							
2 Jan.	Hereford, Barton–Pontypool, Coedygric Junction					33	59
16 Jan.	Hereford, Barton station–Barton (later Barr's Court)					1	7
1855							
20 Aug.	Pontypool Road–Crumlin (Junction)					5	41
3 Sept.	Crumlin (Junction)–Llanhilleth (goods)					1	25
1857							

Table of Opening Dates, Mileage and Gauge

Date	Section of line	B.G.		M.G.		S.G.	
		M	C	M	C	M	C
1 June	Crumlin Junction–Tredegar Junction					3	27
1858							
11 Jan.	Tredegar Junction–Quaker's Yard (Low Level) Junction					7	7
	Mileage, 1 July 1860					52	6

WORCESTER & HEREFORD RAILWAY

Date	Section of line	B.G.		M.G.		S.G.	
1859							
25 July	Henwick–Malvern Link					6	8
1860							
17 May	Worcester, Tunnel Junction–Henwick					1	33
25 May	Malvern Link–Malvern Wells					2	10
	Mileage, 1 July 1860					9	51

ABSORBED RAILWAYS

VALE OF NEATH RAILWAY

Date	Section of line	B.G.		M.G.		S.G.	
1851							
24 Sept.	Neath Jc. with S. Wales Railway–Aberdare	19	0				
1853							
June	Aberdare–Canal Head		41				
2 Nov.	Gelly Tarw Junction–Merthyr	6	23				
1854							
7 Nov.	Gelly Tarw Junction–Dare Junction	2	38				
	Dare Junction–Nantmelyn Colliery	1	15				
1856							
Nov.	Aberdare Valley Railway:						

Date	Section of line	B.G.		M.G.		S.G.	
		M	C	M	C	M	C
	Aberdare, Canal Head–Middle Duffryn Colliery	2	0				
	Dare Junction–Cwmaman Colliery	2	70				
1857							
1 June	Nantmelyn Colliery–Bwllfa Dare Colliery		34				
1861							
23 Aug.	Briton Ferry Dock & Railway, Branch from South Wales Railway		45				
1862							
1 July	Swansea Harbour Railway, North–South Dock		60				
1863							
15 July	Neath Jc.–Wind Street Jc.			7	63		
	East Dock–Swansea Vale Railway				13		
	Swansea Harbour Railway		60		60		
	31 December 1863	35	26	8	56		
1864							
18 Apr.	*Neath Junction–Middle Duffryn*	20	71	20	71		
	Neath Junction–Neath		50		50		
July	*Gelly Tarw Junction–Merthyr*	6	23	6	23		
Nov.	*Dare and Amman Branches*	6	77	6	77		
	31 December 1865		45	43	37		

LLANELLY RAILWAY

Date	Section of line	B.G.		M.G.		S.G.	
1833							
	Llanelly Dock–Dafen (horse traction)					1	70
1839							
1 June	Llanelly Dock–Pontardulais					6	25
1840							

Date	Section of line	B.G.		M.G.		S.G.	
		M	C	M	C	M	C
10 Mar.	Pontardulais–Cwmarnman (Garnant)					9	39
1841							
6 May	Pantyfynnon–Duffryn (Tirydail)					1	23
	Mountain Branch, Duffryn–Cross Hands					4	0
	Garnant–Gwaun-cae-Gurwen					1	75
1842							
June	Bynea and other short branches					1	40
	Cwmarnman–Brynamman					1	67
	31 December 1842					28	19
1853							
1 June	Llanelly Dock–South Wales Railway Station						65
1857							
24 Jan.	Duffryn Junction (Tirydail)–Llandilo					6	75
	31 December 1857					35	79
1858							
1 Apr.	Vale of Towy Railway, Llandilo–Llandovery					11	10
1864							
Nov.	Carmarthen Line, Llandilo Junction–Abergwili Junction with Carmarthen & Cardigan Railway (for goods; for passengers 1 June 1865)					13	20
1867							
14 Dec.	Swansea Line, Pontardulais–Swansea					12	40
	Gower Road–Penclawdd					3	0
	31 December 1867					75	69
1868							
1 Apr.	*Vale of Towy Railway made joint with LNWR*					11	10

Date	Section of line	B.G.		M.G.		S.G.	
		M	C	M	C	M	C
1871							
1 July	*Swansea and Carmarthen Lines taken over by LNWR*					28	60
	31 December 1872					35	79
LLYNVI & OGMORE RAILWAY							
1861							
10 Aug.	Bridgend–Duffryn Llynvi, Tywith	10	11				
	Tondu–Porthcawl Harbour	9	58				
1865							
1 Aug.	*Tondu–Porthcawl Harbour*	9	58	9	58		
		10	11	9	58		
OGMORE VALLEY RAILWAY							
1865							
1 Aug.	Nantymoel–Tondu Junction					7	11
1866							
1 July	Llynvi Valley Railway	10	11	9	58		
	Ogmore Valley Railway					7	11
1 Aug.	*Tondu–Duffryn Llynvi*	7	7	7	7		
1868							
April	*Bridgend–Tondu*	3	4	3	4		
				19	69	7	11
1872							
May	*Bridgend and Porthcawl–Duffryn Llynvi*			19	69	19	69
MONMOUTHSHIRE RAILWAY							
1852							
1 July	Newport, Marshes Turnpike Gate–Pontypool					8	0
1853							

Date	Section of line	B.G.		M.G.		S.G.	
		M	C	M	C	M	C
9 Mar.	Newport, Marshes Turnpike Gate–Mill Street						18
1854							
1 June	Pontypool–Pontnewynydd Canal Head (for goods)					5	71
1855							
May	Newport, Dock Street–Nantyglo, Gate					20	68
	Aberbeeg–Ebbw Vale					6	57
	Pillgwenlly Branch, Courtybella Junction–Old Dock						68
	Loop, Pillbank Junction–Dock Street						42
	Mill Street–Dock Street						76
	Llanarth Street Junction–Salutation Junction						33
Nov.	Risca–Nine Mile Point (passengers 19 June 1865)					2	26
1858							
	Nantyglo Gate–Nantyglo						21
	Cwmtillery Branch						75
1870							
	Cwmfrwydoer Branch					1	25
	Cwmnantdu Branch					1	79
	31 July 1875					51	19

BRISTOL & EXETER RAILWAY (INCLUDING LINES WORKED)

Date	Section of line	B.G.		M.G.		S.G.	
1841							
14 June	Bristol, Harbour Bridge Jc.–Bridgwater	33	30				
	Weston Junction–Weston-super-Mare	1	38				
1842							
1 July	Bridgwater–Taunton	11	45				

Date	Section of line	B.G.		M.G.		S.G.	
		M	C	M	C	M	C
1843							
1 May	Taunton–Beambridge (171 m 72 ch)	8	40				
1844							
1 May	Beambridge–Exeter	22	23				
1847							
28 July	Clevedon Road (Yatton)–Clevedon	3	45				
1848							
12 June	Tiverton Road (Tiverton Junction)–Tiverton	4	60				
	All the above were worked by the Great Western until 1 May 1849	85	41				
1849							
1 May	Bristol & Exeter Railway Company took over	85	41				
1851							
12 May	Exeter & Crediton Railway, Cowley Bridge Junction –Crediton	5	60				
1853							
1 Oct.	Durston–Yeovil, Hendford (goods 26 October)	18	77				
1854							
28 Aug.	Somerset Central Railway, Highbridge Wharf–Glastonbury	12	38				
1857							
2 Feb.	Yeovil, Hendford Junction–Pen Mill GWR	1	38				
1858							
3 May	Somerset Central Railway, Highbridge–Burnham	1	43				
1859							
15 Mar.	Somerset Central Railway, Glastonbury–Wells	5	28				

Date	Section of line	B.G.		M.G.		S.G.	
		M	C	M	C	M	C
Aug.	Bridgwater Docks Branch purchased (worked by horses until November 1867)						48
	31 December 1859	131	53				
1860							
1 June	Yeovil, LSWR Junction–Hendford						74
1861							
30 Aug.	*Somerset Central Railway taken over by SCR*	19	29				
	31 December 1861	112	24				74
1862							
1 Feb.	*Exeter–Cowley Bridge Junction*	1	27	1	27		
	Exeter & Crediton Railway taken over by L & SWR Co.	5	60				
31 Mar.	Watchet Junction–Watchet	14	48				
	31 December 1862	119	65	1	27		74
1866							
11 Sept.	Creech Junction–Chard (goods, March 1867)	12	61				
	31 December 1866	132	46	1	27		74
1867							
18 Apr.	Portishead Jc.–Portishead	9	49				
Nov.	*Highbridge–Durston*	12	6	12	6		
	Durston–Hendford and Yeovil Town	19	75	19	75		
	Bridgwater Docks Branch		48		48		
	31 December 1867	109	46	33	76		74
1868							
12 Nov.	Yeovil Town–Pen Mill		40		40		
1869							
3 Aug.	Yatton–Cheddar	9	65				
Nov.	Dunball Wharf Branch				36		
	31 December 1869	118	71	34	72		74
1870							

Date	Section of line	B.G.		M.G.		S.G.	
		M	C	M	C	M	C
5 Apr.	Cheddar–Wells, Tucker Street	7	57				
	31 December 1870	126	48	34	72		74
1871							
Mar.	Bridgwater Docks Extension				28		
8 June	Norton Junction–Wiveliscombe	7	25				
	31 December 1871	133	73	35	20		74
1873							
1 Nov.	Wiveliscombe–Barnstaple	35	25				
	31 December 1873	169	18	35	20		74
1874							
16 July	Watchet–Minehead	8	12				
	31 December 1874	177	30	35	20		74
1875							
May	*Durston–Taunton*	5	63	5	63		
1 June	*Bristol–Highbridge*	27	6	27	6		
1 July	*Weston Junction–Weston-super-Mare*	1	38	1	38		
15 Oct.	*Yatton–Wells*	17	42			17	42
	31 December 1875	125	41	69	47	18	36
	TOTAL MILEAGE 213 m 44 c						

SOUTH DEVON RAILWAY (INCLUDING LINES WORKED)

1846							
30 May	Exeter, B&ER Stn–Teignmouth	14	78				
30 Dec.	Teignmouth–Newton	5	15				
1847							
20 July	Newton–Totnes (goods, 6 December)	8	55				
13 Sept.	Atmospheric traction, Exeter–Teignmouth						
1848							

Date	Section of line	B.G.		M.G.		S.G.	
		M	C	M	C	M	C
1 Jan.	Atmospheric traction extended to Newton						
5 May	Totnes–Laira Green (goods, 13 September)	21	16				
10 Sept.	Atmospheric traction abandoned						
18 Dec.	Newton–Torquay (Torre) (goods, 6 October 1849)	5	1				
1849							
2 Apr.	Laira Green–Plymouth, Millbay (goods, 1 May)	2	64				
	31 December 1849	57	69				
1853							
May	Laira Junction–Sutton Harbour (horse traction) (closed May 1856 for alteration, re–opened October 1857, locomotive traction from 19 April 1869)	1	62				
	31 December 1853	59	51				
1855							
29 Jan.	*Torquay Branch single line Newton–Aller made Down Main line*	1	5				
	31 December 1855	58	46				
1859							
22 June	South Devon & Tavistock Railway, Tavistock Junction –Tavistock (goods, 1 February 1860)	12	71				
2 Aug.	Dartmouth & Torbay Railway, Torre–Paignton	2	78				
	31 December 1859	74	35				
1861							
14 Mar.	Dartmouth & Torbay Railway, Paignton–Brixham Road (Churston)	2	72				
	31 December 1861	77	27				

Date	Section of line	B.G.		M.G.		S.G.	
		M	C	M	C	M	C
1864							
16 Aug.	Dartmouth & Torbay Railway, Brixham Road–Kingswear	3	63				
	31 December 1864	81	10				
1865							
1 July	Tavistock–Launceston	18	76				
	31 December 1865	100	6				
1866							
4 July	Moretonhampstead & South Devon Railway, Newton–Moretonhampstead	12	13				
1867							
17 June	Exeter City Basin Branch (goods only)		34				
1871							
20 Mar.	*Exeter B&E–City Basin Junction, Mixed Gauge on Down Line only, City Basin Branch*		34		34		
1872							
1 May	Ashburton Jc., Totnes–Ashburton	9	20				
1873							
10 Nov.	Totnes–Quay		62				
	31 December 1873	122	21		34		
1874							
1 July	New single (3rd) line Newton–Aller for Torquay Branch, and 'Torquay Junction' abolished	1	5				
	31 January 1876	123	26		34		
	TOTAL MILEAGE 123 m 60 c						
CORNWALL MINERALS RAILWAY							
1874							
1 June	Fowey–Newquay					24	39

Date	Section of line	B.G.		M.G.		S.G.	
		M	C	M	C	M	C
	Carbus Branch, Bugle Junction–Carbus					1	6
	Retew Branch, Bodmin Road (St Dennis) Junction–Melangoose Mill					2	50
	East Wheal Rose Branch, Newquay (Tolcarn) Junction–Treamble					8	44
	Treloggan Curve						30
	Newquay Harbour Line					1	0
	Cornwall Junction Branch, Bodmin Road (St Dennis) Junction–Drinnick Mill					4	30
	Newquay & Cornwall Junction Railway			3	10		
	Treamble–Gravel Hill					1	9
	(All above for goods and mineral traffic only)						
	30 September 1877			3	10	43	48

NEWQUAY & CORNWALL JUNCTION RAILWAY

Date	Section of line	B.G.		M.G.		S.G.	
1869							
1 July	Burngullow–Drinnick Mill	3	10				

CARMARTHEN & CARDIGAN RAILWAY

Date	Section of line	B.G.		M.G.		S.G.	
1860							
1 Mar.	Myrtle Hill Junction–Carmarthen	1	5				
3 Sept.	Carmarthen–Conwil	6	1				
	Traffic ceased	7	6				
1861							
12 Aug.	Myrtle Hill Junction–Conwil reopened	7	6				
1864							
28 Mar.	Conwil–Pencader	8	10				

Date	Section of line	B.G.		M.G.		S.G.	
		M	C	M	C	M	C
3 June	Pencader–Llandyssil	3	42				
1 Nov.	*Myrtle Hill Junction–Abergwili Junction (for Llanelly Railway)*	1	75	1	75		
1866							
1 April	*Abergwili Jc.–Pencader Jc. (for Manchester & Milford Railway)*	13	54	13	54		
	31 December 1866	3	9	15	49		
1872							
1 June	*Myrtle Hill Jc.–Pencader*			15	49	15	49
	Pencader Junction–Llandyssil	3	9			3	9
	22 August 1881					18	58

TORBAY & BRIXHAM RAILWAY

1868							
28 Feb.	Brixham Road (Churston)–Brixham	2	6				
	31 December 1882	2	6				

FESTINIOG & BLAENAU RAILWAY (Gauge 1 ft 11½ in.)

1868							
30 April	Festiniog–Blaenau Festiniog 3 m 36 ch						
1883							
13 Aug.	Taken over by the Great Western, reconstructed and opened on the Standard Gauge, 10 September 1883						

WATLINGTON & PRINCES RISBOROUGH RAILWAY

1872							

Date	Section of line	B.G.		M.G.		S.G.	
		M	C	M	C	M	C
15 Aug.	Princes Risborough–Watlington					8	66
	31 December 1883					8	66
WHITLAND & CARDIGAN RAILWAY **WHITLAND & TAFF VALE RAILWAY**							
1873							
24 Mar.	Taff Vale Junction (Cardigan Junction) with GWR–Llanfyrnach					10	39
1874							
Oct.	Llanfyrnach–Cryminych Arms					3	55
1877							
	Name altered to WHITLAND & CARDIGAN RAILWAY						
	31 August 1886					14	14
PEMBROKE & TENBY RAILWAY							
1863							
30 July	Pembroke–Tenby					9	37
8 Aug.	Pembroke–Pembroke Dock					2	12
1866							
4 Sept.	Tenby–Whitland					15	57
1868							
1 June	Carmarthen Loop, Towy Bridge–Carmarthen & Cardigan Railway						16
1872							
	Junction at Pembroke Dock–Hobbs Point						51
	30 June 1896					28	13

Date	Section of line	B.G.		M.G.		S.G.	
		M	C	M	C	M	C

NORTH PEMBROKESHIRE & FISHGUARD RAILWAY

Date	Section of line	B.G. M	B.G. C	M.G. M	M.G. C	S.G. M	S.G. C
1876							
	MAENCLOCHOG RAILWAY						
19 Sept.	Narberth Road (Clynderwen)–Rosebush					8	22
1882							
31 Dec.	*The above closed*					8	22
	NORTH PEMBROKESHIRE & FISHGUARD RAILWAY						
1895							
11 April	Clynderwen–Rosebush, and Letterston					17	12

GOLDEN VALLEY RAILWAY

Date	Section of line	B.G. M	B.G. C	M.G. M	M.G. C	S.G. M	S.G. C
1881							
1 Sept.	Pontrilas–Dorstone					10	56
27 May	Dorstone–Hay Junction (with Midland Railway)					7	76
1897							
23 Aug.	*Dorstone–Hay Junction closed*					7	76
1898							
20 April	*Pontrilas–Dorstone closed*					10	56
1899							
1 July	Purchased by Great Western Company and reopened 1 May 1901						

LAMBOURN VALLEY RAILWAY

Date	Section of line	B.G. M	B.G. C	M.G. M	M.G. C	S.G. M	S.G. C
1898							
4 April	Newbury–Lambourn					12	33
	30 June 1905					12	33

Date	Section of line	B.G.		M.G.		S.G.	
		M	C	M	C	M	C
RHONDDA & SWANSEA BAY RAILWAY							
1885							
2 Nov.	Aberavon–Cymmer					7	68
1890							
2 June	Cymmer–Blaen Gwynfy					2	9
2 July	Blaen Gwynfy–Blaen Rhondda					3	6
14 July	Blaen Rhondda–Treherbert Junction (with Taff Vale Railway)						44
1891							
	Aberavon–Port Talbot Dock					1	12
1893							
30 Dec.	Aberavon, Burrows Junction–Briton Ferry Dock					3	12
1894							
14 Dec.	Briton Ferry Junction–Danygraig					6	79
1895							
14 Mar.	Neath Branch					1	19
1899							
7 May	Danygraig–Swansea, Riverside						74
	Sundry short branches					1	60
	1 January 1906					28	63
MANCHESTER & MILFORD RAILWAY							
1866							
1 Jan.	Pencader Junction with Carmarthen & Cardigan Railway–Lampeter					12	27
1 Sept.	Lampeter–Strata Florida					14	73
1867							
12 Aug.	Strata Florida–Aberystwyth					14	5
	30 June 1906					41	25

Date	Section of line	B.G.		M.G.		S.G.	
		M	C	M	C	M	C
PORT TALBOT RAILWAY & DOCKS							
1897							
1 Sept.	Port Talbot, Central–LIetty Brongu (goods; for passengers 14 Feb. 1898)					10	69
1898							
17 Jan.	Aberavon Branch to Rhondda & Swansea Bay Railway						46
14 Feb.	Lletty Brongu–Pontyrhyll Junction with GW Garw Branch					3	12
14 Nov.	Port Talbot, Tanygroes Junction–Tonmawr Junction with South Wales Mineral Railway					5	74
	Blaenavon and Whitworth Branches					2	50
19 Dec.	Port Talbot, Copper Works Junction–Cefin Junction with GWR near Tondu					7	53
	Waterhall Junction–Pyle GWR						75
	Port Talbot Dock Lines					1	68
	31 December 1907					33	47
SOUTH WALES MINERAL RAILWAY							
1861							
June	Briton Ferry Junction with South Wales Railway–West end of Tonmawr Tunnel	5	64				
1862							
	Colliery Branches		40				
1863							
Mar.	Tonmawr Tunnel–Glyncorrwg	6	35				
1872							

Date	Section of line	B.G.		M.G.		S.G.	
		M	C	M	C	M	C
May	*All above converted to Standard Gauge*	12	59			12	59
	31 December 1907					12	59
LISKEARD & LOOE RAILWAY							
1860							
27 Dec.	Moorswater–Looe (passengers, 11 September 1879)					7	3
1901							
25 Feb.	Coombe Junction–Liskeard (branch station) GWR for goods; passengers May 15					2	9
	31 December 1908					9	12
LISKEARD & CARADON RAILWAY							
1844							
28 Nov.	Moorswater–Caradon Mine					5	60
1846							
Mar.	Caradon–Cheesewring Quarries					3	0
	Sundry Branches					4	0
	31 December 1908					12	60

Bibliography

Ahrons, E. L., *Locomotives & Train Working in the Latter Part of the Nineteenth Century,* vols 2 & 4 (Cambridge: Heffer, 1952)

Allen, C. J., *Salute to the Great Western* (London: Ian Allan, 1970)

Allen, G. F., *The Western Since 1948* (London: Ian Allan, 1979)

Barman, C., *The Great Western's Last Look Forward* (Newton Abbot: David & Charles, 1972)

Booker, F., *The Great Western Railway* (Newton Abbot: David & Charles, 1985)

Bourne, J. C., *The History & Description of the Great Western Railway* (London: David Bogue, 1846)

Bryan, T., *The Great Western Railway* (Oxford: Shire Publications, 2011)

Cattell, J. and K. Falconer, *Swindon: The Legacy of a Railway Town* (London: HMSO, 1995)

Chapman, W. G., *Caerphilly Castle* (London: GWR, 1924)

Chapman, W. G., *Cheltenham Flyer* (London: GWR, 1934)

Chapman, W. G., *Locos of the Royal Road* (London: GWR, 1936)

Chapman, W. G., *The King of Railway Locomotives* (London: GWR, 1928)

Chapman, W. G., *The 10.30 Limited* (London: GWR, 1923)

Chapman, W. G., *Track Topics* (London: GWR, 1935)

Chapman, W. G., *'Twixt Rail & Sea* (London: Appleby, 1927)

Clark, R. H. and C. R Potts, *An Historical Survey of Selected Great Western Railway Stations,* vols 1–4 (Oxford: OPC, 1976–85)

Cooke, R. A., *Atlas of the Great Western Railway* (Didcot: Wild Swan Publications, 1997)

Cummings, J., *Railway Motor Buses and Bus Services in the British Isles 1902–1933* (Oxford: OPC, 1978)

Harris, M., *Great Western Coaches from 1890* (Newton Abbot: David & Charles, 1985)

Hawkins, C. and G. Reeve, *Great Western Railway Engine Sheds: London Division* (Didcot: Wild Swan Publications, 1987)

Judge, C. W., *The History of the Great Western AEC Diesel Railcars,* (Oxford: OPC, 1986)

Lyons, E., *An Historical Survey of Great Western Engine Sheds 1837–1947* (Oxford: OPC, 1974)

Lyons, E., *An Historical Survey of Great Western Engine Sheds 1947* (Oxford: OPC, 1985)

Lucking, J. H., *The Great Western at Weymouth* (Newton Abbot: David & Charles, 1971)

Macdermot, E. T., *History of the Great Western Railway,* vols 1 & 2 (London: Ian Allan, 1964)

Maggs, C. G., *Colin Maggs's West of England* (Stroud: Sutton, 1998)

Maggs, C. G., *GWR Principal Stations* (London: Ian Allan, 1987)

Maggs, C. G., *Rail Centres: Bristol* (London: Ian Allan, 1989)

Maggs, C. G., *Rail Centres: Exeter* (London: Ian Allan, 1985)

Maggs, C. G., *Rail Centres: Swindon* (London: Ian Allan, 1983)

Maggs, C. G., *The Bath to Weymouth Line* (Tisbury: Oakwood Press, 1982)

Maggs, C. G., *The Culm Valley Light Railway* (Usk: Oakwood Press, 2006)

Maggs, C. G., *The GWR Bristol to Bath Line* (Stroud: Amberley, 2012)

Maggs, C. G., *The GWR Bristol to Taunton Line* (Stroud: Amberley, 2013)

Maggs, C. G., *The GWR Swindon to Bath Line* (Stroud: Sutton, 2003)

Matheson, R., *The GWR Story* (Stroud: The History Press, 2010)

Measom, G., *The Official Guide to the Great Western Railway* (London: Griffin, Bohn, 1861)

Nock, O. S., *History of the Great Western Railway,* vol. 3 (London: Ian Allan, 1967)

Nock, O. S., *Tales of the Great Western Railway* (Newton Abbot: David & Charles, 1984)

Nock, O. S., *The Great Western Railway in the Twentieth Century* (London: Ian Allan, 1971)

Norris, J., G. Beale and J. Lewis, *Edwardian Enterprise, GWR* (Didcot: Wild Swan, 1987)

Peck, A. S., *The Great Western at Swindon Works* (Oxford: OPC, 1983)

Railway Correspondence & Travel Society, *Locomotives of the Great Western Railway,* vols 1–14 (Long Stratton:

RCTS, 1952–1993)

Robertson, K., *Great Western Railway Halts,* vol. 1 (Pinner: Irwell, 1990)

Robertson, K., *Great Western Railway Halts,* vol. 2 (Bishop's Waltham: KRB Publications, 2002)

Robertson, K., *Odd Corners of the GWR from the Days of Steam* (Stroud: Sutton, 1999)

Robertson, K., *More Odd Corners of the GWR* (Stroud: Sutton, 2003)

Russell, J. H., *Great Western Diesel Railcars* (Didcot: Wild Swan, 1985)

Sekon, G. A., *A History of the Great Western Railway* (London: Digby, Long, 1895)

Semmens, P., *History of the Great Western Railway* (London: George Allen & Unwin, 1985)

Simmons, J. and G. Biddle, *The Oxford Companion to British Railway History* (Oxford University Press, 2000)

Slinn, J. N., *Great Western Way* (Frome: Historical Model Railway Society, 1985)

Timms, P., *Working at Swindon Works 1930 to 1960* (Stroud: The History Press, 2008)

Vaughan, A., *A Pictorial Record of Great Western Architecture* (Oxford: OPC, 1977)

Waters, L., *Britain's Rail Super Centres, London, the Great Western Lines* (London: Ian Allan 1993)

Waters, L., *Rail Centres: Reading* (London: Ian Allan, 1990)

Whitehouse, P. and D. St John Thomas, *The Great Western Railway 150 Glorious Years,* (Newton Abbot: David & Charles, 1985)

Williams, A., *Brunel After* (London: GWR, 1925)

Wilson, R. B., *Go Great Western – A History of GWR Publicity*
  (Newton Abbot: David & Charles, 1970)
Wragg, D., *GWR Handbook* (Sparkford: Haynes, 2010)

About the Author

Colin Maggs is one of the country's foremost railway historians and an authority on the Great Western Railway. He is the author of nearly one hundred railway books, and in 1993 he received the MBE for services to railway history. He lives in Bath.

Index

314